FREE AND INEXPENSIVE LEARNING MATERIALS

Twenty-first Biennial Edition

compiled and published by

GEORGE PEABODY COLLEGE FOR TEACHERS
VANDERBILT UNIVERSITY
Nashville, Tennessee

Norman R. Moore, *Editor*

distributed by

INCENTIVE PUBLICATIONS, INC.
Nashville, Tennessee

Hico
Middle School Library

ISBN: 0-933436-02-5

ISSN: 0733-1886

Library of Congress Catalog Card Number: 53-2471

Printed in the United States of America

Cover by Cynthia Crook

Copies of this publication may be ordered by mail from the distributor. Enclose check or money order for $4.95 per copy plus 10% (minimum $1.00) for shipping and handling. Billing available except for personal orders. Address orders to:

Incentive Publications, Inc.
P.O. Box 120189
Nashville, Tennessee 37212

Foreword

In this edition are descriptions and ordering information for more than 2600 instructional aids. Nearly 1200 items are entirely free upon request. Hundreds more are obtainable for less than a dollar. Only one of every six items costs more than two dollars. Over one-third of the listings herein are new or revised materials since the previous edition in 1981. Also, more than 100 of the 700 distributors of these materials are new additions. Moreover, the distributors collectively have available hundreds of other aids not listed in this volume. Most distributors will furnish free a listing of their offerings upon request.

Entries in this book emphasize materials for direct use by students and for ready use by teachers with groups or classes of students. Most of the items listed are for teaching and learning levels prior to high school. Materials are listed for higher grades, however, including many intended especially for educators.

The educational value of all entries in this edition was evaluated by a staff at George Peabody College for Teachers of Vanderbilt University. Final selections made from the materials reviewed were governed by the following criteria:

Content—The material should be factual, free from exaggerations and propaganda, and carry a minimum amount of advertising.

Timeliness—The information should be of current interest and should supplement that readily found in textbooks.

Utility—The item should be useful as a classroom teaching aid or as a reference. The price, if any, should be low and should represent a genuine value to the purchaser.

In addition, the process used in compiling each edition seeks to assure the availability of the materials listed. Just prior to each publication, all ordering information for each continuing or new entry is verified with the suppliers. All entries in the present volume were so verified within four months of its publication date. Users are advised, however, that it is difficult for many suppliers to estimate their ability to fill orders over a two-year period, especially those which are not publishing firms. Generally speaking, the user should order materials far in advance of the need for them.

Numerous persons contributed to the preparation of this publication. Sincere appreciation is expressed to all who assisted in its many phases. Particular recognition is given to Brenda Buratynski, Lewis Walker, Karen Cunningham, Jeanne Hammonds, and Sue Ann Blackburn. In addition, two historical debts are owed for the current edition. One is to Henry Harap who assembled the first listing of worthwhile teaching aids in 1941 and directed its continual updating through 1959. The other indebtedness is to Marian Tippit whose devotion to overseeing and copy editing most editions from 1960 through 1973 served to keep this series coming off the press. Since its inception, nearly 330,000 copies of the series have been used by teachers, students, librarians, and others in education.

How To Use This Book

LOCATING MATERIALS. All of the educational aids listed in this book are classified under 77 subject headings which parallel subject fields, courses, and unit topics generally taught in elementary and secondary schools. A table of contents of the subject headings, arranged in alphabetical order, directs the user quickly to the materials desired. In addition, the cross-reference index guides the user to related materials within other classifications. The annotation for each aid includes basic information such as the nature of the item, its size, its price, and the full name and address of the distributor. New and revised listings in this edition are designated by a triangle symbol (►) preceding their titles.

GRADE DESIGNATIONS. The annotations given also indicate the school grades for which the material's use is most suited as well as its other characteristics. Coding is used to convey the grade level(s) of the materials where such is not evident from the annotation itself. Those materials developed by publishers for definite grades are indicated by specific designations, for example:

G2 = second grade; G5-6 = fifth and sixth grades; K = kindergarten.

Materials evaluated as being suitable for use within grade groupings are indicated by general designations, as follows:

ps. =	preschool	ms. =	middle school grades (G6-9)
pr. =	primary levels (G1-3)	hs. =	high school grades (G9-12)
el. =	elementary grades (G4-6)	ad. =	advanced levels (colleges, adults, teachers)

Designations for materials which may be applicable to more than one grade grouping may appear as follows:

ps-pr. el-ms. ms-hs. hs-ad. ms-hs-ad. el. to ad.

ORDERING MATERIALS. *The materials listed are available only from the distributors given in each description.* When ordering, observe carefully the supplier's instructions contained in the description for the material desired. Always give the exact reference (title, date, and number as shown) or description (for posters, maps, charts, etc.) of the item desired; print or type your name and full address; and include payment when there is a charge for the material unless post-billing is expressly indicated. In addition, be sure to include return postage or envelope where required by the distributor. Whenever possible, your orders should be placed on school or organizational stationery. Orders should also mention that the item is listed in *Free and Inexpensive Learning Materials* (1983).

Indiscriminate requests for "everything you have" to suppliers of free materials should be avoided. It is permissible, however, to request a list of publications or to describe a teaching assignment and request appropriate materials. General requests such as these, of course, should identify the curriculum areas and grade level of teaching and should indicate class size, if classroom quantities are desired.

Finally, the present edition will be out-of-date after 1984. No orders for items listed herein should be placed beyond 1984.

Table of Contents

Free and Inexpensive Learning Materials

AFRICA

Headline Series. The Foreign Policy Assoc., Inc. 205 Lexington Ave. New York, NY 10016. 64 pp. each. $3.00 each. Analyses of major foreign policy problems by experts. Contains maps, charts, photographs, discussion guide, and bibliography. hs-ad. Titles include:

Conflict in Southern Africa (#240). 1978.

►**Nigeria: Power and Democracy in Africa (#257).** 1982.

Mauritania. Embassy of Mauritania. 2129 Leroy Place., N.W. Washington, DC 20008. Undated. 13 pp. Free. General information on the Islamic Republic of Mauritania in West Africa. hs.

Morocco. Moroccan National Tourist Office. 521 5th Ave. New York, NY 10017; or 408 So. Michigan Ave. Chicago, IL 60605; or 2049 Century Park East, Suite 3762. San Francisco, CA 90067. A variety of full-color brochures, maps, and folders on features of Morocco are available free. el-ms.

South Africa. The South African Consulate General. Information Section. 425 Park Ave. New York, NY 10022. Free. Send for currently available information. ms-hs.

►**To Reach the Village . . .** UNESCO. Room 2401. U.N. Building. New York, NY 10017. 1974. 12 pp. Free. Presents the use of rural newspapers in reaching the backcountry of Africa with information. ms-hs.

Visual Geography Series. Sterling Publishing Co. 2 Park Ave. New York, NY 10016. 64 pp. each. $2.95 each. Orders must be prepaid and include postage. Booklets discuss the land, history, people, government, and economy of each country. Illustrated with photographs and maps. ms. Sample titles are:

Ivory Coast in Pictures

►**Malawi in Pictures**

Tunisia in Pictures

►New and revised listings.

ANIMALS, BIRDS, AND FISH

Animal Friends. Animal Rescue League of Boston. P.O. Box 265. Boston, MA 02117. Bi-monthly. 4 pp. $3.00 annual subscription for 6 issues. The newsletter contains games, information, contests, careers information, and tips. el.

Animals, Birds, and Plants of the Bible. Abingdon. Customer Service Dept. 201 Eighth Ave., S. Nashville, TN 37202. 1971. 63 pp. 95 cents. Payment should accompany all orders; schools and libraries entitled to 25% discount. A glossary-type booklet describing the most common wildlife mentioned in the King James version of the Bible. el-ms.

Audubon—the Birds of America. Huntington Library Publications. 1151 Oxford Road. San Marino, CA 91108. 1978. 33 pp. $2.50 plus 75 cents postage for 1-5 copies. A booklet containing 12 color plates and commentaries from Audubon's collections and a short biography. el-ms.

►**Buffalo: America's Oldest Inhabitant.** National Buffalo Assoc. P.O. Box 706. Custer, SD 57730. Single copy free; enclose self-addressed stamped envelope (#10). Brochure on the Buffalo's history and nutritional value. el-ms.

Cattle Photographs. The Brown Swiss Cattle Breeders' Assoc. Box 1038. Beloit, WI 53511. Free. Five photographs of "Outstanding Brown Swiss" cattle. el-ms.

The Children's Zoo. Eli Lilly and Co. Public Relations Services. 307 E. McCarty St. Indianapolis, IN 46285. 1970. 12 pp. Free in classroom quantities to K-3 teachers; request on school letterhead. Booklets containing illustrations and descriptions of familiar and unusual animals. pr.

►**Endangered Species.** The Center for Action on Engangered Species. 175 W. Main St. Ayer, MA 01432. Request free fact sheet about extinction and list of books, posters, and ideas for teaching units on endangered species. Most items $1.00 to $5.00.

GPO Materials. U.S. Gov't Printing Office. Washington, DC 20402. Lists of many low-cost government publications. Sample titles are:

►**Birds** (SB-177). 1982. 5 pp. Free.

Fish and Marine Life (SB-209). 1980. 9 pp. Free.

Homes for Wildlife: Baths and Feeding Shelters—How to Make and Where to Place Them (Bull. #1). Cranbrook Institute of Science. Box 801. Bloomfield Hills, MI 48013. 1969. 36 pp. $1.50. ms-hs.

Horses. American Quarter Horse Assoc. Dept. F & I. Amarillo, TX 79168. Free. A packet of booklets and pictures about the American quarter horse. Several 16 mm sound films also available. ms-hs.

How to Care for, Train, and Feed Your Dog. Ken-L Ration. Div. of Quaker Oats. Box 3180. Libertyville, IL 60048. 1979. 31 pp. Free. Covers housebreaking, grooming, obedience training, birth control, and health care, el-ms.

How to Know the Birds (E9790). The New American Library. 1633 Broadway. New York, NY 10019. 1957. 168 pp. $2.50. An authoritative guide to recognizing over 200 American birds on sight. ms-hs.

Humane Education. American Humane Education Society. Circulation Dept. 350 S. Huntington Ave. Boston, MA 02130. Teaching aids, animal care booklets, posters, kits, calendars, reprints, and professional publications available. Sample titles are:

Animal Care Booklets. 1977. 11 to 28 pp. each. $1.00 each. Series of five books on birds, dogs, small mammals, horses, and cats. el-ms.

►**The Best of Animals.** 1980. 16 pp. $1.25. A booklet of stories, games, and facts about the world of animals. pr.

The Animal Connections. 1977. 25 pp. $1.00. A teacher's guide to humane education activities in all areas of curriculum. el-ms.

Living With Animals. 1977. 32 pp. $1.50. Illustrated book with 23″ x 29″ coloring poster for discussions and activities on living with animals. el-ms.

►**Macomber Farm Coloring Book.** 1982. 20 pp. $1.25. Contains pictures to color and construct. pr.

Pet Care. Animal Protection Institute of America. P.O. Box 22505. Sacramento, CA 95822. A list of materials and low-cost rental films is available. Sample titles are:

Children's Reading List. 10 pp. Single copy free. A listing of books on animals especially geared for young people. el.

Finding Good Homes for Pets. Single copy free. Advice on selecting good homes and good owners for pets. el-hs.

First Aid for Dogs and Cats. 25 cents. 15 pp. Tips and instructions on basic first aid for shock, hemorrhage, fractures, burns, poisoning, etc. ms-hs.

How to Care for Your Pet. Poster, 23″ x 25″. Full color. $2.00. Contains rules for housing, feeding, and handling of ten common pets, including guinea pigs, tropical fish, mice, and rats. el-ms.

Murphy's Law. Poster, 23″ x 25″. Full color. $2.00. Presents seven problems and precautions concerning dogs; includes dognaping, strays, and hot cars.

Wildlife Under Attack. Poster, 23″ x 35″. Full color. $3.00. Depicts the ten most threatened North American species, the future prospect, and how to help. el-ms.

Recommended Reading. 7 pp. Single copy free. A list of books about animals. pr. to ad.

Pet Care. Animal Rescue League of Boston. P.O. Box 265. Boston, MA 02117. Pamphlets about the care and safety of pet animals. Free; send a self-addressed stamped envelope (#10). Titles include:

►**Cats.** 10 pp. Care and training of pet cats. el-ms.

►**Dogs.** 11 pp. Care and training of pet dogs. el-ms.

►**Small Pets.** 8 pp. Pointers on the care of gerbils, guinea pigs, hamsters, mice, rabbits. el-ms.

►**Why Dogs Bite.** 8-page folder. What to do if you meet a strange dog. pr-el.

Pet Problems. American Veterinary Medical Assoc. 930 N. Meacham Rd. Schaumburg, IL 60196. Single copy free for a self-addressed stamped envelope (#10). A series of leaflets which inform pet owners of common disorders of domestic animals. ms-hs-ad. Titles include:

Canine Heartworm Disease

Canine Distemper

Canine Parvovirus Infection

External Parasites

Feline Panleukopenia

Rabies

►**Thirty Birds: An Introduction.** Audubon Naturalist Society. 8940 Jones Mill Road. Chevy Chase, MD 20815. 1964. 36 pp. 1.00. Contains instructions for beginners in the identification and classification of the most common birds in the east central U.S. el-hs.

Welfare Institute Materials. Animal Welfare Institute. P.O. Box 3650. Washington, DC 20007. An annotated listing of educational materials concerning animals is available free.

Whale Conservation Kit. Project Jonah. P.O. Box 40280. San Francisco, CA 94140. Undated. Booklet, leaflet, and poster. A $3.00 donation to cover postage and printing is requested. Kit gives factual information about man's commercial use of whales, porpoises, and dolphins which may cause their extinction. el-ms.

Wildlife Education Posters. National Bowhunter Education Foundation. Rt. 6, Box 199. Murray, KY 42071. 1977. $4.00 per set to teachers and school administrators when ordered on school stationery. Includes eight 11″ x 17″ color posters and eight black-and-white notebook reductions, one vinyl decal, and one iron-on T-shirt transfer for teaching about animals in their natural settings. Prepared by wildlife biologists. el.

Wildlife Kits. Elsa Clubs of America. P.O. Box 4572. N. Hollywood, CA 91607. $2.00 each. Teaching materials consisting of booklets about endangered wildlife. Sample kits are:

►**America's Endangered Wildlife.** 1982. Six 8-page booklets with stories, pictures to color, and worksheets about such animals as the red wolf, California condor, and sea turtle. pr-el.

►**Marine Mammals of the World.** 1979. Two 30-page booklets with worksheets and details on various marine mammals. pr-el.

►**Wildlife Survival.** Wolf Sancturay. Canid Survival and Research Center. P.O. Box 760. Eureka, MO 63025. Packet. $1.00 postage. Information on wolf behavior, habitat, and survival efforts. el.

ARTS AND CRAFTS

AED Is Where It's Art. Art Education Digest. 10068 Cavell. Livonia, MI 48150. 1979. 18 pp. Free. Catalog. Offers hundreds of art units priced from 10 to 20 cents. Order form included. el-ms-hs.

►**Art Activities** (#130-0). Ann Arbor Publishers, Inc. P.O. Box 7249. Naples, FL 33940. 1976. 57 pp. $3.00. Contains a series of projects that art teachers can use to help foster perceptual skills in children aged 7-10. Illustrated. pr-el.

►**Art and Artists** (SB-107). U.S. Gov't. Printing Office. Washington, DC 20402 1982. 10 pp. Free. A listing of many low-cost government publications which may be used in the classroom.

Card Aids. Teachers Exchange of San Francisco. 28 Dawnview. San Francisco, CA 94131. Add 75 cents to prices for shipping. Titles include:

> **More Time to Draw (Cursive).** Set of 16 cards. 5 3/4″ x 8 3/4″. $1.95. Cards with 32 cartoons that help students use their artistic skills and the cursive alphabet. el.
>
> **More Time to Draw (Manuscript).** Set of 16 cards. 5 3/4″ x 8 3/4″. $1.95. Creative cards with 32 cartoons show how to create drawings from the manuscript alphabet. el.
>
> **Time to Draw.** Set of 20 cards. 5 3/4″ x 6 5/8″. $1.95. Drawing is made easy with creative approach using letters, numbers, and other objects. pr-el.

Catalog of Kodak Educational Materials (Ed 2-1). Eastman Kodak Co. Dept. 412L. 343 State St. Rochester, NY 14650. Free. Contains a listing of educational materials available from Kodak. ad.

Exploring the World of the Arts (SC-4306). World Book, Inc. Merchandise Mart Plaza. Chicago, IL 60654. 1978. 8-page foldout. 20 cents. A guide for the student's independent study. An introduction to the many different arts, architecture, decorative arts, literature, music, drama and motion pictures to be found in *World Book*. ms-hs.

Extension Programs. The National Gallery of Art. Extension Service. Washington, DC 20565. 44 pp. Free. A catalog of color slide programs, films, and videocassettes on various aspects of the visual arts designed to develop awareness and appreciation. Available on a free-loan basis to educational institutions, community groups, and individuals. Borrower must pay return postage (4th class library rate).

Photography. Eastman Kodak Co. Dept. 841. 343 State St. Rochester, NY 14650. Single copies of appropriate literature sent free within continental United States and Canada. A variety of literature mainly about photography and its applications. Describe your specific needs in detail. ad.

Resource Handbooks. Instructor Publications, Inc. P.O. Box 6177. Duluth, MN 55806. 48 pp. each. $2.95 each. Several booklets are available which provide content and instructions for classroom activities and experiences in the art curriculum. Send for free catalog for descriptions. el.

Ricecraft. Rice Council. P.O. Box 740121 Houston, TX 77274. Leaflet. Single copy free. Directions for using rice for mosaics, games, toys, and many other things children like to make. pr-el.

Sterling Salt Fun. International Salt Co. Clarks Summit, PA 18411. 1971. Leaflet. Single copy free; requester *must* send a self-addressed stamped envelope (#10). Contains instructions for making beads, ceramics, maps, and decorations using a combination of salt and other common household items. ms.

►**Such Interesting Things to Do.** Scott, Foresman and Co. 1955 Montreal Road. Tucker, GA 30084. 14 pp. Free. Contains classroom activities that teach such things as detail, hand-eye coordination, writing, and auditory discrimination. ps-el.

Suggestions for Your Art Education Program. Public Relations Manager. Binney & Smith Inc. 1100 Church Lane. P.O. Box 431. Easton, PA 18042. Portfolio of 8 pamphlets. Single copy free. Instructions for common and unusual uses of chalk, crayons, tempera paint, water colors, finger paints, and clay. pr-el.

Why Art Education? The National Art Education Assoc. 1916 Association Dr. Reston, VA 22091. 1980. 5 pp. $1.95 for 1 pack (10 copies). Discusses the value of an art curriculum in the school and how parents can encourage children's interest in art. ad.

ASTRONOMY AND SPACE SCIENCE

Astronomical Photographs. Lick Observatory OP. University of California. Santa Cruz, CA 95064. 1977. 18 pp. 50 cents. Black-and-white photo-illustrated catalogue of astronomical slides and prints. el-ms-hs-ad.

►***Bibliographies.*** National Space Institute. West Wing Suite 203. 600 Maryland Ave., S.W. Washington, DC 20024. Send for information about a series of reference bibliographies on astronomy and space topics, including celestial mechanics, black holes, satellites, space shuttle, and space colonies. hs-ad.

Edmund Materials. Edmund Scientific Co. 7082 Edscorp Bldg. Barrington, NJ 08007. Send for catalog of publications about telescopes and astronomical observation.

►**The Friendly Stars.** Dover Publications. 180 Varich St. New York, NY 10014. 1966. 147 pp. $2.75. A classic for beginning astronomy. Details on how to locate and identify the conspicuous stars of the northern hemisphere. ms-hs.

GPO Materials. U.S. Gov't. Printing Office. Washington, DC 20402. Lists of many low-cost government publications which may be used in the classroom. Sample titles are:

►**Astronomy and Astrophysics** (SB-115). 1981. 11 pp. Free.

►**NASA Educational Publications** (SB-222). 1982. 10 pp. Free.

►**Space, Rockets, and Satellites** (SB-297). 1982. 20 pp. Free.

►**A Guide to the Phases of the Moon.** Jenny Pon. P.O. Box 1845. East Lansing, MI 48823. 1982. 27 pp. $1.50. A study guide with numerous clear illustrations, concept-developing and outside-observing activities, and answers to help observers develop an awareness of where the moon is at any time of the day. ms-hs-ad.

Kits and Packets. Astronomical Society of the Pacific. 1290 24th Ave. San Francisco, CA 94122. A series of informational packets of articles written in non-technical language are available at cost plus mailing. Titles include:

►**Black Holes.** $2.00. Several non-technical articles on various kinds of black holes. Includes further reading list. hs-ad.

►**New Views of Mars.** $1.00. Includes complete photographic map of Mars, a set of 3-D photos (with 3-D glasses for viewing), articles, and reading list. Assembled from recent space-craft data. hs-ad.

Other Materials

►**Index to Mercury Magazine Articles.** 1982. 6 pp. Free for two first-class stamps. A subject index to astronomy articles in the first ten volumes of *Mercury* magazine. Authors include Carl Sagan, Isaac Asimov, and William Kaufmann. hs-ad.

►**Index to N.A.S.A. Astronomy Books.** 1981. 6 pp. Free for two first-class stamps. Provides sources for books published by the space agency during the last 20 years that have gone unpublicized. hs-ad.

►**Update: Debunking Pseudoscience.** 1979. 4 pp. 50 cents. An annotated bibliography covering scientific views of UFO's, astrology, ancient astronauts, the Bermuda Triangle, and other areas of "fringe science." hs-ad.

Meteorites. American Meteorite Laboratory. P.O. Box 2098.Denver, CO 80201. Sample titles are:

Ask a Question About Meteorites. 87 pp. $2.54. Answers questions most commonly asked about meteors, meteorites, meteorite craters, and tektites. Illustrated. ms-hs.

Chips From the Moon. 41 pp. $1.28. Explains the theory that tektites are bits of moon rock landed on our planet. Illustrated. ms-hs.

A Comet Strikes the Earth. 65 pp. $2.41. Presents basic information about meteorites and contains a sample of oxidized meteorite from the Arizona meteorite crater. Illustrated. ms.

Meteorite Crater Study Kit. $3.85. Kit contains samples of the major types of meteoritic material found around the Arizona meteorite crater; also contains *A Comet Strikes the Earth.* ms.

Meteorites Are Valuable for Research—How to Recognize Them. Leaflet. 4 pp. Free. Illustrated.

►**NASA Films.** National Audiovisual Center. General Services Administration. Information Services Section/PR. Washington, DC 20409. 1979. 28 pp. Free. Catalog of 16 mm films available on free loan basis which present phases of the U.S. space program and aspects of space living and experimentation.

Rocketry. Estes Industries, Inc. Robert L. Cannon, Manager of Educational Services. Dept. 165. Penrose, CO 81240. Titles include:

►**Aerospace Education and Model Rockerty** (#2816). 1970. 36 pp. $1.70. A comprehensive teacher's guide on use of model rockerty in learning activities. G4-10.

Alpha Book of Model Rocketry (# 02820). 32 pp. 95 cents. A "first book" for beginners in model rocketry. Includes flight data sheet to record first four missions. ms.

►**Countdown: Mathematics and Model Rockerty** (#2855). 1981. 44 pp. $1.60. A teacher's guide for hands-on and theoretical learning with model rockerty in the mathematics classroom. ms-hs.

Educator's Packet for Model Rocketry (EP-#1452). $1.00 when requested on school letterhead. Contains information on educational applications of model rocketry and on introducing a model rocketry program. Includes Alpha model rocket kit, catalog, teacher's guide, and ordering information.

►**Industrial Arts Teachers Manual for Model Rockerty** (#2810). 1980. 52 pp. $1.20. Outlines specific applications in the study of manufacturing, transportation, research, and construction. ms-hs.

Laws of Motion and Model Rocketry (#02821). 12 pp. 55 cents. Three laws explained in terms which most students of eleven or older can understand. Includes simple experiments and a self-test for each law. ms-hs.

Model Rocket Launch Systems (#02811). 20 pp. 70 cents. Book contains photographs and schematics for easy understanding of the information, including the electrical system of launchers. ms-hs.

►**Space Age Technology** (#2813). 1970. 52 pp. $1.70. Text for mini-course in aerospace education. ms-hs.

Search for Life in the Universe (Vol. 22, No. 10). Center for Information on America. Washington, CT 06793. 1973. 4 pp. 35 cents. Considers the probability of life and civilizations in space and the question of whether attempts to find and communicate with them should be made. hs.

Sky Calendar. Michigan State University. Abrams Planetarium. East Lansing, MI 48824. Monthly publication; mailed quarterly. $5.00 per year; or 13 cents per copy on orders of 50 or more per month. A daily guide to naked-eye astronomy which helps the student watch the sky regularly and notice its changes. ms-ad.

Space Photos. Space Photos. 2608 Sunset Blvd. Houston, TX 77005. 35 mm slides, prints, and posters of all the manned space flights from Gemini IV through Apollo, Skylab, Apollo-Soyez, and the Space Shuttle. Send $2.00 for catalogs.

Space Primer. The Aerospace Corp. Office of Information. P.O. Box 92957. Los Angeles, CA 90009. Rev. 1981. 24 pp. Free. Available in classroom quantities to junior high and high school teachers. An illustrated booklet depicting some fundamentals of space science. ms-hs.

AUDIO-VISUAL

AIT Newsletter. Agency for Instructional Television. Box A. Bloomington, IN 47402. Quarterly. 8 pp. Free to media directors and school administrators. Current information on use of television and related technologies in education. ad.

The American Film Review. The American Educational and Historical Film Center. Eastern College. St. Davids, PA 19087. 1981. 31 pp. Free. A review of films endorsed by a committee of educators for classroom use at all levels.

Bibliographies. National Audio-Visual Assoc. 3150 Spring St. Fairfax, VA 22031. Offers a set of seven bibliographies on AV subjects and two basic tips pamphlets. One set free for a self-addressed envelope (#10) bearing stamps for three ounces. ad. Titles include:

- ►**Basic Tips on Preparing for a Meeting That Uses Slides**
- ►**Basic Tips on Producing and Using Overhead Transparencies**
- ►**Bibliography on Designing A-V and Video Facilities**
- ►**Bibliography on Motion Pictures**
- ►**Bibliography on Still Images for Projection**
- ►**Bibliography on Television and Video**

Educational Films. Modern Talking Picture Service. Film Scheduling Center. 5000 Park St., N. St. Petersburg, FL 33709. Annual catalog available free. Provides a large library of free-loan and rental films.

Federal A/V Materials. National Audiovisual Center. General Services Adm. Information Services Section. Washington, DC 20409. Information about many low-cost rental audiovisual materials and free-loan referrals, when available. Separate lists available for alcohol and drugs, career education, business and government management, consumer education, American history, science, space exploration, vocational education, and other subjects. Titles include:

A List of Audiovisual Materials Produced by the United States Government for Environment and Energy Conservation. 1980. 17 pp. Free.

A List of Audiovisual Materials Produced by the United States Government for Foreign Language Instruction. 1980. 7 pp. Free.

Film List. The Travelers Film Library. 1 Tower Square. Hartford, CT 06115. Free. A descriptive list of free-loan films (16 mm, color, 10 to 58 min.) on topics concerning physical fitness, sports, history, financial planning, and safety. Most films are supplemented with printed materials for classroom use. Borrower pays return postage or shipping costs.

GPO Listings. U.S. Gov't. Printing Office. Washington, DC 20402. Lists of many low-cost government publications. Sample titles are:

Motion Pictures, Films, and Audiovisual Information (SB-073). 1980. 4 pp. Free.

►**Posters, Charts, Picture Sets, and Decals** (SB-057). 1982. 20 pp. Free.

The Overhead Projector in the Mathematics Classroom. National Council of Teachers of Mathematics. 1906 Association Dr. Reston, VA 20091. 1974. 32 pp. $2.00. Emphasizes applications to teaching math and describes techniques for making more effective use of the aid. Extensive bibliography included. ad.

Posters and Prints. Giant Photos. Box 406. Rockford, IL 61105. A large assortment of color posters and pictures are available for 30 cents to $1.50. Send for free brochure.

Records for Children. Enoch Pratt Free Library. Publications. 400 Cathedral St. Baltimore, MD 21201. 1970. 61 pp. 75 cents. An annotated list of activity, story, and music recordings for young children. pr-el.

Reference Lists. National Audiovisual Center. General Services Administration. Information Services Section/PR. Washington, DC 20409. Offers listings of thousands of A-V materials available; many are low-cost rental or free loan. Titles are:

A Reference List of Audiovisual Materials Produced by the United States Government. 1978. 354 pp. Free. Lists over 6000 titles in 30 subject areas.

A Reference List of Audiovisual Materials Produced by the United States Government—Supplement 1980. 1980. 54 pp. Free. Lists over 900 titles in 34 subject areas.

Resource Handbooks. Instructor Publications, Inc. P.O. Box 6177. Duluth, MN 55806. 48 pp. each. $2.95 each. Several booklets are available which provide suggestions and instructions for classroom bulletin boards and displays related to the curriculum. Send for free catalog for descriptions. pr-el.

►**Take a Lesson From TV.** CBS Educational & Community Services. CBS Broadcast Group. 51 West 52 St. New York, NY 10019. 1980. 16 pp. Free. A curriculum project that demonstrates how teachers, students, and their families can use TV for learning in several subject areas. References. el.

Visual Aids Posters. Hayes School Publishing Co., Inc. 321 Pennwood Ave. Wilkinsburg, PA 15221. Color illustrations with text for bulletin boards. Eight pictures per title. $2.50 each. pr-el. Sample titles are:

Dinosaurs and Prehistoric Animals	**Health**
Familiar Animals We Should Know	**Nursery Rhymes**
Good Manners	**Safety**

AUSTRALIA AND NEW ZEALAND

Australia. Australian Information Service. Australian Consulate-General. 636 5th Ave. New York, NY 10020. A variety of free literature is offered; describe your interest with request. U.S. distribution only. ms-hs.

►**New Zealand.** New Zealand Consulate General. 630 5th Ave., Suite 530. New York, NY 10111; or Alcoa Building, Suite 970. 1 Maritime Plaza. San Francisco, CA 94111; or Tishman Building, Suite 1530. 10960 Wilshire Blvd. Los Angeles, CA 90024. Single copy free in U.S. "New Zealand Information Pack" contains a sheet of 30 color pictures to decorate walls or bulletin boards, and a sheet of explanatory captions. Also included are a booklet, "About New Zealand," and an outline map. el-ms.

New Zealand. New Zealand Embassy. 37 Observatory Circle, N. W. Washington, DC 20008. Free to teachers. A teacher's packet containing catalogs of films, "About New Zealand," fact sheets, small flag replicas, and a map. ms-hs.

Visual Geography Series. Sterling Publishing Co. 2 Park Ave. New York, NY 10016. 64 pp. each. $2.95 each. Orders must be prepaid and include postage. Booklets discuss the land, history, people, government, and economy of each country. Illustrated with photographs and maps. ms. Sample titles are:

New Zealand in Pictures

Tahiti in Pictures

BIOGRAPHY

Edison—the Man Who Turned Darkness into Light. Thomas Alva Edison Foundation. Cambridge Office Plaza, Suite 143. 18280 W. Ten Mile Rd. Southfield, MI 48075. 1978. 56 pp. $1.00 each/three for $2.00. Contains text, a photographic section of Edison's accomplishments, and a chronology of significant events in Edison's lifetime. el-ms.

Famous People: Historical, Biographical Book of Birthdays. Louis F. Mlecka, Publisher. P.O. Box 908. Brookville, FL 33512. 1973. 300+ pp. $1.95. Consists of several thousand short biographies of famous people arranged according to date of birth. Compiled for U.S. Bicentennial observance. ms-hs.

Herbert Hoover, Humanitarian. Hoover Presidential Library Assoc., Inc. P.O. Box 696. West Branch, IA 52348. 1960. 200 pp. Free. A biography of an orphaned Quaker boy from Iowa who became a foremost mining engineer and our 31st president. el-ms.

I Know Why the Caged Bird Sings (#22547-2). Bantam Books. 666 Fifth Ave. New York, NY 10103. 1971. 246 pp. $2.95. Maya Angelou's autobiography of a black girl growing up in the South in the 1930s. hs-ad.

Mentor and Signet Books. New American Library. 1633 Broadway. New York, NY 10019. Extensive paperback books in the category of biography are available from this publisher at prices ranging from $1.50 to $2.95. Write for complete listing of titles and prices. Sample titles are:

> **Karl Marx: An Intimate Biography** (ME1897). 1978. 406 pp. $3.50. A balanced, candid, and far-reaching appraisal of the complex and contradictory Karl Marx. hs-ad.
>
> **Mao** (ME1845). 1976. 196 pp. $2.25. A study of the man who led China into the modern world. hs-ad.

Notable Americans. Hoover Presidential Library Assoc., Inc. P.O. Box 696. West Branch, IA 52348. Free to educational institutions requesting on official letterhead. Titles are:

- ►**J. Edgar Hoover, Modern Knight Errant.** 1959. 130 pp. A biographical sketch of the late director of the FBI.
- ►**Charles A. Lindbergh, Aviation Pioneer.** 1970. 189 pp. A biography of the first person to fly across the Atlantic Ocean.
- ►**Lowell Thomas, Adventurer.** 1965. 239 pp. The life story of one of history's greatest travellers and commentators.

Pamphlets. American Foundation for the Blind. 15 W. 16th St. New York, NY 10011. Single copy free. Titles are:

> **Louis Braille.** 12 pp. A brief account of the life of the inventor of Braille communication. el-ms.
>
> **Helen Keller.** 6 pp. A brief record of the achievements of a woman who overcame being a deaf and blind mute. el-ms.
>
> **Helen Keller: An Annotated Bibliography.** 5 pp. Reviews over 30 books about Helen Keller, including ten children's books. ad.

William Penn, Architect of a Nation. Pennsylvania Historical and Museum Commission. William Penn Memorial Museum and Archives Bldg. Box 1026. Harrisburg, PA 17120. 1980. 77 pp. $2.75. Concise account of the influence of the founder of Pennsylvania on the evolution of America. hs-ad.

Will Rogers. Will Rogers Memorial. P.O. Box 157. Claremore, OK 74017. Free. Fact sheets covering various aspects of Will Rogers' life. ms-hs-ad.

BIOLOGY AND NATURE

Adventures With a Microscope. Dover Publications, Inc. 180 Varick Street. New York, NY 10014. 1941. 232 pp. $3.00. Presents 59 interesting investigation using the microscope, with 142 illustrations. ms-hs.

Booklets. Chevron Chemical Co. Public Affairs. P.O. Box 3744. San Francisco, CA 94119. Single copies free to teachers unless priced. Titles are:

> **A Is for Apple.** 1977. 8 pp. A booklet of classroom ideas for teaching about tree and fruit growth. pr-el.
>
> **Celebration of Life: Trees.** 1978. 16 pp. Teacher's Guide. Helps children identify with the world of trees and their influence on their personal lives. el.
>
> **Rural School Garden.** 12 pp. 25 cents. Describes an outdoor garden project at a country school. Covers seed germination, planting, and so on. el.

►**Ecological Super-Posters.** Chevron Chemical Co. Public Affairs. P.O. Box 3744. San Francisco, CA 94119. Set of 6 posters. 24" x 36". Full color. Mailed in tube. $3.00. Posters deal with plants, trees, and insects. Accompanying teacher's guide suggests class experiments in notation, classification, surveying, plant development, and other activities. pr-el.

Experiments for Children. Dover Publications, Inc. 180 Varick St. New York, NY 10014. Contains basic information and a number of experiments ranging from simple to complex. Titles include:

> **Biology Experiments for Children.** 1968. 95 pp. $2.25. el.
>
> **Human Anatomy for Children.** 1968. 95 pp. $2.50. el.

Great Lakes. Sea Grant Institute. Communications Office. University of Wisconsin. 1800 University Ave. Madison, WI 53706. Three booklets. 50 cents each plus 50 cents for postage for each title ordered. Titles are:

►**Educators Guide to Great Lakes Materials** (#600). 1978. 39 pp. An annotated reference to non-fiction, fiction, films, maps, charts, and other materials selected as suitable teaching aids. ms.

►**Fish of Lake Michigan** (#121). 1974. 32 pp. Covers 21 species of fish. hs-ad.

►**Fish of Lake Superior** (#124). 1976. 36 pp. Covers 23 species of fish. Illustrated. hs-ad.

How to Care for Living Things in the Classroom. National Science Teachers Assoc. 1742 Connecticut Ave., N.W. Washington, DC 20009. 1978. 20 pp. $1.50. Suggestions for ways to feed and care for animals and plants in the elementary classroom. ad.

Human Anatomy Atlas. Hammond, Inc. 515 Valley St. Maplewood, NJ 07040. 1960. 36 pp. $2.21. A device for learning the structure of the human body. Illustrated in color. ms-hs.

Humane Education. Animal Welfare Institute. P.O. Box 3650. Washington, DC 20007. Single copy free to teachers and librarians. An annotated listing of educational materials is available free.

Laboratory Animals. National Society for Medical Research. 1029 Vermont Ave., N.W. Washington, DC 20005. Single copy free except as indicated. Titles include:

►**Animal Welfare Act—1976.** 12 pp. Public Law 89-544 reprinted in full with amendments. ad.

►**A Career in Laboratory Animal Science and Technology.** 1972. 4 pp. Describes career opportunities in the field of lab animal science. Notes on preparation and lists of schools and programs are included. hs.

►**Do We Care About Research Animals?** (NIH 79-355). Leaflet. Describes efforts of the National Institutes of Health to aid the care and treatment of lab animals through study of specific animal diseases. ms-hs.

►**Guide for the Care and Use of Laboratory Animals.** (NIH 80-23). Rev. 1978. 70 pp. Covers housing, sanitation practices, provisions for emergency care, euthanasia, and surgery. Appendix includes animal technology programs, federal rules and regulations, and bibliography. ad.

►**Student's Guide—Animals in Biology.** 7 pp. 5 copies free; additional copies 25 cents each. A general guide to the proper care and treatment of laboratory animals. el-ms.

Nature by the Month. The Interstate Printers and Publishers, Inc. 19-27 Jackson St. Danville, IL 61832. 1976. 80 pp. $2.95. Numerous activities can be performed in the home, the classroom and the field to get closer to nature and its many intriguing experiences. el-ms.

1001 Questions Answered About Earthquakes, Avalanches, Floods and Other Natural Disasters. Dover Publications, Inc. 180 Varick St. New York, NY 10014. 1969. 350 pp. $4.00. Violent acts of nature discussed in layman's terms with emphasis on their destructive impact, underlying causes, scientific structures, patterns of behavior, and even some beneficial results. ms-hs-ad.

►***Popular Science Series.*** Illinois State Museum Society. Springfield, IL 62706. Cost vary from 50 cents to $4.50. Nontechnical books on natural history (birds, flowers, fossils, reptiles, etc.) for general reading and field study. Send for complete listing. hs-ad.

Schematic Section of the Human Eye. American Optometric Assoc. Communications Div. 243 N. Lindbergh Blvd. St. Louis, MO 63141. 1979. 2 pp. Single copy free with self-addressed stamped envelope (#10). Diagram of the parts of the human eye with definitions of parts. el-ms.

Southwest Nature Booklets. Southwest Parks and Monuments Assoc. Box 1562. Globe, AZ 85501. Books include detailed illustrations, descriptions, and pictures of wildlife in different areas of the Southwest. Sample titles are:

> **Flowers of the Southwest Deserts.** 1980. 112 pp. $3.50. Contains over 140 of the most interesting and common desert flowers, with 4-page centerfold of flowers in full color. ad.
>
> **Poisonous Dwellers of the Desert.** 1976. 48 pp. $3.00. Tells facts about bites and stings and their treatment, and how to recognize poisonous and harmless animals. ad.

Weeds of the North Central States (B-772). Agricultural Experiment Station. University of Illinois at Urbana-Champaign. Urbana, IL 61801. Rev. 1981. 303 pp. $3.00. Identifies over 200 weeds of economic importance. ad.

BUSINESS EDUCATION

Bibliography on Proprietary Postsecondary Education. Assoc. of Independent Colleges & Schools. 1730 M St., N.W. Washington, DC 20036. 1980. 16 pp. $2.00. A selected list of current and classic titles on postsecondary education of interest to business school educators. ad.

Business in America. American Institute of Cooperation. 1800 Massachusetts Ave., N. W.—Suite 508. Washington, DC 20036. Single copy free. Titles include:

►**Business in Our Community.** Rev. 1982. 24 pp. A guide explaining the business side of any community to satisfy the needs of people. Emphasis is on different methods of doing business in America. ms.

How We Organize to Do Business in America. 1970. 34 pp. Discusses individual ownership, partnerships, cooperatives, and other types of corporations. hs.

The Glossary of Sales and Marketing Definitions. Henry Lavin Associates, Inc. 12 Promontory Drive. Cheshire, CT 06410. 1974. 48 pp. $1.50. A handy guide to commonly-used terms for the layman as well as those engaged in buying and selling occupations. hs.

A Guide to Conducting Meetings (#137-195). Abingdon. Customer Service Dept. 201 Eighth Ave. S. Nashville, TN 37202. 1965. 80 pp. $2.75. Payment should accompany all orders; schools and libraries entitled to 25% discount. Presents the fundamentals to conduct a business meeting in an orderly manner. ms-hs.

NCR Materials. NCR Corp. Customer and Support Education. Special Order Dept. Sugar Camp Education Center. Dayton, OH 45479. Send for free *NCR Educational Publications Catalog.* Orders for single copies must include 50 cents for shipping and handling; orders over $10.00 must include 5%. Educational discount of 20% on orders over $25.00. Titles include:

Basic Business Accounting. 1978. 43 pp. $5.00. Illustrates in detail typical business transactions and how they relate to the general ledger, income statements, and balance sheets. hs-ad.

Financial Terminology. 1973. 48 pp. $3.50. A glossary of over 950 terms for personal and classroom reference in the study of money, banking, and related subjects. hs-ad.

Retail Terminology. 1977. 48 pp. $2.50. A glossary of over 800 terms inherent in the retailing industry, including EDP terms and language. hs-ad.

Policies for Protection. American Council of Life Insurance. Education Services. 1850 K St., N.W. Washington, DC 20006. 1978. 31 pp. Up to 100 copies free to teachers of business education classes. A text-workbook especially for 9th and 10th grade basic business courses; covers life and health insurance policies, how they work, and the economics of personal insurance. hs.

SBA Publications. Lists of free publications are obtainable by writing Small Business Administration offices located in most principal cities. Consult telephone directory. Publications include management aids, technical aids, small business bibliographies, and management research summaries which may be ordered from the SBA or the U.S. Gov't. Printing Office.

Secretarial Guidesheets. Career Advancement Leaflets. c/o Dr. Alan C. Lloyd, Editor. Olsten Temporary Services. Caller Box 1014. Westbury, NY 11590. A series of "how to" guides on punctuation, spelling, proofreading, and other aspects of office communication. Each deals with a single topic. 1-4 pp. each. 8½" x 11". Prepunched for 3-ring notebook. Single copies free for a self-addressed stamped envelope (#10); multiple copies available to teachers. Titles include:

►**How to Arrange Business Letters**

►**How to Avoid Sex Bias**

►**How to Avoid the 100 Worst Spelling Threats**

►**How to File Alphabetically**

►**How to Divide Words**

►**How to Express Numbers**

►**How to Proofread Your Work**

►**How to Space After Punctuation**

►**How to Use the Quotation Mark**

►**How to Use the Super-Coma: The Semicolon**

Stenography, Typing, and Writing (SB-087). U.S. Gov't. Printing Office. Washington, DC 20402. 1982. 4 pp. Free. A listing of many low-cost government publications which may be used in the classroom.

Trademarks. The United States Trademark Assoc. 6 E. 45th St. New York, NY 10017. Single copy free. Titles include:

A Guide to the Care of Trademarks. 1974. 4 pp. Explains the proper use of trademarks. hs.

How to Use a Trademark Properly. 1971. 6 pp. Rules for proper use. hs.

►**Trademark Clearance.** 1982. 4 pp. Explains why new trademarks are cleared before using. hs.

A Trademark Is Not a Copyright or a Patent. 1977. 6 pp. Reflects new copyright law. hs.

Trademarks Promote U. S. Economic Growth. 1973. 4 pp. hs.

Typing Skills. Cleeg Enterprises. 422 Black Hawk Lane. Stratford, CT 06497. Titles are:

Module for Learning Typewriting. 1973. 64 pp. $1.00. Provides most of the essentials for a one-semester course in typing. hs-ad.

Taxonomy of Skills for Typing a Table. 1976. 11 pp. 60 cents. A detailed analysis of all skills needed to type a table or tabulation problem. hs-ad.

CANADA

Booklets. Canadian National Department of Public Relations. P.O. Box 8100. Montreal, Quebec. Canada H3C 3N4. Free; one copy of either title only per request. Available in French and English. Titles are:

►**CN Today.** 23 pp. Includes photographs. ms-hs.

►**Growing Up With Canada.** 1979. 23 pp. History of Canadian railway system. Includes photographs. ms-hs.

British Columbia. Ministry of Tourism. Gov't. of British Columbia. 1117 Wharf St. Victoria, B.C. Canada V8W 2Z2. Inquire about free materials for students and teachers. el-ms-hs.

Canada. Sterling Publishing Co. 2 Park Ave. New York, NY 10016. 64 pp. $2.95; orders must be prepaid and include postage. A Visual Geography Series book which covers the land, history, people, government, and economy. Illustrated with photographs and maps. ms.

►**Canada** (SB-278). U.S. Gov't. Printing Office. Washington, DC 20402. 1981. 8 pp. Free. A listing of many low-cost government publications which may be used in the classroom.

►***Manitoba.*** Travel Manitoba. Dept. 3113. Winnipeg, Manitoba. R3C 0V8. Canada. Free. Request the ''Welcome to Manitoba Canada'' folder.

New Brunswick. New Brunswick Tourism. P.O. Box 12345. Fredericton, New Brunswick. Canada E3B 5C3. Free travel information available.

Newfoundland and Labrador. Dept. of Development. Tourism Div. P.O. Box 2016. St. John's, Newfoundland. Canada A1C 5R8. Inquire about materials free to teachers.

►**Publications Available Outside Canada** (#39). Dept. of External Affairs. External Information Div. Ottawa. Canada K1A 0G2. Rev. 1982. Free. A listing of reference papers, brochures on science and technology, statements on current topics, and other materials available free to persons outside Canada. English and French editions.

Vancouver, British Columbia. Greater Vancouver Convention and Visitors Bureau. 1055 W. Georgia St. P.O. Box 11142 Royal Centre. Vancouver, B.C. Canada V6E 4C8. Free materials about Vancouver and surrounding areas.

Yukon. Yukon Inquiry Centre. Government of the Yukon Territory. Box 2703. Whitehorse, Yukon Territory. Canada. Send for colorful free folders and pamphlets concerning Yukon attractions and government. el-ms.

CAREERS

Note: These entries are arranged alphabetically under four subdivisions which appear in the following order: General, Business, Professional, and Scientific and Technical.

General

Career Communicator. ITT Educational Services. Marketing: Public Relations. 3500 DePauw Blvd. P.O. Box 68888. Indianapolis, IN 46268. Quarterly. Free. Newsletter on job outlook and career education trends. hs.

Career Guidance. Careers, Inc. P.O. Box 135. Largo, FL 33540. Offers a wide variety of materials designed for career awareness, orientation, and exploration. Career Summaries, Job Guides, and Briefs for over 600 career titles give information on duties, working conditions, education, outlook, requirements, and pay. Materials are available in kit files, by subscription, or by individual title. Current catalog and free samples on request.

►**Career World.** Curriculum Innovations, Inc. 3500 Western Ave. Highland Park, IL 60035. Magazine. 9 issues yearly. Sample issue free to teachers. Each issue contains a variety of articles on the latest career information. ms-hs.

Careers for Women. Catalyst. 14 E. 60th St. New York, NY 10022. Offers four series and other publications to women in choosing and planning careers. Send for complete listing. Materials include:

Career Option Series for Undergraduate Women. A series of 12. $2.95 each. Booklets on new career opportunities for women in ten traditionally male-dominated fields, such as accounting, industrial management, and sales. hs.

Career Opportunities Series. A series of 27. $2.00 each. Booklets cover a range of fields, including advertising, fundraising, personnel, real estate, and urban planning. Information on training, career paths, job descriptions, and working conditions. hs.

►**Making the Most of Your First Job** (B4P). 1981. 219 pp. $2.50. Offers advice and insights on surviving one's first job, both personally and professionally, and moving on to advancement and achievement. hs-ad.

►**Marketing Yourself** (B3P). 1981. 185 pp. $3.50. Step-by-step instructions on how to write an effective resume and to conduct oneself confidently in a job interview. hs-ad.

Civil Service Materials. U. S. Civil Service Commission. Washington, DC 20415. The material may also be obtained from the nearest Federal Job Information Center. Free. hs-ad.

►**Experience Exploration** (EESPT). Chronicle Guidance Publs., Inc. Moravia, NY 13118. 1981. 10 pp. $1.00 plus 10% shipping ($1.00 min.). A survey instrument to assess career interests based on evaluation of experiences. G9-14. Request free brochure and sample set (EESS).

Exploring the World of Work (SC-4307). World Book, Inc. Merchandise Mart Plaza. Chicago, IL 60654. 1978. 8-page foldout. 20 cents. A guide for the student's independent study. Helps students realize that there are many kinds of occupations and encourages them to explore in the process of narrowing the field. ms-hs.

Federal Job Information Centers. U.S. Civil Service Commission. Washington, DC 20415. 1981. 8 pp. Free. A directory of local Federal Job Information Centers by state which gives addresses and telephone numbers. hs-ad.

Federal Publications. U.S. Dept. of Labor. Bureau of Labor Statistics. Address to any of these locations: 1371 Peachtree St., N.E. Atlanta, GA 30309; 1603 JFK Federal Bldg. Boston, MA 02203; 230 South Dearborn St. Chicago, IL 60604; 555 Griffin Sq. Bldg.—2nd Flr. Dallas, TX 75202; 911 Walnut St. Kansas City, MO 64106; 1515 Broadway. New York, NY 10036; P.O. Box 13309. Philadelphia, PA 19101; 450 Golden Gate Ave. Box 36017. San Francisco, CA 94102. For cost items, send check or money order payable to the Superintendent of Documents. Titles include:

A Counselor's Guide to Occupational Information, Revised 1980 (BLS Bull. 2042). 1980. 60 pp. $5.00. An annotated listing of federal publications on occupations and careers; overseas jobs; special programs or jobs for minorities, women, veterans, and youth; student financial aid; job search; career education; statistics; and bibliographies. ad.

Exploring Careers (BLS Bull. 2001). A set of 15 booklets. 1979. 28 to 50 pp. each. $2.25 each; $13.00 for set of 15. Designed for middle school and junior high school students to promote career awareness. Contains text, photographs, evaluative questions, suggested activities, and career games. Send for complete listing and order form. Sample booklets are:

Health Occupations

Mechanics and Repairers

Service Occupations

Transportation Occupations

The World of Work and You

►**Occupational Outlook Handbook Reprints, 1982-83 Edition.** A series of 27 leaflets. $2.25 each; $13.00/set. Each reprint describes the nature of the work, training requirements, earnings, and job prospects to 1990 in a group of occupations or industries—for example, printing and publishing occupations. Send for complete listing of reprint titles and order form. ad.

Game Books. Chronicle Guidance Publications, Inc. Moravia, NY 13118. A series of classroom gamebooks that uses pictures, poems, puzzles to stimulate awareness of various occupations. Add 10% of order total for shipping ($1.00 min.). Titles are:

Community Careering (ECP2). 1974. 59 pp. $2.00. Designed for grades 3-4. Instructor's guide $3.00.

Curriculum Careering (ECP3). 1978. 58 pp. $2.00. Designed for grades 5-6. Instructor's guide $3.00.

World of Workers (EW1). 1981. 75 pp. $2.00. Designed for grades 2-3.

How to Get and Keep the Right Job. Carnation Co. Public Relations. 5045 Wilshire Blvd. Los Angeles, CA 90036. Pamphlet. 6 pp. Free. Gives advice for job interviewing and pointers for being a good employee. Also in Spanish. hs.

►**How to Write an Effective Resume.** Cumberland Personnel Service. 1600 Boston Neck Rd. Saunderstown, RI 02874. 1980. 11 pp. $2.00. Gives practical pointers for the preparation of resumes by job-seekers. ms-ad.

Job Fact Sheets. Council for Career Planning, Inc. 310 Madison Ave. New York, NY 10017. Published bi-annually. 2 pp. $1.00 each; sold individually or by subscription. Sheets describe the nature of the job, specific work involved, requisite education, and organizations to contact. Write for free listing of 216 occupations. hs. Sample titles are:

►**Computer Operating Personnel** (#220)

►**Engineering and Science Technicians** (#213)

►**Homemaker-Home Health Aide** (#208)

►**Photographic Laboratory Technician** (#216)

►**Reservation and Passenger Agent** (#221)

►**Telephone and PBX Installer and Repairer** (#211)

►**Job Hunter's Handbook** (#3877). Arco Publishing Co. Educational Div. 219 Park Ave., S. New York, NY 10003. 2nd ed. 1980. 104 pp. $2.25; send payment with order. Covers many aspects of seeking work, such as writing resumes, reading advertisements, using agencies and services, and handling interviews. hs.

Job Prospects. Consumer Information Center. Pueblo, CO 81009. Titles include:

> **Job Service: How It Works for You.** 1979. 10 pp. Free. Explains services for the job-seeker provided by 2,500 public employment offices around the country. hs-ad.
>
> **Occupations in Demand** (531J). Monthly. Free. Lists the number of job openings for over 100 occupations and the cities where they are available. hs-ad.

Military—Air Force. Air Force Opportunities Center. P.O. Box 9339. N. Hollywood CA 91609. Free. Information on career opportunities in the Air Force. hs-ad.

Military—Army. U.S. Army Recruiting Command. Fort Sheridan, IL 60037. Free. A variety of materials describing army opportunities for both men and women. hs-ad.

Military—Coast Guard. U.S. Coast Guard. Commandant (G-PMR-4162). Washington, DC 20590. Free. A variety of information available about the work of the Coast Guard and about careers and opportunities in it for those who want to enlist after high school or college, or to attend the U.S. academy. hs-ad.

Military—Navy. Recruiting Advertising Dept. Navy Recruiting Command. Director of Distribution. 4015 Wilson Blvd. Arlington, VA 22203. Free. A variety of literature available on Navy programs for enlisted and commissioned personnel including educational opportunities in medicine, health, and other professions, and in scientific and technical areas such as nuclear power, electronics, and aviation. hs-ad.

Occupational Briefs. Chronicle Guidance Publications. Moravia, NY 13118. 4 pp. each. $1.00 each plus 10% for shipping ($1.00 min.). A series of career information briefs on 480 occupations; written for high school students. Each brief is coded to the *Dictionary of Occupational Titles.* Send for free listing. hs-ad.

6 Steps to Selecting a Satisfying Career. R.A. ''Dick'' Patton. 4172 Emerald Dr. Decatur, GA 30035. Undated. 6 pp. Free for a self-addressed stamped business envelope (#10). Suggests a method of identifying potential career choices. hs-ad.

Wall Charts. Garrett Park Press. Garrett Park, MD 20896. Series of 25 wall charts 15″ x 17″. $2.00 each; additional copies $1.50 each. Send payment with order. Designed as career education resource for counselors, teachers, and students. Revised and updated on a regular basis. Sample titles are:

> ►**Earnings by Occupation: Profit Making Industries.** 1982. Gives average annual income for many occupations in business and industry. hs-ad.

►**Overseas Employment: Myths and Facts.** 1979. Provides sources of information on job opportunities for Americans abroad. hs-ad.

►**Women in Nontraditional Occupations.** 1980. Presents factual data on women who work in jobs traditionally dominated by men. ms-hs.

Writing Resumes, Locating Jobs, and Handling Job Interviews. Dow Jones-Irwin. A Div. of Richard D. Irwin, Inc. 1818 Ridge Road. Homewood, IL 60430. 1976. 112 pp. $4.95. A personal learning aid to guide the job hunter, including samples, interview guides, and forms used by employment personnel. Includes glossary. hs.

Business

►**The Actuarial Profession.** Society of Actuaries. 208 S. LaSalle St. Chicago, IL 60604. 1982. 20 pp. Free. Explains the work of an actuary and employment opportunities. hs-ad.

Advertising. American Advertising Federation. Information and Education Dept. 1225 Connecticut Ave., N.W. Washington, DC 20036. Send payment with all orders. Titles are:

The Commercial Artist. 1 p. Single copy free. Brief description of the commercial artist's career. hs-ad.

The Copywriter. 2 pp. Single copy free. A brief summary of the job, the qualifications needed, and opportunities. hs-ad.

Jobs in Advertising. 1976. 8 pp. 75 cents. Gives definition of advertising and describes the types of jobs in the field. hs-ad.

Advertising. American Association of Advertising Agencies. 666 3rd Ave. New York, NY 10017. Information to interest young people in advertising careers. Sample titles:

►**Advertising: A Guide to Careers in Advertising.** 1975. 16 pp. $1.00. Describes titles, training, location, and qualifications. hs.

►**Advertising Agencies: What They Are, What They Do, and How They Do It.** 1976. 28 pp. $1.00. An exposition of the agency's role in the advertising and marketing process. hs.

Air Travel. R.A. Patton. 4172 Emerald Lake Dr. Decatur, GA 30035. Titles are:

Air Flight Attendant Acceptance Guide. 1980. 90 pp. $1.75. Inside advice on the airline stewardess career by a former airline employment manager. hs-ad.

Airline Training Schools. Undated. 6 pp. Free for a self-addressed stamped business envelope (#10). Explains qualifications and training needed for airline careers. hs-ad.

Careers in Insurance. Alliance of American Insurers. Communications Dept. Room 2140. 20 N. Wacker Dr. Chicago, IL 60606. 24 pp. Single copies free to counselors requesting on official letterhead; $1.00 to others. Discusses careers in the insurance industry, including underwriters, accountants, claims adjusters, data processers, and others. hs.

►**Careers in Real Estate.** National Assoc. of Realtors. 430 N. Michigan Ave. Chicago, IL 60611. 1975. 5 pp. Free. Delineates career specialities within the real estate field. ms-hs.

►**Careers in the Hospitality Industry.** American Hotel and Motel Assoc. 888 7th Ave. New York, NY 10019. 1979. 16 pp. Free. Discusses opportunities in the lodging industry including professional, management, and skilled positions. hs.

Careers in Trademark Law. The United States Trademark Assoc. 6 E. 45th St. New York, NY 10017. 1977. 20 pp. Free. What trademark attorneys do. hs.

Direct Mail Marketing. The Direct Mail/Marketing Educational Foundation. 6 E. 43rd St. New York, NY 10017. Free. Pamphlets and leaflets describing opportunities in direct mail marketing. hs.

Interior Design Career Guide. American Society of Interior Designers. 1430 Broadway. 22nd Fl. New York, NY 10018. Pamphlet. 6 pp. Single copy free; send stamped, self-addressed envelope (#10); additional copies 25 cents each. Outlines the interior design field. hs.

Newspaper Careers. ANPA Foundation. The Newspaper Center. Box 17407. Dulles International Airport. Washington, DC 20041. Numerous publications on work in the newspaper business. Write for free listing. Titles are:

> **Newspaper Jobs You Never Thought of . . . or Did You?** 1979. 6 pp. Free. Looks at newspaper-related careers in such fields as market research, advertising, labor negotiation, law, engineering, and public relations. hs-ad.
>
> **Newspapers . . . Your Future?** Undated. 7 pp. Single copy free; additional copies 15 cents each. Indicates the range of jobs in the newspaper world. hs-ad.
>
> ►**Your Future in Daily Newspapers.** Rev. 1981. 35 pp. Single copy free; additional copies $1.00 each. Explores broad aspects of the newspaper business and gives practical pointers to those interested in journalism. hs-ad.

►**Newspaper Journalism . . . for Minorities.** Division of Journalism. Box 14. Florida A & M Univ. Tallahessee, FL 32307. 2nd ed. 1982. 22 pp. Single copies free. Two or more copies 75 cents each. A brochure designed to encourage minorities to enter the newspaper business. Includes articles by eleven successful journalists who are members of minority groups. hs.

Photographer. Professional Photographers of America. 1090 Executive Way. Des Plaines, IL 60018. Undated. Pamphlet. Free. hs-ad.

Radio and TV. National Assoc. of Broadcasters. Publications Dept. 1771 N St., N.W. Washington, DC 20036. Two booklets. $1.00 each; bulk rates available. Prepayment is required. Titles are:

Careers in Radio. Rev. 1981. Contains a description of radio jobs with photographs that depict activities at a radio station to encourage interest in radio. hs-ad.

Careers in Television. Rev. 1981. Contains a description of television jobs with photographs that depict activities at a television station to encourage interest in television. hs-ad.

Secretarial Career Kit. Professional Secretaries International. 2440 Pershing Rd. Suite G-10 Crown Center. Kansas City, MO 64108. One kit free. A variety of information helpful in counseling young people who consider a secretarial career. hs-ad.

Textiles. American Textile Manufacturers Institute. 1101 Connecticut Ave., N.W. Washington, DC 20036. Titles are:

Career Awareness Through Textiles. 1974. 4 pp. Single copy free. Resource unit for teachers; an introduction to career awareness for elementary and upper grade teachers.

There's a Career for You in Textiles. 1975. Series of 8 pamphlets. One set free. Describes the variety of opportunities open to young people. hs.

Trucking Industry. American Trucking Associations, Inc. Educational Services. Public Relations Dept. 1616 P St., N. W. Washington, DC 20036. Titles include:

Careers in the Trucking Industry. 1977. 5 pp. Free. Brief descriptions of various occupations related to trucking. hs.

Join the Proud Crowd. Undated. Poster, 18″ x 36″. Free. Depicts and lists many types of careers in trucking. ms-hs.

What's So Special About Paper? American Paper Institute. 260 Madison Ave. New York, NY 10016. Undated. 6 pp. Single copy free. Includes brief history of paper making, how paper is produced, and technology schools to interest students in paper industry careers. hs.

►**Where Shall I Go to College to Study Advertising?** Advertising Education Publications. 3429 55th St. Lubbock, TX 79413. Rev. 1982. 24 pp. 1-9 copies $1.00 each. Prepay orders less than $5.00. Program information on over 90 colleges and universities offering education in advertising. hs.

Professional

Art. The National Art Education Assoc. 1916 Association Dr. Reston, VA 22091. Titles are:

Careers in Art. Undated. 12 pp. $1.30. Indicates the breadth of career fields for those with art skills and advises on steps to take. hs-ad.

►**Job Description in the Business World of Art and Design.** 22 pp. $1.50. Descriptions of a wide range of career possibilities in eleven areas of the commercial art field. ms-hs.

Teaching Art as a Career. Undated. 12 pp. $1.30. Briefly outlines the preparation and career of an art teacher. hs-ad.

Careers in Activity and Therapy Fields (#037-3). American Alliance for Health, Physical Education, Recreation, and Dance. P.O. Box 704. Waldorf, MD 20601. 1976. 36 pp. $1.75. Surveys occupations in 14 different fields; gives nature of work, usual requirements, and sources of information. hs-ad.

Careers in Art. The National Assoc. of Schools of Art and Design. 11250 Roger Bacon Dr., Suite 5. Reston, VA 22090. Undated. 2 pp. 50 cents. Guide to selection of an art school and program of study. hs-ad.

Careers in Music. American Music Conference. 1000 Skokie Blvd. Wilmette, IL 60091. 1980. 139 pp. $2.00. A review of the many career opportunities in music today in business, education, the recording industry, and allied fields. hs-ad.

►**Careers in Music.** National Association of Schools of Music. 11250 Roger Bacon Dr., Suite 5. Reston VA 22090. 4 pp. Single copy free; send self-addressed stamped envelope (#10). Brochure describing opportunities in the field of music. Includes a chart of the qualifications, skills, and training needed. hs.

Careers in Physical Therapy (CI-1). American Physical Therapy Association. 1156 15th St., N.W. Washington, DC 20005. 1978. 18 pp. Single copy 30 cents; quantity rates for additional copies. Information on sources of financial aid for students, approved physical therapy programs, and physical therapy assistant programs. hs.

►**Challenges of Nutrition.** American Institute of Nutrition. Public Nutrition Education Committee. 9650 Rockville Pike. Bethesda, MD 20814. Undated. 4 pp. Single copies free. Pamphlet describing the varied field of work for those prepared in nutrition science. hs.

Children's Books. The Children's Book Council. 67 Irving Place. New York, NY 10003. Two pamphlets. Single copy free for a self-addressed stamped envelope (#10) with first-class postage (1 ounce). Titles are:

►**Illustrating Children's Books** (IB). 8 pp. Some practical suggestions for people who want to illustrate children's books and to know how to submit their work to publishers. Annotated bibliography.

►**Writing Books for Children & Young Adults** (WB). 8 pp. Contains basic information for people who wish to write and publish for these audiences. Annotated bibliography.

Dentistry—a Changing Profession. American Dental Assoc. Council on Dental Education. 211 E. Chicago Ave. Chicago, IL 60611. Rev. 1978. 24 pp. Single copy free. Career-oriented information for those considering the dental profession. hs-ad.

Engineering. Accredition Board for Engineering and Technology. Publications Office. 345 East 47th St. New York, NY 10017. Offers several brochures, reports, and other materials on aspects of the engineer's field. Sample titles are:

►**Is Engineering for You?** Leaflet. Free.

►**Nuclear Engineering: A Challenge for a Promising Future.** Leaflet. Free.

Engineering. American Society of Civil Engineers. 345 E. 47th St. New York, NY 10017. Inquire about currently available materials.

►**Engineering—a Career of Dedication and Responsibility.** National Society of Professional Engineers. 2029 K St., N.W. Washington, DC 20006. 1980. 9 pp. Free. Facts for students considering careers in engineering. hs.

Geography. Assoc. of American Geographers. 1710 16th St., N. W. Washington, DC 20009. Single copy free to individuals; quantity rates available. Sample titles:

Geography as a Discipline. Rev. 1980. 6 pp. Discusses geography in America, various types of careers, and necessary education. hs.

►**Geography: Tomorrow's Career.** 1981. 8 pp. Emphasizes roll of geography as a career field in business, government, planning, and teaching. Indicates academic training required, employment outlook, earnings, and other information about the field. hs.

Getting Started in Writing. Writer's Digest School. 9933 Alliance Rd. Cincinnati, OH 45242. 1977. 18 pp. Free; requester must enclose a self-addressed stamped envelope (#10). Valuable writing tips on manuscript preparation and submission, book contracts, free copyright circulars, and answers to writers' questions. hs-ad.

Journalism Career and Scholarship Guide. The Newspaper Fund, Inc. P.O. Box 300. Princeton, NJ 08540. Updated annually. 132 pp. Single copy free. Provides a listing of over $2.4 million in college scholarships for journalism study and colleges offering degrees in journalism/communications; includes current employment data, where journalism graduates find work, their salaries, and their reactions to their first media jobs. hs-ad.

Landscape Architecture. American Society of Landscape Architects. 1733 Connecticut Ave., N.W. Washington, DC 20009. Single copy free; additional copies priced as shown. hs-ad. Titles are:

Landscape Architecture—a Career (C-02). Undated. 7 pp. 6 cents. Examines the role of the landscape architect within the overall design process.

List of Accredited Programs in Landscape Architecture (C-04). 1979-1980. 4 pp. Free. Lists 37 accredited programs indicating degree and status of accredition.

Women in Landscape Architecture (C-03). Undated. 7 pp. 6 cents. Opportunities for women in the profession are described.

Law as a Career. American Bar Assoc. 1155 E. 60th St. Chicago, IL 60637. 1980. 14 pp. Free. Presents the lawyer's role in society, different types of lawyers, job opportunities, and law school information. hs-ad.

Osteopathy. American Osteopathic Assoc. 212 E. Ohio St. Chicago, IL 60611. Two leaflets on the field and practice of osteopathic medicine. Free. hs-ad. Titles are:

Osteopathic Medicine

What Is a D.O.? What Is an M.D.?

Seven Careers (FIL049). American Foundation for the Blind. 15 W. 16th St. New York, NY 10011. Rev. 1973. 12 pp. Single copy free. Describes careers in social work, rehabilitation teaching, vocational rehabilitation counseling, orientation instruction, and education. hs.

Surgery. American College of Surgeons. 55 E. Erie St. Chicago, IL 60611. Titles include:

Information for High School Students. 1971. 2 pp. Free. Career planning aid. hs.

Modern Surgery. 1978. 24 pp. Free. Outlines how to prepare for a career in surgery and the scope and opportunities of modern surgery. hs-ad.

Veterinary Medicine. American Veterinary Medical Assoc. 930 North Meacham Road. Schaumburg, IL 60196. Single copy free; send self-addressed stamped business envelope (#10). Titles include:

►**Animal Technology.** 1981. 7 pp. Explains duties and training of veterinarian technicians. A current listing of U.S. colleges which offer programs in animal technology is also available free. hs-ad.

►**Today's Veterinarian.** 1981. 22 pp. A booklet to answer questions about veterinarians,what they do, and how they are educated. hs-ad.

What Is a D.O.? Dayton District Academy of Osteopathic Medicine. 405 Grand Ave. Dayton, OH 45405. 1-25 copies free. Discusses the field of osteopathy and its differences from traditional medicine. hs-ad.

Women in Landscape Architecture (C-03). American Society of Landscape Architects. 1733 Connecticut Ave., N.W. Washington, DC 20009. Leaflet. Single copy free. Presents employment opportunities for women. hs-ad.

Scientific and Technical

Archaeology as a Career. Archaeological Institute of America. 53 Park Place. New York, NY 10007. Rev. 1979. 7 pp. $1.00; single copy free to AIA members. Describes the general opportunities in the field; includes further readings and a list of other Institute materials. hs-ad.

A Career in Astronomy. American Astronomical Society. Sharp Laboratory. University of Delaware. Newark, DE 19711. Rev. 1982. 23 pp. 25 cents per copy in coin for handling. Describes educational requirements and opportunities for a career in astronomy. Lists degree programs. Bibliography. hs.

Career Opportunities—Automotive Service. Motor Vehicle Manufacturers Assoc. of the U.S., Inc. 300 New Center Bldg. Detroit, MI 48202. 8 pp. Single copy free; postage and handling charge on bulk orders. Identifies major career facets of the automotive field. hs.

►**Careers in Botany.** The Botanical Society of America. School of Biological Sciences. University of Kentucky. Lexington, KY 40506. 1982. 19 pp. Single copy free; additional copies 25 cents each prepaid. Defines botany, explains the work of botanists, gives career preparation information, and outlines types of employment opportunities. hs-ad.

Careers in Statistics. American Statistical Assoc. 806 15th St., N.W. Washington, DC 20005. Undated. 23 pp. Free. Looks at the work of statisticians, opportunities in different fields, and educational training needed. hs-ad.

Chemistry. American Chemical Society. Education Div. Career Services. 1155 16th St., N.W. Washington, DC 20036. 1982. Packet. Single copy free; additional copies $1.00 each. Six publications designed for high school use. Request "Careers in Chemical Sciences" for complete set. Additional copies of individual titles are priced below. Titles are:

►**ACS List of Approved Schools.** 1982. 8 pp. 25 cents.

►**A Career as a Chemical Technician.** 1981. 6 pp. 25 cents.

►**A Career in Analytical Chemistry.** 1982. 11" x 9" fold-out. 25 cents.

►**A Career in Chemical Engineering.** 1982. 19" x 9" fold-out. 25 cents.

►**Careers in Chemistry: Questions and Answers.** 1982. 6 pp. 25 cents.

►**A Chemistry Project From Start to Finish.** 1982. 13 pp. 50 cents.

Chemistry. American Chemical Society. 1155 16th St., N.W. Washington, DC 20036. Information on careers in the field of chemistry. Listing available on request. Sample titles are:

►**Careers Nontraditional.** 50 cents.

►**Employment Outlook.** 25 cents.

►**Graduate Programs in Chemistry.** 25 cents.

►**Salary Survey.** 25 cents.

Consider a Career in Welding. American Welding Society. 550 NW Le Jeune St. Miami, FL 33135. 1976. 9 pp. Free. Describes skills and aptitudes required for a career in the welding industry and outlines specific job opportunities. hs.

►**Decisions, Decisions, Decisions.** Associated Builders and Contractors. 729 15th St., N.W. Washington, DC 20005. Leaflet. Free. Presents an overview of the construction industry as a career field. ms-hs.

Electronics Careers. International Society of Certified Electronics Technicians (ISCET). 2708 West Berry, Suite 8. Ft. Worth, TX 76109. Two brochures about electronics technicians and professional certification in the field of electronics. Single copies free for a self-addressed stamped envelope (#10). Titles are:

►**CET and ISCET for Professional Electronics Technician**

►**Careers in the Electronics Service Industry**

FBI Careers. Federal Bureau of Investigation. 841 Clifford Davis Federal Bldg. Memphis, TN 38103. Free. A packet of materials on investigative and non-investigative careers within the FBI agency. hs.

Forestry. Forest Service, USDA. 12th and Independence, S.W. P.O. Box 2417. Washington, DC 20013. Various career guides. Titles include:

Career Profiles (FS-308). 1979. 15 pp. Free. Information about forestry, conservation, ecology, and environmental management. hs.

Forestry Schools in the United States (FS-9). 1980. 34 pp. Free. A listing and brief description of college programs in forestry. hs-ad.

Geophysics. Society of Exploration Geophysicists. P.O. Box 3098. Tulsa, OK 74101. Sample titles are:

►**Careers in Exploration Geophysics.** 1974. 16 pp. single copy free to students; additional copies 25 cents each. Pictorial description of the work of an exploration geophysicist. hs.

►**Opportunities in Exploration Geophysics.** 1975. Leaflet. Free. Describes the fields of work of an exploration geophysicist. hs.

►**Geophysics: The Earth in Space.** American Geophysical Union. 2000 Florida Ave., N.W. Washington, DC 20009. 1982. 17 pp. Free. Describes ten areas of study within the field of geophysics and general career opportunities in each of the areas. hs.

The Great American Coal Challenge. National Coal Assoc. 1130 17th St., N.W. Washington, DC 20036. Undated. 25 pp. Free. Outlines opportunities for engineers and other professionals in the coal industry. Lists colleges having mining engineering programs. hs.

A Look into Computer Careers. AFIPS Press. 1815 N. Lynn St., Suite 800. Arlington, VA 22209. 16 pp. Single copy free for a self-addressed stamped envelope (#10); bulk rates available. Covers choices and opportunities in the computer career field, the education and training needed, and guidance pointers. hs.

Mathematics. Mathematical Assoc. of America. 1529 18 St., N.W. Washington, DC 20036. Leaflets. Single copy free; quantity rates available. Titles are:

►**Careers in Mathematics.** Undated. Student's guide to information resources about careers in mathematical sciences. hs.

►**The Math in High School.** 1982. Gives high school mathematics needed for entry into various college studies. hs.

►**You Will Need Math.** Undated. Discusses the mathematical background necessary for various occupations. hs.

Mathematics. American Mathematical Society. P.O. Box 6248. Providence, RI 02940. Titles are:

Careers in Mathematics. 1979. Leaflet. Free. Describes opportunities in government, industry, and education for math specialists. hs-ad.

Seeking Employment in the Mathematical Sciences. 1977. 20 pp. $1.00; additional copies 2 for $1.00. Details types of mathematical employment, preparing for a career, looking for opportunities, and applying for a position. hs-ad.

Metal Casting . . . an Art . . . a Science . . . a Career. American Foundrymen's Society. Golf and Wolf Rds. Des Plaines, IL 60016. 1979. 20 pp. Single copy free; 2-50 copies $1.00 each. Describes vocations for craftsmen, technicians, engineers, chemists, and managers in the industry. hs.

Metallurgy. American Society for Metals. Office of Career Guidance. Metals Park, OH 44073. Several brochures on careers in metallurgy and materials science are available. Free. hs. Sample titles are:

►**A Career in Metallurgy and Materials Science.** 4 pp. Free.

►**Introducing . . . An Exciting New World: The World of Metallurgy and Materials Engineering.** 26 pp. 50 cents. Full-color photographs.

The Metallurgical Engineering Technician. 3 pp.

►**Microbiology in Your Future.** The American Society for Microbiology. 1913 I St., N.W. Washington, DC 20006. 1981. 33 pp. Single copy free; additional copies 50 cents each. Describes types of microbiology and advises on educational planning and employment outlook for the field. hs.

►**Office Machine Computer Occupations** (Bull. 2075-6). Supt. of Documents. Gov't Printing Office. Washington, DC 20402. 1981. $2.75. A reprint from the *Occupational Outlook Handbook* devoted primarily to computer careers. hs-ad.

Physics: A Career for You? American Institute of Physics, Inc. 335 E. 45th St. New York, NY 10017. 1977. 12 pp. Single copy free; multiple copies 60 cents each, prepaid. Basic information about the field of physics. Color photographs. hs.

►**A Rewarding Technical Career in Instrumentation Awaits You.** The Instrument Society of America. 67 Alexander Dr. P.O. Box 12277. Research Triangle Park, NC 27709. Rev. 1981. 10 pp. 1-9 copies 65 cents each; send payment with order. Describes career opportunities in instrumentation. Helpful to high school students interested in the sciences or technologies. hs.

Secretarial Jobs. Assoc. of Independent Colleges & Schools. 1730 M St., N.W. Washington, DC 20036. 1981. 4 pp. each. Free. Leaflets outlining the basic nature of various secretarial occupations. hs-ad. Titles are:

Your Career as a Shorthand Reporter

Your Career as a Legal Secretary

Your Career as a Medical Assistant

Your Career as a Secretary

►**Your Career in Accounting**

So You Want to Be a Forester? The American Forestry Assoc. 1319 18th St., N.W. Washington, DC 20036. Undated. 22 pp. Free. Discusses professional and nonprofessional opportunities in forestry. hs.

What's a Nice Girl Like You Doing in a Man's World? National Association of Trade and Technical Schools. 2021 K St., N.W. Washington, DC 20006. Leaflet. Free. Emphasizes careers opportunities for women in trade and technical fields. Gives sources of career and training information. hs.

Within Your Lifetime. Student Programs. AIAA. 1290 Avenue of the Americas. New York, NY 10104. 16 pp. Single copies free. Examines careers in the aerospace field. Current professionals advise on career preparation. hs.

Women in Aviation. U.S. Dept. of Transportation. Federal Aviation Administration. 800 Independence Ave., S.W. Washington, DC 20591. Sample titles are:

Women in Aerospace (GA-300-113). Undated. 6 pp. Free. Contains true accounts to illustrate the roles women are playing in aerospace. hs.

Women in Non-Traditional Aviation and Space Careers: An Overview (GA-300-140). 1979. 8 pp. Free. Looks at numbers of women presently in aviation and space careers formerly occupied only by men. hs.

►**World of Aviation Maintenance.** Aviation Maintenance Foundation. P.O.Box 739. Basin, WY 82410. Rev. 1982. 22 pp. 50 cents. Describes the role of aviation technicians and lists approved training schools. hs.

►**Your Career as an Appliance Service Technician.** Association of Home Appliance Manufacturers. 20 N. Wacker Dr. Chicago, IL 60606. 1981. 13 pp. 75 cents. Describes the opportunities in appliance servicing and the qualifications needed by a technician. hs.

CHILD CARE AND PARENTING

Baby Care. Johnson & Johnson Baby Products Co. Consumer & Professional Services. Skillman, NJ 08558. Free. Several booklets and free-loan films are available; send for listing. Titles include:

Baby Care Basics. 1980. 48 pp. Booklet covers eating and sleeping habits, cleanliness, illness, and safety precautions. (Spanish version available). hs.

Baby Chart. 1980. Wall chart, 17″ x 22″. Shows the development of a baby from birth to two years on one side; how to give a baby a sponge or tub bath on the other side. (Spanish version available). hs-ad.

Getting to Know Your Newborn. 1980. 18 pp. Explains communication with the newborn. Subjects include crying, eye contact, and playing. hs-ad.

Guide for the First Time Babysitter. 1980. 13 pp. Covers basic topics including safety, emergencies, bedtime, diapering, bathing, feeding, and play. Includes crossword puzzle as a review. ms-hs.

Parenting Insights. 1980. 12 pp. Overview of parenting responsibilities for future parents. References. hs-ad.

Baby Feeding. Consumer Relations Dept. Heinz U.S.A. P.O. Box 57. Pittsburgh, PA 15230. Titles are:

Answering Feeding Questions (BF5613). 1980. 3 pp. Free. hs.

►**Bright Start: A Guide to Infant Feeding** (BF5573R). 1981. 20 pp. Free. hs. 1982. 6 pp. Free. hs.

►**Ingredient Listing and Allergy Information for Heinz Baby Foods** (B16101). 1982. 6 pp. Free. hs.

Planning Baby's Meals (BF5612). 1980. 4 pp. Free. hs.

Planning Meals for the Allergic Infant (BF5603). 1980. 4 pp. Free. hs.

Child Abuse. National Committee for Prevention of Child Abuse. 332 South Michigan Ave., Suite 1250. Chicago, IL 60604-4357. Various booklets and other materials covering subjects such as child abuse, abuse prevention, and parenting. Spanish versions available for some titles. Send for free *NCPCA Catalog* for descriptions and ordering information.

Child Abuse and Neglect. National Center on Child Abuse and Neglect. P.O. Box 1182. Washington, DC 20013. Send for free "Catalog of NCCAN Publication." Sample title:

►**Dennis the Menace: Coping With Family Stress.** 1981. 16 pp. Single copy free. Comic book presentation of how stress can affect relationships between parents and children. el.

Childbearing. Maternity Center Assoc. 48 East 92nd St. New York, NY 10028. Provides teaching aids related to topics such as nurse-midwifery, maternity care, childbearing, and parenthood. Request free list of materials. Titles include:

►**Comfort During Pregnancy.** Leaflet with diagrams. 25 cents. Also in Spanish: **Bienestar Durante el Embarazo.**

►**For the Expectant Father.** Leaflet. 25 cents. hs.-ad.

►**Nurse-Midwifery in Context.** Reprint. 12 pp. 50 cents. hs-ad.

►**Relaxation and Breathing.** Leaflet with diagrams. 25 cents.

►**Children and Television . . . a Primer for Parents.** The Boys Town Center. Boys Town, NE 68010. 1981. 12 pp. Free. Discusses what children may learn from TV and the influence it can have on lives. hs-ad.

►**Divorce.** The Boys Town Center. Boys Town, NE 68010. 1980. Free. 20 pp. A summary of research about the effects of divorce on families. hs-ad.

Early Adolescents: Understanding and Nurturing Their Development. Assoc. for Childhood Education International. 3615 Wisconsin Ave., N.W. Washington, DC 20016. 1978. 40 pp. $2.00 plus 10% for shipping; prepay orders under $10.00. Seven articles about the nature and needs of 10 to 14 year olds and how parents can relate to them. ad.

Eye Care. National Society to Prevent Blindness. 79 Madison Ave. New York, NY 10016. Complete catalog of publications sent on request. Sample titles:

Home Eye Test for Preschoolers. 1975. Single copy free; send 15 cent stamp only. $6.00 per 100. Simple test and instructions for vision screening of 3, 4, and 5 year olds at home. Available in Spanish. ad.

Your Child's Sight (G108). 1975. Leaflet. Single copy free; must send self-addressed stamped envelope (#10). $5.00 per 100. Discusses need for check-ups for children since they often are not aware of an eyesight problem. ad.

►**Feelings and Your Child.** National Mental Health Assoc. 1800 N. Kent St. Arlington, VA 22209. 1981. $2.00 per set; send payment with order. A series of 14 leaflets to help parents deal with potential problem situations in child raising and to identify behaviors that may become troublesome if left unattended. ad.

Infant and Child Care. Professional Communications. Gerber Products Co. 445 State St. Fremont, MI 49412. Free to secondary and college level home economics teachers; request on professional letterhead. Titles are:

►**Feeding Baby.** 1982. 34 pp. Single copy free. Provides information about infant feeding and the introduction of foods to a baby. Includes three fold-out charts. hs.

►**A Handbook of Child Safety.** 1982. 12 pp. Available in classroom quantities. Discusses household hazards children may encounter. hs.

►**Nutrient Values—Gerber Baby Foods.** 1981. Gives tables of nutrient data expressed per 100 grams of product and as percent of the U.S. RDA per jar of product. ad.

►**Things You Should Know About Baby Sitting.** Pamphlet. Available in classroom quantities. Guide to successful baby sitting. ms-hs.

►***La Leche Materials.*** La Leche League International, Inc. 9616 Minneapolis Ave. Franklin Park, IL 60131. Offers books, booklets, and other materials in child care and other topics such as childbirth, breastfeeding, and nutrition. Many cost under $2.00. Send for a free listing. hs-ad.

Marriage. Public Affairs Committee, Inc. 381 Park Ave. S. New York, NY 10016. 50 cents each; bulk rates available. Titles include:

Building a Marriage on Two Altars (#466). 1971. 20 pp. Honest talk about the increasing number of mixed marriages. hs.

New Ways to Better Marriages (#547). 1977. 28 pp. Examines a number of marriage enrichment programs and explains how each helps couples learn to cope with marital problems. hs.

Talking It Over Before Marriage (#512). 1974. 25 pp. Discusses exercises in communication that help young couples judge their compatibility and work out differences before marriage. hs.

Parent Brochures. International Reading Assoc. 800 Barksdale Road. P.O. Box 8139. Newark, DE 19711. Single copy free; send a self-addressed stamped envelope (#10). Titles are:

►**Eating Well Can Help Your Child Learn Better**

►**Studying: A Key to Success . . . Ways Parents Can Help**

Practical Guidance for Space Age Children. Guidance Awareness Publications. Box 106. Rancocas, NJ 08073. 1973. 33 pp. $2.00. Discusses common concerns of parents and teachers in regard to early adjustment to school. ad.

Public Affairs Pamphlets. Public Affairs Committee, Inc. 381 Park Ave. S. New York, NY 10016. 50 cents each; bulk rates available. Sample titles are:

A Death in the Family (#542). 1976. 24 pp. Offers insights and suggestions for constructively dealing with death; includes a special section on explaining death to children. hs-ad.

►**Environmental Hazards to Children** (#600). 1981. 28 pp. Investigates many environmental hazards such as pollution, food additives, contamination, and pesticides. hs-ad.

Helping Children Face Crises (#541). 1976. 24 pp. Suggests methods by which parents can guide children through major crises within the family such as divorce, illness, or death. hs-ad.

Parents and Teenagers (#490). 1973. 24 pp. Gives advice and guidelines for parents, explaining why teenagers behave as they do. hs-ad.

Playmates: The Importance of Childhood Friendships (#525). 1975. 24 pp. Discusses how and why children's relationships with friends prepare them for human companionship throughout life. hs-ad.

►**Teaching Children About Money 1**(#593). 1981. 28 pp. Suggests ways that parents can help children learn the value of money and how to handle it responsibly. Covers other issues of money in child relations. hs-ad.

The Very New Baby: The First Days of Life (#553). 1977. 28 pp. Discusses the importance of prenatal and postnatal procedures, common conditions among newborn babies, and treatments for special problems. hs-ad.

Single Parents. Parents Without Partners. 7910 Woodmont Ave. Washington, DC 20014. Variety of mimeographed materials and leaflets concerning single parents and children. hs-ad. Sample titles are:

Children in a Single Parent's Home. 4 pp. 15 copies for $1.00. Excerpts from literature and a reference list.

For the Never Married Mother. 1972. Pamphlet. 3 copies for 50 cents.

Parents Are Forever. Undated. Pamphlet. 3 copies for 50 cents.

Separation and Divorce: Annotated Bibliography of Selected Literature for Children and Teens. 1979. 15 copies for $1.00.

►**Signals: What Your Child Is Really Telling You** (AE2186). New American Library, 1633 Broadway, New York, NY 10019. 1978. 278 pp. $3.95. A parenting guide on how to recognize, evaluate, and respond to the real problems behind children's troubled behavior. ad.

►**Toys, Games, and Vision.** American Optometric Assoc. Communications Div. 243 N. Lindbergh Blvd. St. Louis, MO 63141. 5-page leaflet. Free for a self-addressed stamped envelope (#10). Discusses toys and games associated with vision development and includes a listing of age-appropriate toys and activities. hs-ad.

►**What Parents Should Know About Child Safety.** Sportshelf. P.O. Box 643. New Rochelle, NY 10802. 1969. 15 pp. $1.00 postpaid. Presents advice for protecting children from accidents and other harm. hs.

CITIZENSHIP

The Constitution of the United States. Dow Jones-Irwin. A Div. of Richard D. Irwin, Inc. 1818 Ridge Road. Homewood, IL 60430. 1975. 120 pp. $4.95. A personal learning aid for understanding the Constitution and its background; includes the Declaration of Independence and the Articles of Confederation. Includes glossary and sample examination. hs.

Education for Citizenship: The Oldest, Newest Innovation in the Schools (Vol. 26, No. 8). Center for Information on America. Washington, CT 06793. 1977. 4 pp. 45 cents; quantity rates available. Discusses what civic education has been, is, and should be to prepare people to live in a democracy. ms-hs.

The Flag of the U. S. A. Dettra Flag Co., Inc. Oaks, PA 19456. 1977. Leaflet. 2 copies free; include a 9″ self-addressed stamped envelope. Contains pictures and information about early American flags and rules for proper use, display, and care of the flag. ms-hs.

►**Immigration, Naturalization, and Citizenship** (SB-069). U.S. Gov't. Printing Office. Washington, DC 20402. 1981. 12 pp. Free. A listing of many low-cost government publications which may be used in the classroom.

►**Open the Door to Opportunity: Become a U.S. Citizen.** Carnation Co. Public Relations. 5045 Wilshire Blvd. Los Angeles, CA 90036. 1982. 9 pp. Free. Describes the many advantages of U.S. citizenship and explains the application process. Also in Spanish. el-ms.

Our Flags. National Flag Foundation. Flag Plaza. Pittsburg, PA 15219. Two pamphlets and a poster about the history and display of our national flag. $1.25 per packet. Order must include self-addressed mailing label. Packet includes:

►**Our Flag: How to Honor It, How to Display It.** 1976. 12 pp. Fold-out. Illustrated. Includes words to the Pledge of Allegiance and The Star-Spangled Banner. el-ms-hs.

►**You Are the Flag: A History of America's Flag.** 1976. 40 pp. Booklet. Depicts many flags flown on this continent and explains their origins. Accompanied by color posters, "You Are the Flag." ms-hs.

United States Flag. Veterans of Foreign Wars. National Headquarters. Broadway at 34th St. Kansas City, MO 64111. Single copy free. Titles include:

Etiquette of the Stars and Stripes. 19 pp. Includes basic history, display, and respect for the flag. ms-hs.

Federal Flag Code. 4 pp. el-ms.

Questions and Answers on the United States Flag. 12 pp. Answers 79 questions concerning proper display and handling of our flag. el-ms.

Ten Short Flag Stories. 8 pp. el-ms.

Your Bill of Rights. 1 p. ms.

COMMUNICATIONS AND MEDIA

The Anatomy of a Newspaper. ANPA Foundation. The Newspaper Center. Box 17407. Dulles International Airport. Washington, DC 20041. Rev. 1980. 44 pp. $1.00; quantity rates available. Describes how a newspaper is put together, from gathering the news to printing and delivery, and discusses how to read and get the most out of a newspaper. ms-hs.

Be Informed on News Media. New Readers Press. Box 131. Syracuse, NY 13210. 1976. 40 pp. $1.20; prepay orders under $10.00. Topics include what becomes news and why, fair vs. biased reporting, TV and radio news and entertainment, and advertising. Includes teacher's guide with resource list. el-ms.

►***Cable TV.*** National Cable Television Assoc. 1724 Massachusetts Ave., N.W. Washington, DC 20036. Write for a listing of NCTA publications.

Copyright Materials. Copyright Office. Library of Congress. Washington, DC 20559. Circulars on copyright laws and procedures. Single copy free. Sample titles are:

- ►**Highlights of the New Copyright Law** (R-99). 1982. 5 pp. Summarizes the important changes to the copyright system made in 1978. hs-ad.
- ►**Copyright Basics** (R-1). 1982. 11 pp. Outlines procedures for obtaining a copyright. hs-ad.

Debate Material. The Foundation for Economic Education, Inc. 30 S. Broadway. Irvington-on-Hudson, NY 10533. One debate packet free to high school debate coach or librarian. A packet of articles, reprints, bibliography, and study questions on the national high school debate topic. hs.

High School Journalism Today. The Interstate Printers and Publishers, Inc. Danville, IL 61832. 1976. 128 pp. $3.95. A compact handbook of practical advice that students can apply in writing and editing school publications. hs.

How to Publish Community Information on an Incredibly Tight Budget (#216). Do It Now Foundation. Institute for Chemical Survival. P.O. Box 5115. Phoenix, AZ 85010. 1976. 22 pp. 65 cents. Contains printing information, terminology, processes, and alternatives which can fit any budget. hs-ad.

►**Introduction to Film Making.** National Council of Teachers of English. 1111 Kenyon Road. Urbana, IL 61801. 1975. 48 pp. $2.50 (members $1.75). A guide for teachers in teaching film production. Includes history, role, types, mechanics, and process in film making. A major portion is devoted to film projects for classes. Bibliography. hs-ad.

►**MediaLog.** The Film Fund. 80 E. 11th St. New York, NY 10003. 98 pp. Free. A guide to television, film, and radio programs supported by the National Endowment for the Humanities over a ten-year period. Describes program content and format and ordering details to help schools, colleges, libraries, and other agencies and groups make local use of over 300 programs on history, literature, philosophy, and other subjects in the humanities. ad.

News Reel. Teacher's Exchange of San Francisco. 28 Dawnview. San Francisco, CA 94131. 1973. $1.25 plus 75 cents for shipping. Dial chart giving 1,000 possible combinations of assignments for understanding the content and relevance of news articles and for critical analysis of reporting. el-ms.

►**Perspectives on Television Studies** (Spring 1978). Journal of the University Film and Video Assoc. Dept. of Cinema and Photography. Southern Illinois University. Carbondale, IL 62901. 1978. 60 pp. $2.50. A journal edition containing seven articles drawn from research exploration. ad.

►**Radio and Television Bibliography.** National Assoc. of Broadcasters. Publications Dept. 1771 N St., N. W. Washington, DC 20036. Rev. 1982. $2.00; prepayment is required. A selective guide to reference material from commercial publishers and other sources on all aspects of broadcasting from programming to audience measurement. hs-ad.

►**Telecommunications** (SB 296). U.S. Gov't. Printing Office. Washington, DC 20402. 1981. 16 pp. Free. A listing of many low-cost government publications which may be used in the classroom.

►**The Television Picture.** CBS Educational & Community Services. CBS Broadcast Group. 51 West 52 St. New York, NY 10019. 1981. 14 pp. Free. Tells the historical development of television and explains how the television business works. References. ms-hs.

►**You Own More Than Your Set.** National Assoc. for Better Broadcasting. 7918 Naylor Ave. Los Angeles, CA 90045. 1982. 50 pp. $4.00. Presents a condensation of ten "white papers" that expose threats to the public interest in TV broadcasting and calls upon the FCC to enforce laws and protect consumers. hs-ad.

CONSERVATION

Cartoon Booklets. Soil Conservation Society of America. 7515 Northeast Ankeny Rd. Ankeny, IA 50021. Series of 11. 16 pp. each. 75 cents each. 2-99 copies of same title 25 cents each. Teacher's guide available with each title at 50 cents each; 2-9 copies of same or mixed titles, 15 cents each. Gives factual information about natural resource problems. G4-7. Write for descriptive brochure. Titles include:

The Earth: Our Home In Space

Help Keep Our Land Beautiful

Plants, How They Improve Our Environment

The Story of Land

Water, the Basis of Life

Catalog of Conservation Films. Film Library. Tennessee Dept. of Conservation. 710 Broadway. Nashville, TN 37203. Free. A descriptive listing of 16 mm conservation films available for free-loan to schools and organizations in Tennessee.

►**Conservation** (SB-238). U.S. Gov't. Printing Office. Washington, DC 20402. 1981. 12 pp. Free. A listing of many low-cost government publications which may be used in the classroom.

Critical Index of Films on Man and His Environment. The Interstate Printers and Publishers, Inc. Danville, IL 61832. 1972. 32 pp. $1.25. Annotated bibliography of selected visual aids for teachers and others on understanding the interrelationships of man and his environment.

Environmental Conservation Education: A Selected Annotated Bibliography. 1977 Supplement. Interstate Printers and Publishers, Inc. 19-27 North Jackson St. Danville, IL 61832. 1978. 27 pp. $1.50. Most recent source list compiled for the Conservation Education Association. pr. to ad.

Plantings for Birds. Soil Conservation Service. Information Div. Washington, DC 20250. Also available from any field or state office of the Soil Conservation Service. Single copy free to teachers. Four materials which explain and illustrate shrubs and trees that will attract birds. el-ms-hs. Titles are:

►**Invite Birds to Your Home—Conservation Plantings for the Midwest** (PA-982). Folded poster.

►**Invite Birds to Your Home—Conservation Plantings for the Northeast** (PA-940). Folded poster.

►**Invite Birds to Your Home—Conservation Plantings for the Northwest** PA-1094). 20 pp.

►**Invite Birds to Your Home—Conservation Plantings for the Southeast** (PA-1093). 16 pp.

Soil Conservation. Soil Conservation Service. Information Div. Washington, DC 20250. Also available from any field or state office of the Soil Conservation

Service. Single copy free to teachers. Offers many materials on soil and water conservation. el-ms-hs. Titles include:

- ►**Conquest of the Land Over 7,000 Years** (AIB-99). 1978. 30 pp.
- ►**Conservation and the Water Cycle** (AIB-326). 1974. Leaflet.
- ►**Early American Soil Conservationists** (MP-449). 1971. 62 pp.
- ►**Know Your Soil** (AIB-267). 1970. 16 pp. Why soil surveys are important.
- ►**The Measure of Our Land** (PA-128). 1969. 22 pp. Explains different types of soils.
- ►**Mulches for Your Garden** (H&G-185). 1978. Leaflet.
- ►**Outdoor Classrooms on School Sites** (PA-975). 1972. 22 pp. How the out-of-doors can be used for creative learning experiences about man's environment.
- ►**Sediment: It's Filling Harbors, Lakes, and Roadside Ditches** (AIB-325). 1967. 16 pp. Tells how soil erosion results in sediment pollution of rivers, harbors, and lakes.
- ►**Soil Erosion: The Work of Uncontrolled Water** (AIB-260). Rev. 1971. 16 pp. Describes various types of soil erosion and their effects upon the land.
- ►**Teaching Soil and Water Conservation: A Classroom and Field Guide** (PA-341). 1970. 29 pp. Practical suggestions for classroom activities and observation out-of-doors.
- ►**Windbreaks for Conservation** (AIB-339). 1969. 30 pp. Discusses the usefulness of windbreaks in reducing erosion and protecting wildlife.

You Can Be a Conservationist. The American Forestry Assoc. 1319 18th St., N.W. Washington, DC 22036. Undated. 16 pp. Free. Discusses soil, water, forests, grasslands, and wildlife conservation. el-ms.

CONSUMER AFFAIRS

Note: These entries appear under the two subdivisions of Consumer Education and Consumer Protection.

Consumer Education

Aerosols (ED005). Johnson Wax. Consumer Services Center. Personal Care Div. P.O. Box 567—Dept. FI 83-A. Racine, WI 53401. Undated. 14 pp. Free; request on postcard. Covers the aerosol packaging of products, how it works, and its uses. hs.

Be Informed Series. New Readers Press. Box 131. Syracuse, NY 13210. $1.20 each; prepay orders under $10.00. Teacher's guide with resource list comes with each title. Sample titles are:

Be Informed on Owning a Car. 1976. 40 pp. Topics covered include saving on fuel, caring for tires, maintaining your car, shopping for repairs, and handling driving emergencies. el-ms.

Be Informed on Personal Insurance . 1978. 40 pp. Topics include social security, life insurance, disability income, health insurance, and retirement income. el-ms.

►**Calculate to Save.** Odin Press. P.O. Box 536. New York, NY 10021. 1978. 204 pp. $2.95. A modern consumers' guide to fighting inflation and saving energy. Demonstrates ways to evaluate energy-saving investments using a simple calculator. hs-ad.

►**Consumer Information** (SB-002). U.S. Gov't. Printing Office. Washington, DC 20402. 1982. 24 pp. Free. A listing of many low cost government publications which may be used in the classroom.

Consumer Information Catalog. Consumer Information Center. Pueblo, CO 81009. Published quarterly. 16 pp. Free. An annotated listing of 200+ selected federal publications aimed at increasing consumer awareness; organized by general topics. More than half are free; most cost items range from $1.00 to $4.50. Order blank provided. Also available in Spanish.

Consumers. Direct Selling Education Foundation. 1730 M St., N.W. Washington, DC 20036. A variety of brochures on consumer education is offered. Some available in Spanish. Sample titles are:

►**At Home with Consumers.** Quarterly newsletter. 6 pp. Free. hs-ad.

►**Promises: Check 'em Out!** or **Promesas: !Compruebelas!** Leaflet. Free. Discusses precautions to take before investing in a personal business opportunity. hs-ad.

►**Questions Every Buyer Should Ask** or **Preguntas Que Todo Comparados Debe Hacer.** Leaflet. Free. Points to check out before making an in-home purchase. hs-ad.

Consumer's Resource Handbook (619J). Consumer Information Center. Pueblo, CO 81009. 1979. 76 pp. Free. A comprehensive guide to how to complain and get results. hs-ad.

►**Current Consumer & Lifestudies.** Curriculum Innovations, Inc. 3500 Western Ave. Highland Park, IL 60035. Magazine. 9 issues yearly. Sample issue free to teachers. Each issue focuses on the life skills students need to get along with others and how to become a well-informed consumer. ms-hs.

Facts About Central Air Conditioning. Council of Better Business Bureaus. 1515 Wilson Blvd. Arlington, VA 22209. 1979. 14 pp. 25 cents. Advice on selecting equipment and a contractor. ad.

►***Food Brochures.*** Food Marketing Institute. Publications Sales. 1750 K St. N.W. Washington, DC 20006. Offers several free consumer information brochures on topics related to food buying. Request publications catalog for descriptions. hs-ad.

Forms in Your Future. Globe Book Co. 50 W. 23rd St. New York, NY 10010. Rev. 1980. 112 pp. $3.56. A text-workbook that gives students experience in reading and filling out 24 actual forms they will encounter in life—mail orders, income tax, checks and deposits, and various applications. Teaching guide included. hs.

Insurance. Insurance Information Institute. Education Department. 110 William St. New York, NY 10038. Student materials designed for use by those who teach or study the topic of property and liability insurance in high schools and colleges, but especially for consumer education, business education, driver education, and home economics. Free in quantities, except as indicated. Titles include:

►**Automobile Insurance Leaflet**

►**Careers in Property and Liability Insurance**

►**Educator's Guide to Teaching Auto and Home Insurance.** One to a teacher.

►**Home Insurance Leaflet**

►**Insurance Insights.** Newsletter for educators.

►**Risk Management and Business Insurance.** One to a teacher. Request accompanying educator's guide.

►**Sample Insurance Policies**

►**Wall Chart on Auto Insurance.** 23″ x 36″. One to a classroom.

►**Wall Chart on Home Insurance.** 22″ x 36″. One to a classroom.

Life Insurance. The Bankers Life. Consumer Services. 711 High St. Des Moines, IA 50307. Single copy free; additional copies 20 cents each. Titles include:

►**How Much Life Insurance Do I Need?** 16 pp.

►**How to Choose a Life Insurance Plan.** 20 pp.

►**How to Select the Right Life Insurance Company.** 1976. 31 pp.

►**Insurance Handbook.** 26 pp.

Pamphlets and Guides. State Farm Insurance Cos. Public Relations Dept. 1 State Farm Plaza. Bloomington, IL 61701. Free in classroom quantities. hs-ad. Titles include:

Accident Report Guide. 4 pp. An information blank to make it easier to gather data at the scene of an accident and to complete required reports.

Finding the Right Home for You. 1973. 20 pp. A guide consisting of three evaluation forms to be used to compile and compare detailed information on prospective houses.

A Guide to Renting an Apartment. 36 pp. Designed to anticipate problems in renting an apartment. Includes an easy-to-use rating system.

Inventory. 12 pp. Presents methods of knowing the contents of your home and having adequate protection in case of theft.

What Is Auto Insurance? 5 pp. Introduces what anyone who owns a car needs to know about car insurance, types of coverage, costs, and the like.

Questions and Answers About Advertising. American Advertising Federation. Educational Services. 1225 Connecticut Ave., N.W. Washington, DC 20036. 1975. 6 pp. 75 cents; quantity rates available. Brief answers to twenty questions of general interest. hs.

State Farm Pamphlets. State Farm Insurance Co. Public Relations Dept. 1 State Farm Plaza, Bloomington, IL 61701. Titles are:

Life Insurance Buyers Guide. 1977. 8 pp. Free. hs-ad.

What Is Auto Insurance? Undated. 5 pp. Free. hs-ad.

What Is Home Insurance? Undated. 5 pp. Free. hs-ad.

Where the Rubber Meets the Road. The Firestone Tire and Rubber Co. Public Relations Dept. 1200 Firestone Pkwy. Akron, OH 44317. 1981. Leaflet. Free. A guide to tires, tire safety, maintenance, and performance. hs-ad.

Consumer Protection

Consumer Credit. Board of Governors of the Federal Reserve System. Publication Services. Room MP-510. Washington, DC 20551. Several short pamphlets on aspects of consumer credit for classroom use. Free in quantities. hs-ad. Sample titles are:

Alice in Debitland. 1980. 16 pp.

Consumer Handbook to Credit Protection Laws. 1980. 44 pp.

The Equal Credit Opportunity Act and Age. 1977. 5 pp.

The Equal Credit Opportunity Act and Women. 1977. 7 pp.

Fair Credit Billing. 1976. 5 pp.

How to File a Consumer Credit Complaint. 1978. 5 pp.

If You Use a Credit Card. 1979. 4 pp.

What Truth in Lending Means to You. 1980. 5 pp.

FDA Leaflets. Food and Drug Administration. Office of Consumer Affairs. HFE-88. 5600 Fishers Lane. Rockville, MD 20857. Leaflets. Single copies free. hs-ad. Sample titles are:

Antibiotics and the Foods You Eat (FDA 80-2125)

Foodborne Illness (FDA 80-2044)

Toxic Shock Syndrome and Tampons (FDA 82-4025)

We Want You to Know About Cooking Utensils (FDA 80-2123)

We Want You to Know About Microwave Oven Radiation (FDA 80-8121)

We Want You to Know About Preventing Childhood Poisonings (FDA 75-7001)

We Want You to Know What We Know About Cosmetics (FDA 79-5011)

X-Rays: Get the Picture on Protection (FDA 79-8088)

Fly-Rights (615J). Consumer Information Center. Pueblo, CO 81009. 1979. 28 pp. Free. Consumer booklet from the Civil Aeronautics Board on air fares, reservations, delayed and cancelled flights, overbooking, and air line safety. hs-ad.

Home Buying. American Land Title Assoc. 1828 L. St., N.W. Washington, DC 20036. Free. Pamphlet materials which explain how land title insurance protects real estate ownership. hs-ad. Titles include:

►**Closing Costs and Your Purchase of a Home**

►**Things You Should Know About Home Buying and Land Title Protection**

Making Products Safer (#524). Public Affairs Committee, Inc. 381 Park Ave. S. New York, NY 10016. 1975. 28 pp. 50 cents. Focuses on injury, disability, and death related to hazardous products and the role of the consumer and government in assuring greater safety, and advises on what to do if harmed. hs-ad.

Product Safety. U.S. Consumer Products Safety Commission. Consumer Information Div. Washington, DC 20207. Numerous materials are available free on various common products, their hazards, and their safe use. Send for *Catalogue of Publications* for a complete listing.

►**Your Credit Rights.** Federal Reserve Bank of Minneapolis. Office of Public Information. Minneapolis, MN 55480. 1982. 96 pp. Free. An instructional unit of six sections on using credit and consumer credit protection. Includes learning activities and instructions, key concepts, vocabulary, answer key, and masters for making student handouts and transparencies. hs-ad.

Your Right to Write. Clorox Co. Consumer Services. P.O. Box 24305. Oakland, CA 94623. 10 pp. Up to 25 copies free. Explains how and why to write companies about their products or services to register a complaint, request information, or submit an idea. hs-ad.

DENTAL HEALTH

ADA Instructional Aids. American Dental Assoc. Bureau of Health Education and Audiovisual Service. 211 E. Chicago Ave. Chicago, IL 60611. Free brochure, *Learning About Your Oral Health*, available to teachers, nurses, administrators, and curriculum specialists. Describes a K-12 dental health curriculum; and curriculum guides, posters, overhead transparencies, spirit masters, oral hygiene kits, and audio-visuals offered by the ADA.

Clean Teeth Club. Lever Brothers Co. Consumer Education Dept. 390 Park Ave. New York, NY 10022. Free. One wall poster and classroom quantities of individual toothbrushing charts. pr-el.

Nutrition Aspects. Direct requests to the Dairy Council office in your area. If not served by area Council, send to: National Dairy Council. 6300 N. River Rd. Rosemont, IL 60018. Request a free annotated catalog of a variety of materials for grades K-12, consumers, and health professionals. Several items are available on the nutritional aspects of good dental health. ad.

Oral Hygiene. American Academy of Periodontology. Suite 924. 211 E. Chicago Ave. Chicago, IL 60611. Titles include:

> **Consumer's Guide to Periodontal Disease.** 1979. 4 pp. Single copy free for a self-addressed stamped envelope. Describes the cause of periodontal disease and gives helpful hints on treatment. hs-ad.
>
> **Effective Oral Hygiene.** 11 pp. 35 cents. Shows how to keep teeth clean and in good health. pr-ad.
>
> **Facts About Periodontal Disease.** 6 pp. 30 cents. Describes various types of diseases of the mouth and teeth. hs-ad.
>
> **How's Your PDIQ?** 1976. 3 pp. 15 cents. A pamphlet and quiz on causes, symptoms, and treatment of periodontal disease. el-ms-hs.

►**Preventing Tooth Decay** (NIH 82-1196). National Caries Program. National Institute of Dental Research. Westwood Bldg., Rm. 549. 5333 Westbard Ave. Bethesda, MD 20205. 1981. 40 pp. Free. A guide for implementing self-applied fluoride in school settings. Includes sample pamphlet and order forms for free posters and free-loan films. el-ms-hs.

Teeth. Office of Scientific and Health Reports. National Institute of Dental Research. Bldg. 31—Room 2C34. Bethesda, MD 20205. Single copy free; classroom quantities free to teachers. Titles are:

> **RX for Sound Teeth** (#79-793). 1979. Foldout. Illustrated guide for cleaning, brushing, and flossing teeth. el-ms-hs.
>
> **Tooth Decay** (#80-1146). 1980. 5 pp. Causes and prevention of tooth decay are discussed. el-ms-hs.

What You Should Know About Your Teeth. Sportshelf. P.O. Box 643. New Rochelle, NY 10802. 1968. 15 pp. $1.00 postpaid. Discusses common oral health problems and ways to avoid them. ms-hs.

Yes, You Can Teach Dental Health (#213-9). American Alliance for Health, Physical Education, Recreation, and Dance. Publications Sales. P.O. Box 704. Waldorf, MD 20601. 1976. 46 pp. $3.95; 10% discount on 10 or more copies. A teacher resource for use in planning and conducting an approach to dental health instruction which is correlated with other K-12 classroom subjects.

DISEASES AND DISABILITIES

Birth Defects. March of Dimes Birth Defects Foundation. 1275 Mamaroneck Ave. White Plains, NY 10605; or request from your local March of Dimes office. A variety of materials on the prevention of birth defects is available. Single copy free. hs-ad. Sample titles are:

Be Good to Your Baby Before It Is Born. 29 pp.

Birth Defects: Tragedy and Hope. 14 pp.

Drugs, Alcohol, and Tobacco Abuse During Pregnancy. Leaflet.

Genetic Counseling. 22 pp.

Recipe for Healthy Babies. Leaflet.

Blindness. The American Foundation for the Blind. 15 W. 16th St. New York, NY 10011. Various pamphlets and leaflets. Single copy free. Sample titles are:

Dog Guides for the Blind. Briefly tells about dog guides and the selection and training of both user and dog. hs-ad.

Facts About Aging and Blindness and Visual Impairment. Basic information about old age and blindness. hs-ad.

Facts About Blindness. Basic information concerning blindness. ms-hs.

How Does a Blind Person Get Around? 1973. 20 pp. An explanation for the general public of orientation and mobility training of the blind. hs-ad.

Servicios, Informativos Hacia los Cjegos y la Ceguedad. 1974. 12 pp. Basic information in Spanish about services for the blind in the United States and how to find these services. hs-ad.

Cancer. Several booklet and pamphlet materials are available from the local unit of the American Cancer Society in each state. For addresses write American Cancer Society, Inc. 777 3rd Ave. New York, NY 10017.

Cancer. National Cancer Cytology Center. 88 Sunnyside Blvd. Plainview, NY 11803. Free. Educational leaflets on cytology tests for the detection of various types of cancer. hs.

Diabetes. American Diabetes Assoc. 2 Park Ave. New York, NY 10016. Send for free listing of pamphlets, booklets, and other patient education materials, including 6-page pamphlet entitled "Who We Are, What We Do." hs-ad.

►**Diseases in Humans** (SB-008). U.S. Gov't. Printing Office. Washington, DC 20402. 1981. 24 pp. Free. A listing of many low-cost government publications which may be used in the classroom.

Epilepsy. Epilepsy Foundation of America. Materials Service Center. 4351 Garden City Dr., Suite 406. Landover, MD 20785. Various materials on epilepsy are offered. Titles include:

►**Questions and Answers About Epilepsy.** 1982. 15 pp. 10 cents. Pamphlet giving general information in question-answer format. hs.

Recognition and First Aid for Those With Epilepsy. 1979. 12 pp. 20 cents. Medical definition, causes of epilepsy, types of seizures, and information on handling seizures. hs-ad.

►**Everything Doesn't Cause Cancer.** U.S. Public Health Service. National Institutes of Health. Bldg. 31, Rm. 10A18. Bethesda, MD 20205. 1980. 12 pp. Free. Booklet of questions and answers about cancer causing agents.

Facts Everyone Should Know About Diabetes. Household Grocery Products Div. Alberto-Culver Co. 2525 Armitage Ave. Melrose Park, IL 60160. Undated. Leaflet. Free. Defines diabetes and discusses how it can be controlled. ms-hs.

Hearing Loss. A.G. Bell Assoc. for the Deaf. Publications Sales. 3417 Volta Place, N.W. Washington, DC 20007. Two brochures. Free for a self-addressed stamped envelope (#10). Titles are:

►**Hearing Alert!** 1978. Introduces the problem of hearing loss to parents and suggests where to go for help.

►**Listen! Hear! For Parents of Hearing-Impaired Children.** 1982. Advises parents on what they can do to help normal development.

Hearing Problems. Maico Hearing Instruments. 7375 Bush Lake Rd. Minneapolis, MN 55435. Two wall charts, 9″ x 11″. Free. Titles are:

Sound Levels and Human Response. Shows noise level of various everyday sounds and their effect on hearing. el-ms.

Where Hearing Losses Occur. Shows cross-section of ear with labeled parts where hearing damage can occur. el-ms.

Heart Disease. American Heart Assoc., Inc. National Center. 7320 Greenville Ave. Dallas, TX 75231. Send for teacher resources list. Single copies of most items are available free from your local Heart Association.

Leaflets. National Easter Seal Society. 2023 W. Ogden Ave. Chicago, IL 60612. Several free leaflets on different aspects of handicapping conditions are available. Free catalog of other Society publications upon request with self-addressed stamped envelope (#10).

MSD Pamphlets. Health Information Services. Merck Sharp and Dohme. West Point, PA 19486. Offers several pamphlets on various health problems. 25 cents each; send payment with order. ms-hs-ad. Titles include:

►**Arthritis, a Common Chronic Disease.** 4 pp.

►**Facts About Pheumococcol Pneumonia.** 4 pp.

►**High Blood Pressure.** 4 pp.

►**Saving Your Sight From Glaucoma.** 7 pp.

Multiple Sclerosis. National Multiple Sclerosis Society. 205 E. 42nd St. New York, NY 10017. Pamphlets discussing the nature of MS, an incurable disease of the central nervous system. Single copy free; additional copies as priced. Also available through local chapters. Titles are:

Emotional Aspects of MS. 1980. 12 pp. 10 cents. hs-ad.

Living With MS. 1978. 16 pp. 8 cents. hs-ad.

Mental Health and MS. 1953. 15 pp. 9 cents. hs-ad.

MS: Enemy of Young Adults. 1978. 6 pp. 5 cents. ms-hs.

►**Someone You Know Has Multiple Sclerosis—a Book for Families.** 1982. 31 cents.

What Everyone Should Know About Multiple Sclerosis. 1980. 15 pp. 10 cents. ms-hs.

Public Affairs Pamphlets. Public Affairs Committee, Inc. 381 Park Ave. S. New York, NY 10016. 50 cents each; quantity discounts. Titles include:

Arthritis: Everybody's Disease (#562). 1978. 24 pp. Describes the symptoms of arthritis' many forms that affect 30 million Americans, and explains what is known about causes and treatment. hs-ad.

The Brain and Aging: The Myths, the Facts (#591). 1980. 28 pp. Explains senility and the dangers of mistaking similar symptoms caused by other conditions. hs-ad.

Cataracts and Their Treatment (#545). 1977. 24 pp. A discussion of the causes of blindness by cataracts, how blindness can be avoided through surgery, and how vision is regained afterward. hs-ad.

Glaucoma—Diagnosis, Treatment, Prevention (#568). 1979. 28 pp. Explains how common forms of glaucoma cause needless loss of vision which proper examinations could prevent. Covers signs and symptoms and how glaucoma is related to other vision problems. hs-ad.

►**Low Back Pain—What It Is, What Can Be Done** (#601). 1982. 28 pp. Explains how different back conditions may be treated and outlines exercises for muscles and joints. hs-ad.

What Can We Do About Limited Vision? (#491). 1973. 28 pp. Outlines some measures in prevention, detection, and rehabilitation to assist persons with visual disabilities to maximize their vision. hs-ad.

What Do We Know About Allergies? (#486). 1972. 28 pp. How desensitization, medication, and preventive measures offer relief to the millions of people with allergic reactions. hs-ad.

Respiratory Disorders. American Lung Assoc. 1740 Broadway. New York, NY 10019. Teachers may secure free materials from local associations.

DRIVER EDUCATION

Allstate Leaflets. Allstate Insurance Company. Advocacy Programs Div. Allstate Plaza, F-3. Northbrook, IL 60062. Free. hs-ad. Titles include:

Does Driver Education Make Sense?

The Drunk Driver May Kill You (L746-4). 14 pp.

►**Passive Restraints: Ready When You Are** (L1101-10). 30 pp. Explains the safety features of air cushions in cars. Illustrated. hs-ad.

AAA Materials. American Automobile Assoc. 8111 Gatehouse Rd. Falls Church, VA 22047. Materials available only from local AAA Club offices; request prices.

Federal Materials. U. S. Dept. of Transportation. Federal Highway Administration. Washington, DC 20590. Write for list of current publications related to driver education. Sample titles are:

►**Driver License Administration Requirements and Fees.** 1982. 48 pp. Free. A report on administrative requirements and qualifications needed to obtain driver licenses in all states and territories and other state and federal regulations. hs-ad.

►**License Plates.** 1982. Free. Fold-out chart showing examples of car license plates and data on their regulation in all states and territories. hs-ad.

►**New Driver.** Curriculum Innovations, Inc. 3500 Western Ave. Highland Park, IL 60035. Magazine. 9 issues yearly. Sample issue free to teachers. Each issue contains a variety of articles on driving and traffic safety. hs.

Open Your Eyes to Vision in Driving Safety. American Optometric Assoc. Communications Div. 243 N. Lindbergh Blvd. St. Louis, MO 63141. Leaflet. Single copy free for a self-addressed stamped envelope (#10). Stresses the importance of visual skills in safe driving. hs-ad.

Practical Driving Tips. American Trucking Assoc., Inc. Public Relations Dept. Educational Services. 1616 P St., N. W. Washington, DC 20036. Free in classroom quantity. Titles are:

> **Practical Driving Tips.** Undated. 13 pp. A collection of driving tips for motorists for conditions such as heavy traffic, freeways, and various weather factors. hs-ad.
>
> ►**Sharing the Road With a Truck.** Leaflet. Explains some special driving situations of truck drivers and gives tips to motorists for driving near trucks. hs.

Tips. Consumer Information Center. Pueblo, CO 81009. Titles include:

> **How to Deal With Motor Vehicle Emergencies** (506J). 1979. 30 pp. Free. How to handle emergencies like brake or steering failure, blowouts, or overheating. hs-ad.
>
> **Winter Driving Tips** (508J). 1976. 12 pp. Free. How to prepare for winter driving and how to react to hazardous driving conditions. hs-ad.

►**What You Should Know About Motor Oil.** Quaker State Oil Refining Corp. P. O. Box 989. Oil City, PA 16301. Rev. 1982. 34 pp. Free. A booklet about the design and function of motor oil. hs-ad.

DRUGS

Alcohol. NIAAA National Clearinghouse for Alcohol Information. P.O. Box 2345. Rockville, MD 20852. A variety of pamphlets and booklets. Request the current publications order form ENCAS 7304. Single copies free. Titles include:

> ►**Facts About Alcohol and Alcoholism** (PH 106). 1980. 47 pp. Concise source of information on alcohol use, misuse, the illness of alcoholism, and other associated factors. hs-ad.
>
> ►**Is Beer a Four Letter Word?** (PH 95). 1980. 58 pp. Suggestions for a youth-initiated alcohol abuse prevention program. ms-hs.

Alcohol. Public Affairs Committee, Inc. 381 Park Ave. S. New York, NY 10016. 50 cents each; quantity rates available. Titles include:

Drinking on the Job: The $15 Billion Hangover (#544). 1977. 28 pp. Tells why alcohol-related absenteeism and production loss are a major economic cost and describes some measures to treat alcoholism. hs-ad.

Understanding and Dealing With Alcoholism (#580). 1980. 28 pp. Discusses alcoholism as a disease, its causes and effects, and the many different approaches to its treatment. hs-ad.

You and Your Alcoholic Parent (#506). 1974. 28 pp. Helps teenagers to understand an alcoholic parent's illness and ways to ease the situation for themselves and their family. hs-ad.

►**Alcohol Abuse.** The Cottage Program International. 736 South 500 East. Salt Lake City, UT 84102. Free. A packet of materials on establishing an alcohol prevention program in a community. ad.

►*Alcohol Education.* The National PTA. 700 North Rush St. Chicago, IL 60611-2571. "How-to" materials for use by parents, teachers, students, and community groups are available. Free publications listing. Sample title is:

►**Poster Series.** Set of 8. 14″ x 18″. $4.00 per set. Photos and text focus on youth and typical alcohol-related settings. ms-hs.

Alcohol Packet. American Council on Alcohol Problems. 6955 University Ave. Des Moines, IA 50311. Free. An assortment of leaflets and reprinted articles. ms-hs. Titles include:

►**Alcohol Facts—5 Ways Drinking Can Hurt You**

America's Worst Drug?

Half Drunk Drivers Are Dangerous Too!

What You Need to Know About Alcohol for Your Health and Safety

Alcoholism. Alcoholics Anonymous World Services, Inc. P.O. Box 459. Grand Central Station. New York, NY 10163. Booklets and pamphlets on the recovery from alcoholism. Titles include:

44 Questions and Answers About the AA Program of Recovery From Alcoholism (P-2). Rev. 1978. 33 pp. 20 cents. hs-ad.

►**A Message to Teenagers** (F-9). Pamphlet. Free in quantity. Contains a simple quiz to help one tell when drinking is becoming a problem. ms-hs.

It Happened to Alice (P-39). 1968. 24 pp. 15 cents. Comic book format. el.

What Happened to Joe (P-38). 24 pp. 15 cents. Comic book format. el.

Alcoholism. National Council on Alcoholism, Inc. 733 3rd Ave. New York, NY 10017. Send payment with orders under $25.00. Quantity rates available. Sample titles are:

►**The Alcoholic Is a Sick Person Who Can Be Helped.** 1979. 3 pp. 20 cents. The who, where, and why of the alcoholic and how you can help him.

►**Do's and Don'ts for the Wives of Alcoholics.** 14 pp. 35 cents. Includes 15 practical suggestions. hs-ad.

►**How to Know an Alcoholic.** 1981. 12 pp. 35 cents. Dramatic description of an alcoholic based on personal experience. hs-ad.

►**13 Steps to Alcoholism.** 980. 16 pp. 25 cents. A graphic presentation of the progressive pattern of alcoholism.

►**What Are the Signs of Alcoholism?** 3 pp. 20 cents. Lists 26 questions useful in detecting alcoholism. Also indicates stages of disease. hs-ad.

►**What You Need to Know About You, Your Baby and Drinking.** 1982. 3 pp. 20 cents. Describes the fetal alcohol syndrome. Geared toward teen-aged girls. ms-hs.

AAA Materials. American Automobile Assoc. 8111 Gatehouse Rd. Falls Church, VA 22047. Materials available only from local AAA club offices; request prices.

AMA Materials. American Medical Association. Order Dept. P.O. Box 821. Monroe, WI 53566. Inquire about available materials.

Booklets. Hazelden Literature. P.O. Box 176. Center City, MN 55012. Offers numerous inexpensive materials for alcohol and drug education. Send for complete catalog and order form. Include item number with title. Add 75 cents postage for orders under $20.00. Titles include:

Alcohol: Facts for Decisions (#5035). 1974. 40 pp. $1.50. el-ms.

Marijuana (#1089). 1979. 49 pp. $2.50. ms-hs.

Phencyclidine ("Angel Dust") (#1942). 1979. 20 pp. $1.15. ms-hs.

Thinking About Drinking (#1435). 1975. 31 pp. 85 cents. ms-hs.

What Everyone Should Know About Alcohol (#4810). 15 pp. 75 cents. ms-hs.

►**Catalog of Publications.** National Council on Alcoholism, Inc, 733 3rd Ave. New York, NY 10017. 50 pp. Free. Contains descriptions of numerous books, pamphlets, kits, audio-visual aids, and other materials on alcoholism. Entries are organized by topics or fields, such as families, women, youth, aging, clergy, medical, and counseling.

►**Clearing the Air.** U.S. Public Health Service. National Institute of Health. Bldg. 31, Rm 10A18. Bethesda, MD 20205. 1981. 36 pp. Free. A guide to help smokers quit smoking. ms-ad.

Do-It-Now Materials. Do It Now Foundation. P.O. Box 5115. Phoenix, AZ 85010. Free listing of materials sent on request. ms-hs. Sample titles are:

Amyl/Butyl Nitrate and Nitrous Oxide (#142). 1979. 7 pp. 20 cents. Discusses the implications of the rising popularity of two inhalants.

Cause and Defect: Fetal Alcohol Syndrome. 1978. 9 pp. 20 cents. Explains the dangerous effects on unborn fetuses when the mother drinks alcohol regularly or in excess.

Marijuana: Information (#118). 1980. Leaflet. 15 cents. A report on the findings from marijuana research.

P.C.P.: Dream Turned Nightmare (#116). 1980. 6 pp. 15 cents. Leaflet describing one of the most unknown problems in street drugs.

Sniffing: A Parent's Perspective (#106). 1980. 6 pp. 15 cents. A discussion of the facts about sniffing paint, aerosol products, glue, gasoline, petroleum products, and cryogenics to dispell misconceptions.

Substance Abuse and Safety (#128). 1979. Leaflet. 15 cents. Discussion of chemical use and its relationship to accidents.

Valium & Librium: The Pharmaceutical War Against Anxiety (#134). 1976. 8 pp. 20 cents. Pamphlet describes benefits and dangers involved in regular use of valium and librium, emphasizing non-drug alternatives.

Drug Booklets. Public Affairs Committee, Inc. 381 Park Avenue S. New York, NY 10016. 50 cents each; quantity rates available. Titles are:

Children and Drugs (#584). 1980. 24 pp. Offers basic facts—what drugs are, how used, effects, dangers, slang terms—and practical guidance. ad.

Drugs—Use, Misuse, Abuse (#515). 1974. 20 pp. Discusses family lifestyle and parents' own drug habits as strong factors influencing drug abuse by children. ad.

What You Should Know About Drug Abuse (#550). 1977. 28 pp. Discusses many reasons that drug abuse remains a serious social problem. hs-ad.

►**Drugs, Demons & Disaster: Can We Save Our Kids?** America's Future. 514 Main St. New Rochelle, NY 10801. 1981. 30 pp. Free to students and teachers for school use; 50 cents to others. A booklet written by two parents on the effects and dangers of drugs. hs-ad.

Health Series. New Readers Press. Box 131. Syracuse, NY 13210. $1.75 each; prepay orders under $10.00. 8-page student exercises available for each title at 28 cents each. Sample titles are:

Alcohol: Facts for Decisions. 1974. 40 pp. Presents facts about alcohol to enable responsible drinking decisions. el-ms.

►**Drugs: Facts for Decisions.** Rev. 1983. 32 pp. Presents facts about the use and abuse of commonly used drugs. el-ms.

Tobacco: Facts for Decisions. 1978. 32 pp. Presents information about smoking and methods of quiting. el-ms.

GPO Materials. U.S. Gov't. Printing Office. Washington, DC 20402. Lists of many low-cost government publications which may be used in the classroom. Sample titles are:

►**Alcoholism** (SB-175). 1982. 12 pp. Free.

►**Drug Education** (SB-163). 1982. 12 pp. Free.

►**Publicaciones en Espanol** (SB-130). 1981. 4 pp. Free.

K-4 Guides. American School Health Assoc. P.O. Box 708. Kent, OH 44240. Two unit guides for teaching about alcohol and tobacco in the early childhood years. $1.50 each (members $1.00). Titles are:

Introducing Alcohol Education in the Elementary School K-4. 1978. 13 pp.

Introducing Tobacco Education in the Elementary School K-4. 1978. 19 pp.

Prevention. National Clearinghouse for Drug Abuse Information. National Institute on Drug Abuse. P.O. Box 416. Kensington, MD 20895. Single copy free. Sample titles are:

Deciding About Drugs: A Woman's Choice (ADM 80-820). 1979. 28 pp. A pamphlet written for women by women on coping with stress and using drugs. ad.

Drug Abuse Films (ADM 80-914). 1980. 26 pp. An annotated list of 16 mm films and ordering sources. Indexes films by topic and intended audience. Contains several low-cost rental and free-loan films. ad.

For Parents Only: What You Need to Know About Marijuana (ADM 80-909). 1980. 28 pp. Presents the latest scientifically accepted information about marijuana's effects on children's physical and mental health. ad.

Primers. Do It Now Foundation. P.O. Box 5115. Phoenix, AZ 85010. Send for catalog of drug, alcohol, and health publications. Prepay and include 50 cents for postage with orders under $5.00. Titles include:

Drug Abuse: A Realistic Primer for Parents (#204). 1980. 20 pp. 60 cents. Presents drug abuse to parents in a way that will not turn them off. ad.

Drugs: A Primer for Young People (#212). 1976. 26 pp. 75 cents. Designed to help children deal with peer group pressure to experiment with drugs. el.

►**Questions and Answers About Drug Abuse.** Prudential Insurance Co. P.O. Box 36. Newark, NJ 07101. 1981. 28 pp. Free. A pamphlet of specific information about the substances most commonly abused. ms-hs-ad.

Smoking. American Lung Assoc. 1740 Broadway. New York, NY 10019. Free materials on the effects of smoking on one's health and that of others. Send for current catalog.

Smoking—a Habit That Should Be Broken (#573). Public Affairs Committee, Inc. 381 Park Ave. S. New York, NY 10016. 1979. 28 pp. 50 cents. Examines the Surgeon General's report on the dangers of smoking, particularly for teen-agers, women, and industrial workers. Protection for the nonsmoker and "psychological inoculation" against starting are covered. hs-ad.

►**Steering Clear: Helping Your Child Through the High-Risk Drug Years.** Winston Press. 430 Oak Grove, Suite 203. Minneapolis, MN 55403. 1982. 112 pp. $4.95. Explains alcohol, marijuana, and several other popular drugs, their widespread use, and some approaches on avoiding and coping with the problem. hs-ad.

EARLY CHILDHOOD EDUCATION

Activity Books. Milliken Publishing Co. 1100 Research Blvd. St. Louis, MO 63132. Publisher offers a wide assortment of books of duplicating masters for the basic curriculum areas at economical prices. Send for K-3 catalog.

Activity Hints. Academic Therapy Publications. 20 Commercial Blvd. Novato, CA 94947. Payment should accompany all orders and include 10% handling charge (minimum $1.50); U.S. currency only. California residents must include sales tax. Official purchase orders over $15.00 may be billed. Sample titles are:

Activities for Developing Auditory Perception (#111-6). 1975. 64 pp. $2.50. A multisensory manual of exercises to strengthen memory, discrimination, comprehension, localization, and other auditory skills. pr-el.

The Effect of Affect (#166-3). 1977. 64 pp. $3.00. Presents more than 100 classroom activities to develop better relationships, self-esteem, and decision making among primary age children. pr.

Bibliography of Materials for Equal Early Education. Non-Sexist Child Development Project. Women's Action Alliance, Inc. 370 Lexington Ave. New York, NY 10017. 1980. 8 pp. Free.

►**Catalog of Classroom Aids** (SC-6300L). World Book Inc. Merchandise Mart Plaza. Chicago, IL 60654. 1982. 5 pp. Free. A listing of articles, posters, guides, learning aids for use with *World Book,* and other teaching aids.

Clean and Neat Is Hard to Beat. The Soap and Detergent Assoc. Consumer Affairs Dept. 475 Park Ave. S. New York, NY 10016. Complete packet, $1.00; or 60 cents for one record; 40 cents for two posters; and 20 cents for the guide. A preschool instructor's packet to encourage children to develop good personal habits; includes one 45 rpm record of ten songlets, a guide and a week's supply of lesson plans, and two posters that emphasize cleanliness.

►**Early Childhood & Day Care.** Children's Book & Music Center. 2500 Santa Monica Blvd. Santa Monica CA 90404. Rev. bi-annually. 48 pp. $1.00. A catalog of recordings, books, and rhythm instruments for children of all ages. Several items less than $5.00. Titles are arranged under 10 headings and indexed. ps-pr.

►**Free Stuff for Kids.** Meadowbrook Press. Deephaven, MN 55391. Rev. 1983. 120 pp. $2.95 plus 50 cents for shipping. Contains over 250 items children can receive by mail for a self-addressed stamped envelope or a small fee. Items include information on sports, pets, and hobbies; free badges, buttons, games, kits, puzzles; and coloring and comic books. pr.

Grow With Books. Enoch Pratt Free Library. Publications Dept. 400 Cathedral St. Baltimore, MD 21201. 1979. 27 pp. 75 cents. A list of books for parents or other caring adults to read with children aged two to five. ps.

Guide Books. The Play Schools Assoc., Inc. Room 615. 19 W. 44th St. New York, NY 10036. Sample titles are:

> **Play With Puppets.** 1971. 52 pp. $1.50. Tells how to make simple effective puppets for 5- and 6-year-olds to stimulate oral expression and interaction.
>
> **Materials and Equipment for Learning in Play Activities.** 1973. 15 pp. 50 cents. A list of supplies and program ideas for many types of recreation. Arranged according to age groups. ps-pr-el.
>
> **Music Is Fun for Children.** 1971. 32 pp. $1.50. Suggestions for music and movement in children's educational and play program. Bibliography and list of recordings. ps-pr.
>
> **There Was a Little Boy.** 1968. 40 pp. $2.00. A one act play showing the need for communication between child and parent. hs-ad.

NAEYC Publications. National Association for the Education of Young Children. 1834 Connecticut Ave., N.W. Washington, DC 20009. Request free annotated listing of books, posters, and brochures. Sample titles are:

> ►**A Guide to Discipline.** 1978. 32 pp. $1.75

More Than Graham Crackers: Nutrition Education and Food Preparation with Young Children. 1979. 100 pp. $4.15.

►**Number in Preschool and Kindergarten: Educational Implications of Piaget's Theory.** 1982. 92 pp. $3.85.

"Name Game" Coloring Books. Spelling B. 3796 Midvale Ln. Huntington Valley, PA 19006. 1976. 24 pp. each. $1.50 each plus $1.00 postage (total). Six coloring books in which an animal, object, number, or shape is formed by the letters spelling its name. ps-pr. Titles include:

A to Z Things to Color

Shapes to Color

Numbers to Color

Zoo Animals to Color

Picturebook Learning. Ann Arbor Publishers, Inc. P.O. Box 7249. Naples, FL 33940. Titles are:

Benji the Bug. 1973. 21 pp. $2.50. Picturebook designed to teach directionality concepts. pr.

Finton the Fish. 1974. 29 pp. $2.50. Picturebook designed to teach visual discrimination. pr.

Itty the Inchworm. 1974. 31 pp. $2.50. Picturebook designed to teach motor coordination for children. pr.

Roxy the Robin. 1974. 48 pp. $3.00. Picturebook designed to teach sequence relationships for children. pr.

Sesame Street. Community Education Services. Children's Television Workshop. 1 Lincoln Plaza. New York, NY 10023. ps-pr. Titles include:

The Muppet Gallery. 1978. 26 pp. $1.00. 25 copies or more 80 cents each. The muppets illustrate social skills such as co-operation, resolving conflicts, and entering social groups. Contains "read-aloud" stories and activities.

Sesame Street Activities. 1976. 65 pp. $2.00; 25 or more copies $1.60 each. A manual of children's activities based on the entertainment approach to teaching used on T.V.'s "Sesame Street." Spanish version also available.

►**Sesame Street Fire Safety Resource Package.** 1982. 36 pp. $2.00. A teaching resource designed to introduce fire safety education to adult caregivers of preschoolers. Contains activities, skits, and songs with fire safety messages. Spanish version available.

Teacher Aids. Assoc. for Childhood Education International. 3615 Wisconsin Ave., N.W. Washington, DC 20016. Send for publications list. Add 10% to prices for shipping. No billed orders under $10.00; prepay in U.S. currency. Sample titles are:

Art Guide—Let's Create a Form. 1969. 54 pp. $2.50. Contains activities and suggestions for encouraging creative expression through art. ad.

Bits and Pieces—Imaginative Uses for Children's Learning. 1967. 72 pp. $4.00. Describes the recycled use of odds and ends for creative learning in the classroom. ad.

►**Functions of Folk and Fairy Tales** (#096-0). 1981. 24 pp. $2.00. Articulates the value of fantasy in the lives of children. Includes selective reading lists for children, teachers, and parents. ad.

►**Teacher Idea Exchange.** Scholastic, Inc. 50 W. 44th St. New York, NY 10036. 1981. 46 pp. $1.50. Contains more than 100 teaching ideas developed over many years by "See-Saw" teachers. K-1.

Traffic Safety. American Automobile Assoc. 8111 Gatehouse Rd. Falls Church, VA 22047. Materials available only from local AAA Club offices; request prices.

ECOLOGY

Air Pollution. American Lung Assoc. 1740 Broadway. New York, NY 10019. Several materials which present the effects of air pollution on the environment and on one's health are available free. Send for catalog.

Be Informed Series. New Readers Press. Box 131. Syracuse, NY 13210. $1.20 each; prepay orders under $10.00. Each includes teacher's guide with resource list. Titles are:

Be Informed on Pollution 1974. 40 pp. Topics include the balance of nature, major forms of pollution, causes of pollution, and possible solutions. el-ms.

Be Informed on Population 1974. 24 pp. Topics include population growth and its effect, population resources and pollution, and the politics of population control. el-ms.

►**Becoming an Environmentalist.** Cottonwood Publishing Co. P.O. Box 1222. Walla Walla, WA 99362. 1976. 58 pp. $2.45; school discount available. A humorous account of how one family adjusted its lifestyle to conserve energy and to ecological living. el-ms-hs.

►**Charlie Brown Clears the Air.** U.S. Environmental Protection Agency. Public Inquiries Center. PM-211-B. Washington, DC 20460. 1979. 30 pp. Free. Charlie Brown and friends express their concern about pollution. Captions and dialog with each illustration. ps. to ms.

The Continuing Campaign for Cleaner Air (#572). Public Affairs Committee, Inc. 381 Park Ave. S. New York, NY 10016. 1979. 24 pp. 50 cents. Explains air pollution and its harmful effects, discusses the status of the Clean Air Act, and clarifies economic issues of cleanup and control. hs-ad.

Ecological Super Posters. Public Relations Dept. Chevron Chemical Co. P.O. Box 3744.San Francisco, CA 94119. 6 full-colored posters, 24" x 36", on heavy paper. $3.00 per set. Posters representing ecological concepts with accompanying "Teaching Tips" guide to experiments in notation, classification, tabulation, surveying, field visits, living cycles, and plant development. el.

Environmental Materials. Ecology Center. 2701 College Ave. Berkeley, CA 94705. A self-addressed stamped envelope must accompany requests for free leaflets. hs-ad. Titles include:

Backyard Composting. 17 pp. 50 cents. Details for aerobic composting.

Pesticides. Leaflet. Free.

Ten Things You Can Do to Solve the Solid Waste Problem. Leaflet. Free.

►**Water Conservation in the Garden.** Leaflet. Free.

Water: A Selected Bibliography. Leaflet. Free.

Environmental Projects. Keep America Beautiful. 99 Park Ave. New York, NY 10016. Free. A variety of materials for community and school projects to protect and improve the environment. hs-ad.

EPA Materials. U.S. Environmental Protection Agency. Office of Public Affairs (A-107). Room 301. West Tower. Washington, DC 20460. Send for current listing of available publications.

GPO Materials. U.S. Gov't. Printing Office. Washington, DC 20402. Lists of many low-cost government publications which may be used in the classroom. Sample titles are:

►**Air Pollution** (SB-046). 1981. 5 pp. Free.

►**Environmental Education and Protection** (SB-088). 1981. 13 pp. Free.

►**Noise Abatement** (SB-063). 1981. 3 pp. Free.

►**Salvage and Recycling** (SB-159). 1981. 3 pp. Free.

Hazardous and Solid Waste. Environmental Action Foundation. The Dupont Circle Bldg., Suite 724. Washington, DC 20036. Titles are:

Exposure. Tabloid. Monthly. 8-12 pp. Sample copy free. Reports on citizen activity on waste and toxic substances issues in communities and workplaces around the country. Technical aspects are translated into lay language. hs-ad.

Waste and Toxic Substance Resource Guide. Updated every 6 months. 32 pp. $2.00. Lists books, pamphlets, films, packets, and educational materials on issues concerning solid waste, hazardous waste, and toxic exposure. Resources cover such topics as recycling technologies, dump sites, and model legislation. hs-ad.

Meecology.® McDonald's Corporation. 16 mm film. Color. Sound. 20 min. Available for showing through local McDonald's restaurants; ask for the Community Relations Representative. Available for purchase from: Dennis Films, Inc. 161 E. Erie St. Chicago, IL 60611. Shows children ages 6 to 12 how to become personally involved in improving the environment at home and in the community. Includes teacher discussion kit. pr-el.

Pollution. Center for Information on America. Washington, CT 06793. Editions in the Vital Issues series. Titles are:

Noise: The Most Ubiquitous of All Pollutions (Vol. 28, No. 3). 1978. 4 pp. 45 cents. Is harmful noise an increasing danger? The U.S. census disclosed that citizens generally considered noise a worse neighborhood problem than even crime. hs.

Solid Waste Matter—What to Do About It? (Vol. 24, No. 6). 1975. 4 pp. 35 cents. Outlines the ubiquitous problem of solid waste matter and explains how one state's solution is being implemented. hs.

Pollution. League of Women Voters Education Fund. 1730 M St., N.W. Washington, DC 20036. Sample titles are:

►**Blueprint for Clean Air** (#222). 1981. 8 pp. 75 cents. Basic background information on the Clean Air Act. Outlines the sources and effects of air pollution, the status of air quality controls, and previews the upcoming debate over CAA renewal. hs-ad.

►**Blueprint for Clean Water** (#639). 1982. 24 pp. 75 cents. Covers the Clean Water Act's history and track record, different types of water pollutants, and the economics of pollution control. hs-ad.

Getting in the Swim: How Citizens Can Influence Water Quality Planning (#188). 1977. 6 pp. 40 cents. Explains how community leaders and citizens can influence water quality planning. Includes some examples of citizen participation. hs-ad.

Recycling. Reynolds Metals Co. Recycling Public Relations Manager. Dept. VU. 6603 W. Broad St. Richmond, VA 23261. Titles include:

Reynolds Aluminum Recycling Program: Questions and Answers. 1977. 10 pp. Free. ms-hs.

Reynolds Aluminum Presents Michael Recycle. 1979. 8 pp. Free. Comic book. pr-el.

Resource Recovery. Committee of Tin Mill Products Producers. American Iron and Steel Institute. 1000 16th St., N. W. Washington, DC 20036. 1979. 20 pp. Free. Reports on the conversion of solid waste into energy, and the new processes for recycling steel cans. Lists sources of further information. ms-hs.

Sierra Club Materials. Information Services. Sierra Club. 530 Bush St. San Francisco, CA 94108. Many articles and teaching packets are available on subjects such as environment, pollution, public lands, natural resources, population, and wildlife; request current literature list. el-ms.

Sound and Noise. Motor Vehicle Manufacturers Assoc. of the U.S., Inc. 300 New Center Bldg. Detroit, MI 48202. Undated. 24 pp. Free. A booklet to acquaint the reader with the general principles of sound. Glossary. Illustrated. ms-hs.

The Story of Environment and Industry. U.S. Steel Corp. Education & Training. Rm. 727. 600 Grant St. Pittsburgh, PA 15230. 1977. Free. Large foldout. Presents aspects of land, water, and air pollution related to industry. ms-hs.

Suggestion Sheets. Keep America Beautiful, Inc. 99 Park Ave. New York, NY 10016. Two-page sheets on learning activities or on individual and group actions related to protecting the environment. 1-5 copies free; additional copies 5 cents each. Titles are:

> **Community Clean-up Campaign Check List.** ms-hs.
>
> **Pollution Pointers for Elementary Students.** el.
>
> **You Take the First Step: Ways to Improve the Environment.** More than 5 copies one cent each. hs-ad.

►**Teaching About Spaceship Earth.** (Int. #71). Global Perspectives in Education, Inc. 218 East 18th St. New York, NY 10003. 1971. 53 pp. $2.25 postpaid. A space travel story that provides a classroom simulation for learning environmental concepts. el-ms.

The Web of Life (MW1644). New American Library. 1633 Broadway. New York, NY 10019. 1953. 128 pp. $1.95. A short and simple study of how all living things fit together into a single pattern. Illustrated. ms.

What Can I Do? American Forestry Assoc. 1319 18th St., N.W. Washington, DC 20036. Undated. 16 pp. Free. Tells how individuals can help stop pollution and improve the quality of life. ms-hs-ad.

Wildlife. Wildlife Management Institute. 709 Wire Bldg. 1000 Vermont Ave., N.W. Washington, DC 20005. Various materials about wildlife, ecology, and management. Titles include:

> ►**The American Landscape: 1776-1976, Two Centuries of Change.** 1976. 91 pp. $2.50. A look at the changes in the natural resource base and their causes. hs-ad.
>
> **Helping Wildlife: Working With Nature.** 1977. 26 pp. $1.00. Guide for teaching basic ecological concepts of natural resources and wildlife management. Illustrated. References. ms-hs.
>
> ►**Placing Wildlife Management in Perspective.** 29 pp. 50 cents. Discussion of the roles and emphasis in wildlife resource management. ms-hs.
>
> **Wildlife: The Environmental Barometer.** Pamphlet. Single copy free. Summaries the influence of habitat, man, and pollution.

The World Around You: Environmental Education Packet. The Garden Club of America. Conservation Committee. 598 Madison Ave. New York, NY 10022. One packet free to teachers, librarians, learning centers, etc.; additional packets $2.00 each; individual articles or leaflets are available for a self-addressed stamped (37 cents) envelope. Contains six articles on such environmental subjects as public lands, toxic substances, national parks, and endangered species for upper grades; three activity leaflets and three wall charts for elementary grades. Looseleaf. el-ms-hs.

ECONOMICS

Amoco Teaching Aids. Amoco Educational Services. Public Affairs—MC 3705. P.O. Box 5910-A. Chicago, IL 60680. 7 pp. Free. A listing of educational and classroom materials on energy, conservation, economics, and careers. ad.

Basic Concepts. National Schools Committee for Economic Education, Inc. 143 Sound Beach Ave. Old Greenwich, CT 06870. Request catalog. Titles include:

How We Live and Work. 1979. 96 pp. $3.50 to teachers. A teacher's guide for economic education in grades 7-12. Includes student activities and references to teaching resources. ms-hs.

Introducing the World of Work. 1977. 60 pp. $3.00 to teachers. A manual for teaching economic concepts in the elementary grades. Includes source lists of books, films, and filmstrips. el.

►**You Choose.** 1982. 32 pp. $1.00. A student workbook in which cartoon characters tell a story of going into business to earn enough money for what they most want. Illustrated. G3-5.

CED Publications. Committee for Economic Development. 477 Madison Ave. New York, NY 10022. Prepay orders under $50.00; add 10% to total order for shipping (min. 65 cents). Titles include:

►**Employment Policy for the Hard-to-Employ: The Path of Progress** (#110). 1982. 11 pp. $1.00. Urges Congress to redesign federal training and jobs programs to strengthen the role of local business leaders and that of the Private Industry Councils. hs-ad.

Fighting Inflation and Rebuilding a Sound Economy (#071). 1980. 26 pp. $3.00. Offers a long-term strategy for reducing inflation and rebuilding American industry and the economy. Urges special attention to defense and energy issues. hs-ad.

Jobs for the Hard-to-Employ: New Directions for a Public-Private Partnership (#066). 1978. 112 pp. $3.00. Calls for a commitment to reducing structural unemployment without inflation through national policy. Urges actions for the transition of the hard-to-employ from income support and subsidized jobs into permanent, private-sector employment. hs-ad.

►**Reforming Retirement Policies.** (#073). 1981. 66 pp. $5.00. Calls for changes in Social Security, employer pensions, and individual saving and investment that can develop a retirement system to care for retirees and also promote noninflationary economic growth. hs-ad.

CEP Reports. Conference on Economic Progress. 2610 Upton St., N.W. Washington, DC 20008. Send for complete listing. Sample titles are:

Goals for Full Employment and How to Achieve Them Under the "Full Employment and Balanced Growth Act of 1978." 1978. 103 pp. $2.00. An explanation of the proposed legislation, founded upon discussion of U.S. economic developments, basic problems, and national programs and policies since the Korean war. hs-ad.

"Liberal" and "Conservative" National Economic Policies and Their Consequences, 1919-1979. 1979. 149 pp. $3.00. An historical analysis which reviews U.S. economic developments over six decades, evaluates effects of national policies, and offers alternative policies. hs-ad.

Money, Credit, and Interest Rates: Their Gross Mismanagement by the Federal Reserve System. 1980. 112 pp. $3.00. A comprehensive examination of "Fed" policies and their consequences, from 1953 to 1980, and proposals for alternative policies. hs-ad.

►**Delicate Bonds: The Global Semiconductor Industry.** Pacific Studies Center. 222B View St. Mountain View, CA 94041. 1981. 26 pp. $2.00. Describes the impact of the silicon chip and other electronic components on international economic relations. hs-ad.

►**Economics for Young Americans.** Chamber of Commerce of the U.S. Special Projects Div. 1615 H St., N.W. Washington, DC 20062. Brochure. Free. Describes a prepared economics education program that may be purchased by schools or local patrons. ms-hs.

►**Economics of the Environment.** American Iron and Steel Institute. 1000 16th St., N.W. Washington, DC 20036. 1977. Single copy free to teachers. Explores and defines the costs of pollution and pollution control. Includes sound cassette, filmstrip, and teaching guide. hs.

Economics Unit Outline. American Trucking Assoc. Inc. Public Relations Dept. Educational Services. 1616 P St., N.W. Washington, DC 20036. Rev. 1974. 12 pp. One free to teacher. A complete outline for teacher use in introducing basic economic concepts using the trucking industry. G4-9.

Federal Reserve. Public Information Center. Federal Reserve Bank of Chicago. Box 834. Chicago, IL 60690. Single copy free. Titles include:

Economic Perspectives. Bimonthly. 16 to 32 pp. Contains survey and in-depth articles on banking, business, agriculture, and international economic matters. hs-ad.

Two Faces of Debt. Rev. 1979. 34 pp. Discusses debt within the public and private sectors and its essential role in economic prosperity. hs-ad.

Federal Reserve. Federal Reserve Bank of Kansas City. Research Div. Kansas City, MO 64198. Single copy free. Titles are:

Economic Review. Subscription free. An economic journal with emphasis on banking, business, and agriculture. hs-ad.

Energy and American Agriculture. 1980. 41 pp. A report dealing with the reassessment of the use of energy in food and fiber production; discusses possible alternative sources and conservation. hs-ad.

Farm Real Estate Values: What's Happening and Why. 1979. 36 pp. Treats issues raised about the demand for farm land by farm operators and non-farm investors, including who is buying farm land and how it is being financed. hs-ad.

International Trade and American Agriculture. 1976. 59 pp. Reviews the history of U.S. agricultural exports, points out the issues involved, and states the case for international trade. hs-ad.

►**Issues in Monetary Policy: II.** 1982. 136 pp. Contains reprints of ten articles from the *Economic Review* devoted to monetary policy issues. Especially prepared as a resource for college students, banking school students, and others interested in policy analysis. ad.

►**Modeling Agriculture for Policy Analysis in the 1980s.** 1981. 222 pp. Discusses the increasing complexity of agricultural policy issues, and how they have become increasingly intertwined with other economic and political issues. ad.

►**Monetary Policy Issues in the 1980s.** 1982. Discusses monetary policy in this decade, touching on such topics as the effect of U.S. policies on foreign countries and the selection of monetary targets. ad.

►**Western Water Resources: Coming Problems and the Policy Alternatives.** 1980. 324 pp. Focuses on water supply issues and problems in our western states that will confront the nation in coming years. ad.

Federal Reserve. Federal Reserve Bank of Minneapolis. Office of Public Information. Minneapolis, MN 55480. Sample titles are:

Employment and Unemployment. 1978. 28 pp. Free. Considers concepts and measures of, and trends and cyclical movements affecting, employment and unemployment. Includes a section on policy proposals. ad.

Goals and Objectives of the Introductory College-level Course in Economics. 1976. 42 pp. Free. Eight leading economics educators offer suggestions for a systematic evaluation of teaching objectives. ad.

Ford Foundation Materials. Ford Foundation. Office of Reports. 320 E. 43rd St. New York, NY 10017.

►**The Search for a New Economic Order.** 1982. 44 pp. Free. A report describing the main areas of economic research supported by the Ford Foundation in the 1970s, with particular emphasis on the work in the international economics. hs-ad.

►**Ford Foundation Publications and Films.** 24 pp. Free. Annotated list of pamphlets, reports, reprints, and films prepared by or for the Foundation.

►**The Freeman.** The Foundation for Economic Education, Inc. 30 South Broadway. Irvington-on-Hudson, NY 10533. Free. 64 pp. A digest-size, monthly journal of ideas on current economic and consumer issues. hs-ad.

Futures Trading. The Chicago Board of Trade. Literature Services. LaSalle at Jackson. Chicago, IL 60604. Free in limited quantities. Titles include:

►**Action in the Marketplace: Commodity Futures Trading.** 1982. 25 pp. Covers the Exchange, auction, clearing, ticker symbols, hedging, and speculation. hs-ad.

►**Financial Futures: The Delivery Process.** 1982. 33 pp. Explains the delivery process on CBT financial futures market. Topics include procedures for actual delivery, function of delivery, and CBT Clearing Corporation. hs-ad.

►**A Guide to Financial Futures.** 1982. 60 pp. An introduction to the interest rate futures market. Discusses hedging, spreading, and basis and includes trading examples. hs-ad.

►**Speculations in Futures.** 1979. 51 pp. Describes normal and invested markets, forecasting, risk, accounts, and trading. hs-ad.

Grain Reserves: What Are the Initiatives for Them? (Vol. 27, No. 10). Center for Information on America. Washington, CT 06793. 1978. 4 pp. 45 cents. Discusses the formulation of a grain reserve policy to help anticipate a poor harvest while protecting grain farmers from low prices and consumers from severe food price inflation. hs.

Illustrated Booklets. Wheelabrator-Frye Inc. Liberty Lane. Hampton, NH 03842. Titles are:

Alice's Big Story. 1979. 17 pp. Free. A fictional television anchorperson uncovers a cause of inflation—waste. el-ms.

►**The Money Machine.** 1980. 17 pp. Free. An account of the function of the Federal Reserve in creating money written in storybook form. Cartoon illustrations. el-ms.

►**The Surrey.** 1981. 17 pp. Free. The benefits of international cooperation and the dangers of protectionism are described in storybook form. Cartoon illustrations. el-ms.

Journey Through a Stock Exchange. American Stock Exchange. Publications Dept. 86 Trinity Pl. New York, NY 10006. 1970. 24 pp. Single copy 50 cents (free to teachers using school letterhead); additional copies 25 cents each. Booklet explains the workings of a stock exchange as seen through the eyes of a 12-year-old. Color illustrated. el-ms.

Leaflet Series. Amoco Educational Services. MC-3705. P.O. Box 5910-A. Chicago, IL 60680. Free in classroom quantities. el-ms-hs. Titles include:

Basic Economic Concepts. 5 pp. A leaflet defining seven economic concepts.

►**Energy and Economics.** 4 pp. Teacher's guide with test. For use with "This Business of Energy."

Freedom of Choice. 3 pp. A leaflet discussing ten economic freedoms.

It's a Great System. 8 pp. Outlines the American private enterprise, free market system and how it works.

This Business of Energy. 7 pp. A leaflet reviewing the economics of energy.

What Is a Business? 2 pp. A leaflet on how business affects the individual.

The Mochans. Amoco Teaching Aids. P.O. Box 1400K. Dayton, OH 45414. 1976. $1.00. A 10-page booklet, 10 duplicating masters for student activity, pre- and post-tests, and teacher's guide with suggested lesson plans and various classroom activities. Covers key economic concepts including means of exchange, methods of production, scarcity of resources, and economic stability. A film, "The Kingdom of Mocha," (16 mm, color-sound, 26 min.) is available for free loan from Modern Talking Picture Service. G7-12.

Periodicals. Public Information Center. Federal Reserve Bank of Chicago. Box 834. Chicago, IL 60690. Free in quantities. Titles are:

►**Midwest Update.** Monthly. 2 pp. Summary of economic conditions in major sectors of the midwest states' economy. hs-ad.

►**On Reserve: News for Economic Educators.** 3 issues yearly. 2-4 pp. each. Explores economic or consumer education topics, suggests supplemental reading materials and teaching activities, and relates news of regional economic education programs. hs-ad.

Policy Issues. National Federation of Independent Business. Education Dept. 150 W. 20th Ave. San Mateo, CA 94403. Offers editions from the Public Policy Discussion Series. Each edition contains an essay by a noted economist on a current public issue of concern to independent businesses. Free for classroom use to teachers using school letterhead. Titles include:

►**Entrepreneurship: Starting a Small Business.** 1980. 7 pp. hs-ad.

Inflation and the Burden of Taxation. 1979. 5 pp. hs-ad.

►**Minimum Wage and Minority Employment Opportunities.** 1978. 5 pp. hs-ad.

►**Small-Business Performance in the Regulated Economy.** 1981. 5 pp. hs-ad.

►**Social Security: The Case for Comprehensive Reform.** 1979. 6 pp. hs-ad.

►**Prices, Wages, and the Cost of Living** (SB-226). U.S. Gov't. Printing Office. Washington, DC 20402. 1981. 20 pp. Free. A listing of many low-cost government publications which may be used in the classroom.

Resource Materials. Federal Reserve Bank of Richmond. Bank and Public Relations Dept. Richmond, VA 23261. Sample titles are:

►**Essays on Inflation.** 1982. 206 pp. Free. Contains 25 articles which summarize major issues in the contemporary inflation problem. ad.

The Federal Reserve Today. 1980. 23 pp. Free. Explains the structure, service functions, and monetary policy of the Federal Reserve System. hs.

►**Instruments in the Money Market.** 1981. 148 pp. Free. A compilation of twelve new articles on various money market instruments. ad.

Keys for Business Forcasting. 1980. 32 pp. Free. Describes in nontechnical language the key statistics and techniques used in appraising economic conditions. hs-ad.

The Relevance of Adam Smith. 1977. 16 pp. Free. Uses passages from the *Wealth of Nations* to show the widespread use of Adam Smith's ideas in debates over public policy. ad.

Series for Economic Education. Federal Reserve Bank of Philadelphia. Public Services Dept. P.O. Box 66. Philadelphia, PA 19105. 8 to 13 pp. Free. Booklets designed for easy understanding of the major features, trends, and problems of our national economy. el-ms. Titles include:

Economic Man vs. Social Man

Inflation and/or Unemployment

The Growth of Government

The Mystery of Economic Growth

Teaching Economics. Joint Council on Economic Education. 1212 Avenue of the Americas. New York, NY 10036. Request checklist for an annotated listing of a variety of teaching and testing materials offered by the Council. Sample titles are:

Audiovisual Materials for Teaching Economics (#288). 3rd ed. 1980. 176 pp. $4.00. Annotates more than 600 AV items for economic education in kindergarten through college. Describes the process for choosing the entries, lists items by grade level, and gives addresses of distributors. ad.

A Framework for Teaching Economics: Basic Concepts, Part I (#253). 1977. 56 pp. $3.50. Presents the basic concepts and generalizations for teaching economics. Summarizes the structure and substance of economics as understood by the majority of economists and economic educators. ad.

A Guide to Games and Simulations for Teaching Economics (#283). 3rd ed. 1979. 93 pp. $2.50. Annotates 130 items with emphasis on the construction, selection, evaluation, and use of games and simulations. Also lists catalogs, journals, and newsletters in the field and their publishers. ad.

Strategies for Teaching Economics: Intermediate Level (#258). 1978. 126 pp. $6.00. Detailed directions for activities on economic topics plus eight simulations, including five based on the mini-society instructional system. G4-6.

Strategies for Teaching Economics: Primary Level (#257). 1977. 142 pp. $6.00. Directions for using a number of activities to teach six key economic topics. Provides overview of each topic for teachers and indicates grade levels for each activity. G1-3.

Understanding the Money Muddle (XX, No. 9). American Institute for Economic Research. Great Barrington, MA 01230. 1980. 20 pp. $2.00. Presents a view of the economic problems caused by inflating the value of money. hs-ad.

►**"What's the Difference?"** National Federation of Independent Business. Education Dept. 150 W. 20th Ave. San Mateo, CA 94403. 1982. Wall chart, 22″ x 17″; teacher's guide, 16 pp. Free. Chart shows comparative standard of living and other economic data for U.S., U.K., U.S.S.R., France, and West Germany. Teacher's guide suggests lessons and activities which use the chart. hs.

Worldwatch Papers. Worldwatch Institute. 1776 Massachusetts Ave., N.W. Washington, DC 20036. Titles are:

►**Microelectronics at Work: Productivity and Jobs in the World Economy** (#39). 1980. 64 pp. $2.00. Discusses why advances in microelectronics have raised complex issues and problems for nearly all national economies. hs-ad.

►**Productivity: The New Economic Context** (#49). 1982. 47 pp. $2.00. Asserts that productivity gains made by new technology will not necessarily improve the standard of living. New ways to distribute the benefits need to be found. Wiser use of energy, land, and raw materials is a sign of a healthier economy in the long run. hs-ad.

►**Six Steps to a Sustainable Society** (#48). 1982. 63 pp. $2.00. Argues that the global economy is threatened by the deterioration of biological systems in much of the world and suggests policies for correction. hs-ad.

You and the Investment World. New York Stock Exchange. School and College Relations. 11 Wall St. New York, NY 10005. Rev. 1979. 48 pp. Single copies free. Describes how stocks and bonds are bought and sold; the structure, history, and function of the American corporation and of the New York Stock Exchange; how investment promotes economic growth; and helpful suggestions for the future investor. Request also accompanying teacher's manual of supplementary resources and teacher-tested classroom practices. hs-ad.

EDUCATION

ACEI Publications. Assoc. for Childhood Education International. 3615 Wisconsin Ave., N.W. Washington, DC 20016. Add 10% for postage and handling. Send payment with orders under $10.00; no Canadian currency. Publications concerned with children 2-12 years old. Free publications list sent upon request. Sample titles are:

The Most Enabling Environment: Education Is for All Children. 1979. 64 pp. $4.00. A bulletin on mainstreaming to meet the needs of classroom teachers, special education teachers, and parents.

Teachers as Curriculum-Makers or Curriculum Making in 9 Easy (?!!) Steps. 1979. 8 pp. 75 cents. Outlines nine steps to sound curriculum implementation and associated precautions. References.

Art Education. The National Art Education Assoc. 1916 Association Dr. Reston, VA 22091. Titles include:

►**Standards for Art Teacher Preparation Programs.** 24 pp. $1.30. Guidelines for college programs which prepare art teachers. ad.

►**Youth Art Month.** 12 pp. $1.50. Practical suggestions for organizing community observances of Youth Art Month, each March, to promote the values of art in the schools.

Arts and Education. The Arts, Education, and Americans, Inc. Box 5297. Grand Central Station. New York, NY 10163. A membership organization offering books, audio-visuals, and monograph reports. Sample titles are:

►**Arts in the Curriculum** (Monograph 8). 1981. 20 pp. $2.00. Provides practical answers to the question, "What does it mean to infuse or integrate the arts into the (school) curriculum?" ad.

►**Arts in the Classroom: What One Elementary Teacher Can Do** (Monograph 10). 1981. 24 pp. $2.00. Suggests how teachers can incorporate the arts in classroom activities to make learning richer and more exciting. ad.

Citizen Guides. Council for Basic Education. 725 15 St., N.W. Washington, DC 20005. Two fold-out leaflets. 50 cents each. Titles are:

►**How Effective Are Your Schools: A Checklist for Citizens.** Provides a list of questions for use in assessing six key aspects of a school. ad.

►**Where Can I Go for Help: A Resource Guide for Improving Schools.** Identifies organizations that help or advise citizen action groups and cites selected publications. ad.

Classroom Pointers. The Boys Town Center. Boys Town, NE 68010. Three fold-out leaflets. Free. Titles are:

►**Discipline in the Classroom.** Covers setting rules, being friendly and firm, not using corporal punishment. Includes student progress report. ad.

►**Parents Guide to the Periodic Progress Report.** Discusses parent roles and building relationships with child and teacher. ad.

►**What to Do if Your Child Is an Underachiever in School.** Briefly explains the "why" and "what to do" to parents. ad.

►**Communication Quarterly.** Institute for Research on Teaching. College of Education. Michigan State University. East Lansing, MI 48824. Two issues yearly. 4 pp. Free subscription. A newsletter on research developments in the field of education and teaching. ad.

Creating Climates for Growth. The Hogg Foundation for Mental Health. The University of Texas, Austin, TX 78712. 1975. 35 pp. $1.00. Discusses ways of teaching by considering feelings which exist in the teaching-learning process.

Current Topics. Educational Testing Service. Publications Order Services, Dept. E01. Princeton, NJ 08541. Wide selection of booklets available. Write for free publications listing. Sample titles are:

►**Making the Public Schools Work.** 1982. 24 pp. Free. Booklet discusses education, teacher competencies, and funding in urban schols. ad.

►**Focus: New Vistas in Special Education.** 1980. 20 pp. Free. Booklet touches on PL 94-142, the educational openings for special children, and the I.Q. testing controversy. ad.

ERIC References on Urban and Minority Education (ED 162013). ERIC Clearinghouse on Urban Education. P.O. Box 40. Columbia Univ. 525 W. 120th St. New York, NY 10027. 1977; 1980. 11 pp. Free. Bibliographies on various aspects of urban and minority education; Fact Sheets which synthesize the literature in discrete areas; an Information Bulletin (3 times yearly); and the Equal Opportunity Review (1966-1982). ad.

►**ERIC/IR Update.** ERIC Clearinghouse on Informational Resources. Syracuse University. School of Education. Syracuse, NY 13210. Newsletter. Twice yearly. 4 pp. Free subscription by request. Provides reviews of ERIC and other resources of current interest. ad.

GPO Materials. U.S. Gov't. Printing Office. Washington, DC 20402. Lists of many low-cost government publications which may be used in the classroom. Sample titles are:

►**Teachers and Teaching Methods** (SB-137). 1981. 12 pp. Free.

►**Vocational and Career Education** (SB-110). 1982. 23 pp. Free.

IRT Publications Catalog. The Institute for Research on Teaching. Michigan State Univ. East Lansing, MI 48824. Revised yearly. Free. A special issue of *Communication Quarterly* lists and describes numerous research reports available at cost and through ERIC.

Kids' Stuff Teacher's Plan Book (#60-9). Incentive Publications, Inc. 2400 Crestmoor Rd. Nashville, TN 37215. 1978. 56 pp. $3.95. Features a 17-month calendar, special occasion stickers, and monthly teaching ideas. pr-el.

Montessori Approach. American Montessori Society. 150 5th Ave. New York, NY 10011. Several pamphlets and informational pieces on Montessori education and directories of Montessori children's schools and of accredited teacher training programs are available. Single copies free; must send self-addressed envelope (#10) with first-class postage affixed.

NAEP Materials. National Assessment of Educational Progress. 700 Lincoln Tower. 1860 Lincoln St. Denver, CO 80295. Numerous publications related to the national project to assess basic learning skills are available through the NAEP office, some at no charge. Send for free *Publications List*.

NEA Catalog. National Education Assoc. Publications Order Dept. Academic Bldg. Saw Mill Road. West Haven, CT 06516. Free. Catalog of publications and audiovisual materials listing inservice training and curriculum resource materials produced by the National Education Association.

Occasional Papers. Council for Basic Education. 725 15th St., N.W. Washington, DC 20005. Periodic reports available to non-members. $2.00 each; 20% discount on 20 or more copies. Titles include:

The Education of Gifted and Talented Students: A History and Prospectus (#27). 1979. 38 pp.

Improving Curriculum Management in the Schools (#30). 1980. 26 pp.

Minimum Competency Testing: Guidelines for Policymakers and Citizens (#29). 1980. 25 pp.

Parent Rights and Responsibilities. National Committee for Citizens in Education. Suite 410. Wilde Lake Village Green. Columbia, MD 21044. Single copy free for a self-addressed stamped envelope (#10); quantity rates available. Titles are:

Annual Education Checkup. Rev. 1978. Card. Guide to help parents review a child's school progress. Spanish edition available.

Parent Rights Card. Rev. 80. Lists 21 rights parents have in a child's education under federal and state law. Spanish edition available.

►**Special Education Checkup.** 1981. 6-page leaflet. Guide to parents of children in special education.

Penguin Books. Viking-Penguin, Inc. 625 Madison Ave. New York, NY 10022. Sample titles are:

The Great American Writing Block. 1979. 187 pp. $3.95. Examines the decline in writing ability among students and proposes approaches and techniques for treating the problems.

The World of the Gifted Child. 1979. 202 pp. $4.95. Discusses the unique needs of the child of high ability or creativity, types of schooling, and enrichment activities.

Publications Catalog. American Federation of Teachers. 11 Dupont Circle, N.W. Washington, DC 20036. Free. An annotated listing of the Federation's publications on topics of interest to professional educators.

Resources for Decision Making. The Psychological Corp. 757 3rd Ave. New York, NY 10017. Revised annually. Free. Listing of psychological and educational tests available. Also contains annotated listings of editions in the *Test Service Bulletins* and *Test Service Notebooks* series on various topics in testing and measurement which are available at no charge.

Schooling. America's Future. 514 Main St. New Rochelle, NY 10801. Free to students and teachers for school use; 50 cents to others. Titles are:

►**The Art of Choosing a College.** 1981. 23 pp. Examines criteria that should guide prospective students and their parents in selecting a suitable college. hs-ad.

►**Why Our Public Schools Are Failing.** 1982. 22 pp. Addresses a few central issues about conditions in our public schools and suggests corrective actions. ad.

Sex and Youth: A Symposium. American Library Assoc. Young Adult Services Div. 50 E. Huron St. Chicago, IL 60611. 1978. 52 pp. $2.00. Challenges educators and librarians to provide sex education and information to young people.

►**Sex Education in the Public Schools.** American School Health Assoc. P.O. Box 708. Kent, OH 44240. 1981. 124 pp. $4.50. Practical articles by over 25 professionals on how to implement programs, train teachers, gain community support, and deal with the opposition. ad.

Teacher-Tested Alternative for Use in Classroom Management. Guidance Awareness Publications. Box 106. Rancocas, NJ 08073. 1980. 134 pp. $3.00. Details over 100 specific techniques presented to help the classroom teacher provide a classroom climate most conducive to learning.

Television. ERIC Clearinghouse on Informational Resources. Syracuse University. School of Education. Syracuse, NY 13210. Titles are:

►**Children's Television: The Best of ERIC** (IR-20). 1977. 76 pp. $3.50. Contains synopses of 112 studies, programs, or papers subsumed under 14 questions regarding TV viewing and children's learning. ad.

►**Instructional Television: The Best of ERIC** (IR-12). 1976. 35 pp. $2.00. An annotated bibliography of documents relative to instructional uses of TV. Organized by general categories. ad.

Testing Materials. CTB/McGraw-Hill. A Div. of McGraw-Hill Book Co. Del Monte Research Park. Monterey, CA 93940. Titles include:

CTB/McGraw-Hill Catalog. Annual 1982. 184 pp. Free. Gives the uses and descriptions of several types of tests available and illustrations of scoring reports.

Glossary of Measurement Terms. 1973. 23 pp. Single copy free; additional copies $2.50 each. Defines terms encountered in test manuals and in the literature of mental measurement.

Parent's Guide to Understanding Tests. 1980. 8 pp. Single copy free with self-addressed stamped envelope (legal size). Describes kinds of tests, uses of tests, and test scores in layman's language.

►**Toward Self-Discipline: A Guide for Parents and Educators** (#089-8). ACEI. 3615 Wisconsin Ave., N.W. Washington, DC 20016. 1981. 48 pp. $4.00 plus 10% for postage and handling; 10% discount to members. No billed orders under $10.00. Describes roles and guidelines for parents, teachers, and principals for correcting and preventing discipline problems. ad.

Violence in Our Schools (#586). Public Affairs Committee, Inc. 381 Park Ave. S. New York, NY 10016. 1980. 24 pp. 50 cents prepaid. Describes crime and violence in schools and reports on efforts to cope with the problem, including case accounts of some successful programs.

►**What Are You Doing Here? or Schooldays for the Teacher** (OP6). Council for Basic Education. 725 15 St., N.W. Washington, DC 20005. 1979. 38 pp. $2.00. Presents insights gained about the "separate world" of students by a teacher who became a student in her high school. ad.

►**You Can Control Your Class** (#236-6). Ann Arbor Publishers, Inc. P.O. Box 7249. Naples, FL 33940. 1978. 53 pp. $3.50. Presents principles and techniques to motivate students to develop inner controls rather than relying on external pressures. ad.

ENERGY

API Materials. American Petroleum Institute. Educational Services. 2101 L St., N.W. Washington, DC 20037. Single copy free to teachers. Titles are:

> **Conservation Tip Sheets.** Undated. 8 pp. Suggests ways of gaining energy efficiency in the home and in driving. Includes conservation quiz. ms-hs.
>
> ►**Looking for Energy? A Guide to Information Resources.** 1982. 36 pp. Reference list of various information on energy-related topics classified into eleven subject areas, such as conservation, supplemental sources, and exploration and production. Includes 47 sources of materials. hs-ad.

Conservation. Amoco Educational Services. MC-3705. P.O. Box 5910-A. Chicago, IL 60680. Leaflets. Free in classroom quantities. Titles are:

> ►**Energy Savers.** 1980. 7 pp. Reviews 11 ways to reduce home energy costs. hs-ad.
>
> ►**Mileage Maker Tips.** 1980. 4 pp. Reviews ways the motorist can save gasoline. ms-hs.

Critical Mass Energy Project. Critical Mass Resources. P.O. Box 1538. Washington, DC 20013. Provides a monthly journal and various reprints and other publications related to nuclear power, safety, economics, and weapons. Prices vary from 50 cents to $2.50, quantity rates available. 15% charge for shipping. Resources listing is free. Sample title is:

> ►**Atomic Power Today** (NP-1). 1981. 12 pp. 50 cents. An updated reprint of testimony submitted by Ralph Nader to the House Interior Committee. hs-ad.

Earthbeats (#1). Communications Office. University of Wisconsin. Sea Grant Institute. 1800 University Ave. Madison, WI 53706. 1977. 10 pp. Free. A newspaper edition devoted to energy conservation, including a version of the household energy game. ms-hs.

Electricity. Edison Electric Institute. Contact your local electric company to obtain materials prepared by the Institute. Single copies free. Titles include:

> **Coal—Answers to Your Questions** (01-078011). 48 pp. Discusses coal and what is being done to make it more economic and cleaner as a fuel. hs.

Energy Research—Answers to Your Questions (01-7846). 53 pp. Discusses 30 questions about research into new ways of obtaining energy. hs.

Nuclear Power—Answers to Your Questions (01-418001). 48 pp. Discusses fears concerning the use of nuclear power to produce electricity. hs.

Energy Alternatives. Citizen's Energy Project. 1110 6th St., N.W.—Suite 300. Washington, DC 20001-3687. Booklets, posters, and reports on current energy issues and trends. Request free listing of descriptions and prices for each title. el-hs. Sample titles are:

►**Gashol and Alcohol Fuels.** 1981. 30 pp. $3.00. Discusses aspects of alternative fuels for combustion engines. hs-ad.

►**Passive Solar Energy.** 1981. 20 pp. $2.00. A review of the history, potential, problems, and model programs. Includes resource list. hs-ad.

►**Small-Scale Fossil Fuels.** 1981. 20 pp. $2.00. Presents some options for home heating. hs-ad.

►**Solar Power Satellites.** 1980. 18 pp. $1.50. A critique of proposals to use satellites to collect solar energy. hs-ad.

►**Energy Education.** (Intercom #98). Global Perspectives in Education, Inc. 218 East 18th St. New York, NY 10003. 1980. 32 pp. $2.50. Contains an overview of the debate issues, using energy studies in school, decision-making simulation, and a selected resource listing. hs-ad.

►**Energy Films.** The Maxima Corp. c/o DOE-TIC Film Library. P.O. Box 62. Oak Ridge, TN 37830. Catalog. 17 pp. Free. Gives descriptions of films on energy topics from the Technical Information Center Film Library of the U.S. Dept. of Energy. el-ms-hs.

Energy: How and Where Should We Get It? From Coal; From Nuclear Power? How Do They Compare? (Vol. 26, No. 10). Center for Information on America. Washington, CT 06793. 1977. 4 pp. 45 cents. Compares the feasibility of coal mining and nuclear reactors for producing electricity. hs.

Energy Kits. Amoco Teaching Aids. P.O. Box 1400K. Dayton, OH 45414. Each packet includes teacher's instructions, duplicating masters for student activities, and suggested lessons. Send payment with order. Titles include:

Energy Adventure. 1981. $1.00. Contains 28 pages of teaching and resource material with 7 masters and 10 exhibits in the form of maps, charts, graphs, and illustrations. Eight separate sections review energy history, petroleum, natural gas, coal, electricity, alternative sources, conservation, and economics. G10-12.

The Energy Crisis. 1978. 50 cents. Reviews causes and possible solutions to our energy problems. Teacher's instructions, 3 pp.; 5 masters. G4-6.

Living With Energy. 1978. 50 cents. Provides information about energy supply, alternate sources, and conservation. Teacher's instructions, 3 pp.; 5 masters. G7-10.

►**Energy Management for the Future.** Energy, Mines and Resources Canada. Communications Branch. 580 Booth St. Ottawa, Ontario. Canada, K1A OE4. 1979. 127 pp. Free. A sourcebook of ideas and activities for energy conservation learning. Includes study units, reproducible activity sheets, filmstrip scripts, an energy game, order forms, and more. el-ms-hs.

►**The Energy Problem** (SC-4300). World Book, Inc. Merchandise Mart Plaza. Chicago, IL 60654. 1982. 8-page foldout. 20 cents. A guide for the student's independent study. An investigation into the different forms and sources of energy used in our homes and factories and for transportation and communication. How can we continue to meet our increasing energy needs in the years ahead? ms-hs.

Energy Statistics and Information. U.S. Department of Energy. Energy Information Administration (EIA). National Energy Information Center, E1-22. Room 1F-048 Forrestal Bldg. Washington, DC 20585. Several publications free to all requestors; all publications free to school, public, and academic libraries. Sample titles are:

►**EIA Publications Directory—a User's Guide** (DOE/EIA-0149). Semiannual. 275 pp. Free. A directory which contains abstracts of all EIA publications, with indices by subject, title, and report number. hs-ad.

►**EIA Publications—New Releases** (DOE/EIA-0204). Monthly. 24 pp. Free. A monthly current awareness newsletter that lists newly-published EIA publications and current news about EIA products and services. hs-ad.

►**Energy Data Contacts Finder** (DOE/EIA-0259). Quarterly. 4 pp. Free. Lists names and telephone numbers of energy data specialists by their subject speciality. hs-ad.

►**Energy Factsheets** (DOE/EIA-0240). Irregular. 1 p. Free. One-page summaries that feature EIA statistics and analyses on a variety of topics such as the solar industry, coal as an energy source, energy tax incentives, and fossil fuel reserves. hs-ad.

Reference Materials. Three periodic statistical reports. Free to libraries only. Order on letterhead from: Sup't. of Documents. U.S. Gov't. Printing Office. Washington, DC 20402. Titles are:

►**International Energy Annual** (DOE/EIA-0219). Annual. 110 pp. Reports annual data, by country and world region, on the production, reserves, supply, disposition, and prices of major energy sources. hs-ad.

►**Monthly Energy Review** (DOE/EIA-0035). Monthly. 110 pp. Provides a complete overview of the nation's energy supply and demand picture by month. hs-ad.

►**Weekly Petroleum Status Report** (DOE/EIA-0208). Weekly. 36 pp. Contains weekly data on the petroleum supply situation. hs-ad.

Energy: The Next Twenty Years: An Overview. Ford Foundation. P.O. Box 559. Naugatuck, CT 06770. 1979. 67 pp. $2.00; payment must accompany order; include $1.00 per order for shipping. Summarizes a report on the world's energy options conducted by 19 scientists and scholars. Treats seven major energy realities and offers nine recommendations for energy policy. ad.

►**How Safe Is New Mexico's Atomic City?** Southwest Research and Information Center. P.O. Box 4524. Albuquerque, NM 87106. 1980. 62 pp. $2.50 postpaid. Reports on an investigation of radiation control at Los Alamos Scientific Laboratory. hs-ad.

Key Elements of a National Energy Strategy (#064). Committee for Economic Development. 477 Madison Ave. New York, NY 10022. 1977. 24 pp. $1.65 prepaid. Calls for an energy strategy based on six fundamental principles including conservation, nuclear energy, research, and the market system. hs-ad.

Natural Gas. American Gas Assoc. 1515 Wilson Blvd. Arlington, VA 22209. Numerous materials available free from local gas companies or above address. Request catalog, *Natural Gas Teaching Aids,* for listing. Sample titles are:

►**Natural Gas Energy** (N00585). 1982. Booklet. Tells the story of natural gas: exploration, production, transmission, distribution, storage, and household and commercial uses. Color illustrations. ms-hs.

►**Natural Gas Energy.** (N00590). 1982. Color poster to complement booklet. ms-hs.

Natural Gas Serves Our Community (N00160). A cutout kit. Consists of 28 four-color pictures on pasteboard depicting the story of gas from the gas fields to the community and an illustrated text. el-ms. Also available for lower grades.

Filmstrips. 35 mm. Color. With teacher's guide. Sample titles are:

America's Changing Energy Story (N81110). 48 frames with cassette. An overview of the energy picture in the U.S. today and future needs. ms-hs.

More to Come (N81090). 46 frames with cassette. Shows how scientists and technologists estimate energy resources still to be found. Develops concepts of potential supply and proved reserve. G4-8.

►**The Next Step.** Breeder Reactor Corporation. P.O. Box U. Oak Ridge, TN 37830. Three formats with script: 16 mm film, videotape (½″ or ¾″), and 35 mm slides with cassette tape. Free-loan. Presents the history and development of the nuclear breeder reactor at the Clinch River Plant. hs-ad.

►**The Nuclear Option: A Question of Survival.** America's Future. 514 Main St. New Rochelle, New York 10801. 1980. 21 pp. Free to students and teachers for school use; 50 cents to others. Describes the contributions of nuclear power to U.S. energy independence and some of the public fears about nuclear energy. hs-ad.

Nuclear Power. American Nuclear Society. Public Communications Dept. 555 N. Kensington Ave. LeGrange Park, IL 60525. Offers a set of materials for a self-addressed 9″ x 12″ envelope bearing first-class postage for 7 ounces. Titles are:

►**Earth.** 1982. 28 pp. Stresses the importance of electricity in today's lifestyle and supports nuclear energy as a safe source. Illustrated. ms.

►**Energy's Future Rests in Your Hands.** 1981. Fold-out leaflet. Contains information on nuclear power, including economics, safety, radiation, and waste disposal. References. ms-hs-ad.

►**Nuclear Energy Facts: Questions and Answers.** 1980. 36 pp. Covers 32 common questions about nuclear energy. References. ms-hs-ad.

►**Source Energy Equivalents.** A simulated pellet of uranium attached to 3½″ x 5½″ card illustrating the amount of oil, coal, wood, or gas needed for equal energy production. el-ms-hs.

►**Nuclear Power Controversy.** Union of Concerned Scientists. 1384 Massachusetts Ave. Cambridge, MA 02238. Leaflet. Up to 25 copies free. Request free publications list of books, reports, sideshows, brochures, and posters concerning research into the pros and cons of nuclear power. ms-hs.

Nuclear Power Packet. The Women's International League for Peace and Freedom. 1213 Race St. Philadelphia, PA 19107. $2.00. Contains several pamphlets and other materials on the dangers of nuclear power plants. ms-hs.

Oil. Amoco Educational Services. MC-3705. P.O. Box 5910-A. Chicago, IL 60680. Single copies free unless otherwise noted. Also request *Amoco Teaching Aids* for a complete listing of materials offered. Titles include:

►**Catalysts and Crude.** 1980. 22 pp. Describes aspects of petroleum refining. Illustrated. ms-hs.

Oil in Depth. 1978. 30 pp. Story of petroleum exploration, development, and production. Reviews geology, geophysics, leasing, drilling, and advanced recovery. ms-hs.

Our Energy Future. 1978. 5 pp. Classroom quantities free. Leaflet reviews twelve alternative energy sources, research, and environment. el-ms.

►**Petroleum Facts.** 1982. 5 pp. Classroom quantities free. Contains statistics on segments of the oil industry. ms-hs.

►**Petroleum From Fossil to Flame.** 1982. 8 pp. Teacher's guide with test. Reviews all aspects of petroleum. ms-hs.

►**Petroleum Industry Careers.** 1980. 5 pp. Classroom quantities free. Identifies many of the industry's 3000 occupations and their levels of training. hs.

►**That Amazing Maze—a Refinery.** 1978. 3 pp. Classroom quantities free. A simple overview of oil refining. el-ms.

Renewable Energy. Conservation and Renewable Energy Inquiry and Referral Service. Box 8900. Silver Springs, MD 20907. Offers brochures, factsheets, bibliographies, and other information on alternative energy sources and conservation. Titles include:

►**Renewable Energy: An Overview** (FS 175). 1982. 4 pp. Free.

►**Solar Energy and Your Home: Questions and Answers** (FS 176). 1982. 4 pp. Free.

►**Wind Energy Systems** (FS 135). 1982. 4 pp. Free.

Bibliographies. Several annotated bibliographies of non-technical readings are offered. Sample titles are:

Energy Education Materials. 1980. 6 pp. Free. el-ms-hs-ad.

Solar Energy Reading List for Children. 1980. 2 pp. Free. pr-el.

Solar Energy Reading List for Young Adults. 1980. 2 pp. Free. ms-hs.

Save Energy and Have Fun . . . With Textiles. American Textile Manufacturers Institute. 1101 Connecticut Ave., N.W. Washington, DC 20036. 1977. 36 pp. Single copy free. A booklet filled with energy-saving ideas for the home and many projects ideal for the classroom. el-ms.

Solar Energy. Tennessee Valley Authority. Information Office. 400 W. Summit Hill Dr. Knoxville, TN 37902. Offers numerous brochures and factsheets on solar energy and conservation. Free to teachers and school libraries. Sample titles are:

►**Introduction to Solar Energy.** 8 pp. Explains basic terms, concepts, and systems. el-ms.

►**Solar Energy in the Home.** 6 pp. Describes the benefits of basic types of solar systems. ms-hs.

►**The Squeeze Toward Global Energy Cooperation** (#398). League of Women Voters Education Fund. 1730 M St., N.W. Washington, DC 20036. 2 pp. 1981. 20 cents. Describes the mounting pressure from an unrelieved energy crisis in developing countries and its impact on global cooperation. hs-ad.

►**The Story of Petroleum.** Shell Oil Co. Public Affairs Dept. P.O. Box 2463. Houston, TX 77001. 1982. 56 pp. Free. An illustrated booklet covering such subjects as exploration, production, manufacturing, and petrochemicals. hs.

Sunpowered Hot Dog Cooker. Energy Management Center. District School Board. P.O. Box 190. Port Richey, FL 33568. 3 pp. 25 cents. Directions for making a small solar device from common materials. May be duplicated. el.

Teaching Modules. Energy Management Center. District School Board. P.O. Box 190. Port Richey, FL 33568. Guides for three-week modules of energy education in the elementary classroom. Titles are:

Let's Learn About Energy (Module A). 1978. 54 pp. 90 cents. Covers forms of energy, uses man makes of them, simple machines, and whether energy has been used wisely. G4.

Nature's Energy (Module B). 1978. 63 pp. 90 cents. Examines the nature of solar energy and fossil fuels and how all living things consume energy. G4.

Man and Energy (Module C). 1978. 52 pp. 90 cents. Explores the production and use of electricity and how its dependence on fossil fuels creates needs for conservation and alternative energy sources. G4.

Utilities and Nuclear Power. Environmental Action Foundation. Dupont Circle Bldg., Suite 724. Washington, DC 20036. Titles are:

►**Accidents Will Happen: The Case Against Nuclear Power.** 1979. 339 pp. $3.50 postpaid. Presents 20 essays, contributed by senators, physicians, lawyers, and organizers confronting industry claims that nuclear power is inexpensive, safe, and a needed energy source. Includes the incidents at Three Mile Island and Browns Ferry. hs-ad.

►**Power Line.** Tabloid. Monthly. 8-12 pp. Sample copy free. A national journal on energy and electric utilities written for citizens on issues such as nuclear economics, alternative energy sources, and energy pricing. hs-ad.

Utility Action Guide. Updated every 6 months. 20 pp. $2.00. Lists studies, articles, legal briefs, expert testimony, and books for people working to reform electric utilities, fight nuclear power, and promote alternative sources of energy. hs-ad.

Worldwatch Papers. Worldwatch Institute. 1776 Massachusetts Ave., N.W. Washington, DC 20036. Booklets dealing with the conservation and future of energy supplies. Titles are:

Energy and Architecture: The Solar and Conservation Potential (#40). 1980. 64 pp. $2.00. Examines the prospects for passive solar design, conservation, and retrofiting in producing energy-efficient buildings by the year 2000. hs-ad.

Energy: The Solar Prospect (#11). 1977. 79 pp. $2.00. Discusses solar resources in the form of wind power, water power, biomass, and direct sunlight in present and future applications. ad.

Nuclear Power: The Fifth Horseman (#6). 1976. 68 pp. $2.00. Examines nuclear energy in terms of economics, safety, adequacy of fuel supplies, ecology, and security. ad.

►**Rivers of Energy: The Hydropower Potential** (#44). 1981. 55 pp. $2.00. Makes the case that hydropower, if developed, could satisfy most of the world's electricity needs. hs-ad.

The Solar Energy Timetable (#19). 1978. 40 pp. $2.00. Contends that most of the world's energy could come from the sun by 2025 through the massive use of solar collectors and wind turbines. hs-ad.

►**Wind Power: A Turning Point** (#45). 1981. 56 pp. $2.00. An exposition on how wind power could supply 20-30% of the electricity for many countries by the early 2000s. hs-ad.

EUROPE

Austria. Austrian National Tourist Office. 545 5th Ave. New York, NY 10017. Regional offices: 3440 Wilshire Blvd. Los Angeles, CA 90010; 200 East Randolph Dr. Suite 7023. Chicago, IL 60601; 1007 N. W. 24th Ave. Portland, OR 97210. Free. Brochures describing and illustrating in colorful pictures the republic of Austria. Color posters are available upon special request.

Austria. Austrian Information Service. 31 East 69th St. New York, NY 10021. Free. Pamphlets and brochures on the economy, art, literature, painting, Austrian folklore, fine foods, music, scenery, and other aspects of Austria.

►**Belgium Historic Cities.** Belgian National Tourist Office. 745 5th Ave. New York, NY 10151. 1981. 42 pp. Free. A listing of main attractions, city maps, and yearly events of several cities. ms-hs.

►**Britain in Brief.** British Information Services. 845 3rd Ave. New York, NY 10022. 1978. Free; teacher requests only. Information about geography, people, culture, and government of Britain. Color photos. el-ms-hs.

Bulgaria. Embassy of the People's Republic of Bulgaria. 2100 16th St., N. W. Washington, DC 20009. Free. Pamphlets and booklets on Bulgaria.

Denmark. Consulate General of Denmark. Danish Information Office. 280 Park Ave. New York, NY 10017. Free general information on Denmark available for teachers, students, colleges, and libraries. Please specify. Limited quantities to U.S. residents only. No posters. Materials include:

►**Denmark Today.** 1979. 120 pp. Free. Tells about life, economy, culture, and government in Denmark. Illustrated with pictures and two maps. ms-hs-ad.

►**Denmark.** Free. Packet of fact sheets on Denmark ranging from foreign policy to furniture. ms-hs-ad.

Denmark. Ministry of Foreign Affairs. Denmark. Christiansborg Slot. DK-1218 Copenhagen K, Denmark. Materials include:

►**Danish Journal.** Newsletter. 12 pp. Free subscription. hs-ad.

►**How the Danes Live.** 1981. 56 pp. Single copy free. A special issue of the *Danish Journal* in magazine format. hs-ad.

Estonia. Consulate General of Estonia. 9 Rockefeller Plaza. New York, NY 10020. Send for free material on Estonia and list of other items available.

European Community. European Community Information Service. 2100 M St., N.W.—Suite 707. Washington, DC 20037. Free. Several materials available on the unity of European countries. Maps, histories, fact sheets, and study guides sent upon request as supplies permit. Publication catalogs available. Sample titles are:

►**European Community Facts.** 1981. 33 pp. ms-hs.

►**Steps to European Unity.** 1981. 70 pp. A chronology of progress. ms-hs.

►**Working Together: The Institutions of the European Community.** 1979. 36 pp. hs-ad.

Finland. Consulate General of Finland. Finland House. 540 Madison Ave. New York, NY 10022. General information, brochures, booklets, and maps about Finland. Free. Titles include:

Focus on Finland. 1979. 32 pp. A booklet of general information and color pictures. ms-hs.

►**Letter About Finland.** Brochure. Brief information on aspects of life in Finland. Photographs. el.

Posters. 1975. 13″ x 20″. Set of 6. A series of posters with narratives depicting the resources, climate, geography, history, and culture of Finland.

Finland. Embassy of Finland. 3216 New Mexico Ave. N. W. Washington, DC 20016-2782. Send for available current publications.

Finland. Finnish Tourist Board. 75 Rockefeller Plaza. New York, NY 10019. Single copies free. Titles include:

Finland Free Loan Films. Brochure describing tour films; 16 mm, color-sound, 10 to 30 min. User pays only return postage. Includes booking form.

►**Finland Vacation Guide.** 32 pp. A booklet describing the main areas to visit in scenic Finland. Illustrated. el-ms.

France. Cultural Services of the French Embassy. 972 5th Ave. New York, NY 10021. Free when requested on school letterhead. An informational packet on French culture and education.

Germany. German Information Center. 410 Park Ave. New York, NY 10022. A variety of free literature on contemporary Germany.

Germany. Goethe Institute Atlanta. German Cultural Center. 400 Colony Square. Atlanta, GA 30361. Numerous materials available free to German teachers in southeastern states. Write for information on free loan films, slides, tapes, and cassettes, and free brochures, maps, and posters.

Greece. Embassy of Greece. Office of Press and Information. 2211 Massachusetts Ave., N.W. Washington, DC 20008. A variety of materials is free to students.

Ireland. Irish Tourish Board. 590 Fifth Ave. New York, NY 10036. Titles are:

►**A Touch of Ireland.** 1981. 31 pp. Free. Booklet full of color pictures, Irish history, tour, recreation, and hotel information. el. to ad.

►**Ireland: Travelers Guide 1982.** 63 pp. Free. Information on weather, maps, currency, and traditions. el. to ad.

Italy. Italian Gov't. Travel Office. 630 5th Ave. New York, NY 10111. Free. Color brochures on travel to Italy, other highlights, and general information.

Latvia. Latvian Legation. 4325 17th St., N. W. Washington, DC 20011. Free materials available. Two titles are:

Latvia. Rev. 1976. 58 pp. Free. A history of Latvia, with sections dealing with its arbitrary incorporation into the Soviet Union. hs-ad.

Latvian Information Bulletin. Published quarterly. 6 pp. Free subscription. Newsletter oriented to political events and actions of importance to Latvia. hs-ad.

Netherlands. Free and inexpensive materials available upon request to the Consulate-General of the Netherlands at any of the following addresses: 3 Illinois Center. 303 E. Wacker Dr. Chicago, IL 60601; Suite 610. Post Oak Bank Bldg. 2200 S. Post Oak Road. Houston, TX 77056; 1 Rockefeller Plaza, 11th Floor. New York, NY 10020; 712 International Bldg. 601 California St. San Francisco, CA 94108; Central Plaza, Suite 509. 3460 Wilshire Blvd. Los Angeles, CA 90010; or The Royal Netherlands Embassy. Press and Cultural Section. 4200 Linnean Ave., N.W. Washington, DC 20008.

Norway. Norwegian Information Service. 825 3rd Ave. New York, NY 10022. Materials free to teachers and students.

Poland. Embassy of Polish People's Republic. Press Office. 2640 16th St., N. W. Washington, DC 20009. A variety of free material on Poland.

Portugal. Centro de Turismo de Portugal. Portugese National Tourist Office. 548 5th Ave. New York, NY 10036; or 919 N. Michigan Ave., Suite 3001. Chicago, IL

60611; or 3440 Wilshire Blvd., Suite 616. Los Angeles, CA 09910. Write nearest office for free literature.

Scandinavian Countries. Scandinavian National Tourist Offices. 75 Rockefeller Plaza. New York, NY 10019. Send for free packet of colorful materials.

Sweden. Swedish Information Service. 825 3rd Ave. New York, NY 10022. Send for free literature on Sweden. Indicate class level and special emphasis. Include self-addressed mailing label.

Switzerland. Swiss National Tourist Office. 608 5th Ave. New York, NY 10020. Send for free "Teachers Pack" of material on Switzerland. Includes booklets, fact sheet, and map.

Visual Geography Series. Sterling Publishing Co. 2 Park Ave. New York, NY 10016. 64 pp. each. $2.95 each. Orders must be prepaid and include postage. Booklets discuss the land, history, people, government, and economy of each country. Illustrated with photographs and maps. ms. Sample titles are:

East Germany in Pictures

France in Pictures

Poland in Pictures

Spain in Pictures

FAR EAST

China. Information and Communication Div. Coordination Council for North American Affairs in New York. 159 Lexington Ave. New York, NY 10016. Free. Atlas-type maps of Taiwan and the Republic of China, "Questions and Answers About the Republic of China," large wall posters, and a series of leaflets on such topics as language, paper-cutting art, music, festivals, silk, and Kung Fu.

China. China Books and Periodicals. 2929 24th St. San Francisco, CA 94110. Also branches at: 125 5th Ave. New York, NY 10013; 174 W. Randolph St. Chicago, IL 60601. A variety of books and periodicals in English imported from China are available. Write for free catalog. Sample titles are:

China: A General Survey. 1979. 252 pp. $4.95. A concise introduction to the history and geography of China. Photographs. el-ms-hs.

Quotations From Chairman Mao Tse-tung. 1968. 312 pp. $1.95. The original handbook of the Chinese Red Guards. hs-ad.

Indonesia. Embassy of the Republic of Indonesia. Information Div. 2020 Massachusetts Ave., N. W. Washington, DC 20036. Write for free publications. Titles include:

Focus on Indonesia. Quarterly. 30 pp. Free. Magazine on current events and conditions. hs.

History and Geography of Indonesia. 29 pp. Free. Describes Indonesia's growth to statehood and its geographic characteristics. hs.

Japan. Consulate General of Japan. 1830 International Trade Mart. No. 2 Canal St. New Orleans, LA 70130. Free. Several publications on aspects of modern Japan. Titles include:

Facts About Japan. 1975-1977. 4 pp. or 8 pp. each. Topical pamphlets on geography, music, sports, education, government, literature, and other features. hs.

The Japan of Today. 1980. 141 pp. Gives information on the government, economy, social conditions, and cultural life of Japan. hs-ad.

►**Japan Today.** 1981. 32 pp. Concise editon of *The Japan of Today.*

►**Japan.** Japan National Tourist Organization. 1519 Main St., Suite 200. Dallas, TX 75201. Free. Packet includes a color-illustrated brochure of attractions, a Tokyo guide, and maps of Tokyo and Japan. el. to ad.

Malaysia. Embassy of Malaysia. 2401 Massachusetts Ave., N.W. Washington, DC 20008. Titles include:

Malaysia in Brief. Undated. 271 pp. Free. A 4″ x 6″ data book on the history, people, government, and economy. Illustrated. el-ms.

Malaysian Panorama. Quarterly. 24 pp. Free. Magazine featuring the industry, beauty, festivals, and events of Malaysia. Color photos. el-ms-hs.

Pakistan. Embassy of Pakistan. Information Div. 2315 Massachusetts Ave., N.W. Washington, DC 20008. Free. Two series of pamphlets. Titles are:

Facts About Pakistan. 4 pp. each. Several pamphlets on subjects such as customs and ceremonies, festivals, handicrafts, and cuisine. ms-hs.

Pakistan. Several fold-out pamphlets on different places of interest such as Lahore, Peshawar, Rawalpindi, Karachi, and northern areas. ms-hs.

Thailand. Royal Thai Embassy. Office of the Information Counselor. 2300 Kalorama Rd., N.W. Washington, DC 20008. Write for free brochures, posters, and other materials.

Visual Geography Series. Sterling Publishing Co. 2 Park Avenue. New York, NY 10016. 64 pp. each. $2.95 each. Orders must be prepaid and include postage. Booklets discuss the land, history, people, government, and economy of each country. Illustrated with photographs and maps. ms. Sample titles are:

Korea in Pictures

The Philippines in Pictures

Thailand in Pictures

FOODS AND BEVERAGES

Apple Notebook. Washington State Apple Commission. P.O. Box 18. Wenatchee, WA 98801. Undated. 4 pp. Up to classroom quantities free to home economics teachers only. Contains apple variety chart, nutritional information, apple terms, recipes, and hints on purchasing, storage, and care of apples. ms-hs.

Baked Goods. ITT Continental Baking Co. Consumer Affairs Dept. P.O. Box 731. Rye, NY 10580. Send for a list of free materials on bread, food additives, food labels, and other subjects. ms-hs.

Dairy Foods. Direct requests to the Dairy Council office in your area. If not served locally, send to: National Dairy Council, 6300 N. River Rd., Rosemont, IL 60018. Request free annotated catalog of a variety of booklets, posters, films and filmstrips for grades K-12, consumers, and health professionals. Teacher's guides, reference materials, and multi-media packages are also available. Several materials explain milk, cheese, yogurt, butter, ice cream, and other dairy foods.

Figs. California Dried Fig Advisory Board. P.O. Box 709. Fresno, CA 93712. Titles include:

> **California Figs—Naturally Good! Naturally Good for You!** 4 pp. Up to 10 copies free. Points out the nutritional value of figs. hs.
>
> **California Figs. S-O-O-O Good. So Good for You!** Leaflet. Single copy free; up to 25 copies free to teachers. A selection of recipes using figs and information about their nutritional value. hs.

►**Food, Diet, and Nutrition** (SB-291). U.S. Gov't Printing Office. Washington, DC 20402. 1982. 19 pp. Free. A listing of many low-cost government publications which may be used in the classroom.

►**The Fruit Lovers Guide.** Beecham Products. Consumer and Public Affairs. Dept. E-1. P.O. Box 1467. Pittsburgh, PA 15230. Undated. 22 pp. Free. Contains recipes to retain the color and flavor of fresh fruits and hints for freezing and canning. hs.

Fruits. California Tree Fruit Agreement. P.O. Box 255627. Sacramento, CA 95825. Write on school letterhead. Brochures available in limited quantities related to California nectarines, pears, peaches, and plums. Includes recipes and tips on buying and storage. el-ms-hs.

Fruits—Citrus. Sunkist Growers. P.O. Box 7888, Van Nuys, CA 91409. Sample titles are:

> **Build a Better You With Fresh Citrus** (#8311). Rev. 1978. 16 pp. Free. Brochure for youngsters and adults on good health facts and snacking tips. Includes a leader's guide. hs.
>
> **Fresh Citrus Handbook** (#8512). Rev. 1980. 12 pp. Free. Covers seasonal availability, sizes, storage, uses and nutritional value of fresh citrus fruit. hs.

The Inside Story of Fresh Citrus Fruit (#8516). 16 pp. Free. Answers questions about citrus fruit including garnishes, basic preparation tips, measurement equivalents for each variety with metric conversions, and recipes. hs.

To Market, To Market (#8804). 1973. Single copy free to teachers. A game for learning about the growing and marketing of citrus fruits. el.

World of Work as It Relates to the Citrus Industry (#8802). 1973. 8 pp. Single copy free to teachers. Provides a unit outline with classroom activities for teaching about our dependency on others for our food. el-ms.

Grapes: The Natural Snack. California Table Grape Commission. P.O. Box 5498. Fresno, CA 93755. 4 pp. Free for a self-addressed, stamped, business-size envelope. Facts on grapes and the different ways they can be used as snacks or recipe ingredients. ms-hs.

Guides and Recipes. Advertising Stock Dept. Heinz U.S.A. P.O. Box 57. Pittsburgh, PA 15230. Each item free for one label from Heinz vinegar. Titles are:

►**Heinz Guide to Successful Pickling** (VV5751). 1981. 32 pp. hs.

The Heinz Vinegar Almanac (VV4768). 1977. 15 pp. hs.

►**H. J.'s Family Meat Loaf** (M16105). 1982.

A Salad Tour of the United States (DV4650). 1976. 19 pp. hs.

Hawaii's Sugar Islands. Hawaiian Sugar Planters' Assoc. P.O. Box 1057. Aiea, HI 96701. 1979. 16 pp. Free. Booklet describes sugarcane growing and sugar production. Color photographs. el.

The Ideal Beef Steer. American Hereford Assoc. Hereford Dr. P.O. Box 4059. Kansas City, MO 64101. 1 p. Single copy free. Chart shows cuts of beef and the parts of the cow from which they come. ms-hs.

Lettuce. California Iceberg Lettuce Commission. P.O. Box 3354. Monterey, CA 93940. Free to teachers. Lesson plans, wall charts, and recipe leaflets for teachers. Also, a 14-minute film for loan through Modern Talking Picture Service, Film Scheduling Center, 5000 Park St. N. St. Petersburg, AL 33709. ms-hs.

Macaroni. National Pasta Assoc. P.O. Box 1008. Palatine, IL 60067. Leaflets. Single copies free; must send self-addressed stamped envelope. Basic cooking instructions, recipes, and nutritive information. ms-hs. Titles include:

Macaroni Products: Versatile Foods

Nutritive Values of Macaroni, Spaghetti, and Egg Noodle Products

Pasta Primer

12 Award-Winning Pasta Recipes

Meat. National Live Stock & Meat Board. 444 N. Michigan Ave. Chicago, IL 60611. A variety of pamphlets, teaching kits, charts, and recipes are available. Request *Catalog of Literature and Audio-Visual Aids.* Sample titles are:

►**Any Way You Cut It . . . It's Beef for the Classroom** (17-720). 1982. 4 pp. $2.50 each. A detailed lesson plan for use in a 3-day unit on meat cooking; includes a wall chart, seven handouts, and *Basics About Beef* booklet. hs.

Basics About Beef (17-208). 1979. 16 pp. 75 cents each; 10-99 copies 40 cents each. Booklet covers all aspects of buying, storing, preparing, and serving beef. hs.

►**Focus on Pork** (17-207). 1981. 16 pp. 75 cents each; 10-99 copies 40 cents each. Booklet covers procedures for purchasing, storing, preparing, and serving pork. Includes chart of pork cuts. hs.

►**And the Winner Is . . . Ground Beef** (17-103). 1982. 6 pp. 40 cents each; 10-99 copies 30 cents each. Emphasizes consumer buying principles and the storage, cookery, and nutritive value of ground beef. Teacher's Guide with every 30 copies. hs.

Meat Guide. Armour and Co. Consumer Service Dept. Greyhound Tower. Phoenix, AZ 85077. 1976. 31 pp. Single copy free. Information on meat processing and grading, and on the purchasing, storage, and preparation of meat. Chart illustrations. hs.

Meat Products. Oscar Mayer & Co. Consumer Affairs. P.O. Box 8940 FI. Madison, WI 53708. Titles are:

Dietary Fitness, a Meat Lover's Guide. 1979. 6 pp. Free. Presents the role of meat in the diet including comparisons with other popular diet foods. ms-hs.

►**Making Foods Safe.** 1978. Kit. Free. Five activity masters and teacher's guide. A unit for learning about food composition, processing and distribution, and about safe food habits at home. G3-5.

►**Sausage I.D.** Rev. 1982. 4 pp. Free. A chart and text explaining types of sausages and their selection and serving. Spanish version also available. hs.

Fact Sheets. 2 pp. each. Free. hs. Titles are:

Freshness Dating

Nitrate, Nitrite, and Nitrosamines

Read the Label

More Fun With Coffee. Nat'l. Coffee Assoc. of U.S.A., Inc. 120 Wall St. New York, NY 10005. 1967. 33 pp. Free; limit of one per order while supply lasts. Booklet of recipes using coffee. hs.

►**Nutrition and Chocolate.** Consumer Information Dept. Hershey Foods Corporation. Park Blvd. Hershey, PA 17033. Free. Packet of information on such topics as chocolate and acne, snacking, the story of chocolate and cocoa, and nutritional values. el-ms.

Peanuts. National Peanut Council. 1000 16th St., N.W.—Suite 700. Washington, DC 20036. Free. Pamphlets, leaflets, recipes, teaching guides, activity folders, wall charts, and more. Sample titles are:

The Peanut Fun & Fact Folder. 1980. Gives facts on peanuts and suggested classroom activities. Includes four activity sheets for duplication. pr-el.

The Peanut Story. 1980. 14 pp. Overview of the history, production, and food and non-food uses of peanuts. ms-hs.

Pickles. Pickle Packers International, Inc. P.O. Box 606. St. Charles, IL 60174. Titles are:

►**Perk Up Meals With Pickle Power.** Leaflet. Up to 20 copies free to teachers. Features recipes using pickles. hs.

Stop, Save Pickle Liquid. Leaflet. 1-6 copies free to teachers or librarians; additional copies 4 cents each. Features recipes using pickle liquid. hs.

Sweet & Dill Pickle Salad Cubes. Leaflet. Up to 30 copies free to teachers. Features recipes using pickle cubes. hs.

Pineapple. Castle & Cooke. Box 2990. Honolulu, HI 96802. Information about pineapple growing, harvesting, and canning. Also offers 35 mm slide sets for purchase. Titles are:

Facts on Pineapple. 1976. 4 pp. Free. el-ms.

The Story of Pineapple in Hawaii. 1979. 16 pp. Free. el-ms.

Raisins. California Raisin Advisory Board. P.O. Box 5335. Fresno, CA 93755. Free. Recipes on request. ms-hs.

Rice. Rice Council. P.O. Box 740121. Houston, TX 77274. Send for free folders and booklets containing pictures and recipes for rice dishes. Titles include:

American Rice in the Diet. 8″ x 11″ notebook-size leaflet. Shows the importance of rice in a balanced diet. Contains cooking hints and recipes. hs.

Facts About American Rice. 8″ x 11″ notebook-size leaflet. Background facts on the production and processing of rice. ms-hs.

The Fourth R. 8″ x 11″ notebook-size booklet. Classroom quantities upon request from teachers. Designed to teach elementary students the history, production, and processing of American rice. el-ms.

Recipes. Clorox Co. Consumer Services. P.O. Box 24305. Oakland, CA 94623. Titles include:

►**Guide to Great Barbecues.** 32 pp. Up to 25 copies free. A booklet from Kingsford charcoal covering types of barbecue grills, care and cleaning, basic utensils, how to grill, rotisserie cooking, grilling with foil, cooking in the coals, and numerous recipes. ms-hs.

►**Make It Easy.** 25 pp. 50 cents. A booklet of recipes, time-saving tips, and cooking shortcuts featuring Kitchen Bouquet gravy aid. ms-hs.

Roquefort Chefmanship Recipes. Roquefort Assoc. P.O. Box 2908. 41 E. 42nd St. New York, NY 10017. 1970. 39 pp. Free in quantities for classroom use. A small book of handy recipes using Roquefort cheese for snacks with salads, dinner dishes, and desserts. ms-hs.

Sauer Kraut. The National Kraut Packers Assoc. P.O. Box 606. St. Charles, IL 60174. Titles are:

Put Some Kraut in Your Life. Undated. 31 pp. 50 cents. A variety of recipes illustrated with color pictures. hs.

Sauer Kraut Recipe Book. Leaflet. Up to 30 copies free to teachers. Features recipes using sauer kraut. hs.

Spices. American Spice Trade Assoc. P.O. Box 1267. Englewood Cliffs, NJ 07632. Many pamphlets, folders, and reprints on spices are available. Most priced between 25 cents and $1.00. Sample titles are:

A History of Spices. 16 pp. 75 cents prepaid. hs.

A Glossary of Spices. 20 pp. $1.00. An illustrated encyclopedia of spices. hs.

►**The Story of Colombian Coffee.** Colombia Information Service. 140 E. 57th St. New York, NY 10022. 22 pp. Free. Tells the story of the coffee bean from planting to processing. el.

10 Short Lessons in Canning and Freezing. Kerr Glass Manufacturing Corp. Consumer Products Div. Box 97. Sand Springs, OK 74063. 1980. 21 pp. Single copy free; additional copies 10 cents each. hs. Spanish version available.

Thoughts on Peanuts. Growers Peanut Food Promotions. 109 S. Main St. Rocky Mount, NC 27801. 1974. 15 pp. Free to teachers for two first-class stamps. Information on peanut growing, uses of peanuts, and recipes. Includes 11″ x 17″ wall chart of the peanut plant. el.

Tuna. Tuna Research Foundation, Inc. 1101 17th St., N.W.—Suite 603. Washington, DC 20036. Free. el-ms. Titles include:

►**Education Kit.** Contains six activity masters and teaching notes covering tuna, tuna fishing, and the tuna industry. pr-el.

►**Everybody in the Kitchen With Tuna.** 23 pp. A recipe book; includes brief history of the tuna industry. hs.

Tuna News. A newsletter which covers various aspects of the tuna industry.

Yogurt. The Dannon Co., Inc. P.O. Box 1975. Long Island City, NY 11101. Titles are:

►**Yogurt and You.** Dept. A. 1981. 15 pp. Free. Offers nutrition information, guide to yogurt selection, history of yogurt, and recipes. Spanish version available. el-ms-hs.

►**The Yogurt Way to Diet.** Dept. B. 50 cents. Single copy free to professionals who request on letterhead. Offers nutrition information, menus, calorie counter, and tips for weight control. el-ms-hs.

FOREIGN RELATIONS AND TRADE

Discussion Guides. Center for Information on America. Washington, CT 06793. Publications in the Vital Issues series. 4 pp. each. 45 cents each. Sample titles are:

American-African Cooperation: What Are the Problems and Prospects? (Vol. 26, No. 5). 1977. Outlines various issues involved in achieving better relations between the U.S. and African nations. hs.

World Law: What Does It Mean? What Could It Do for the World? (Vol. 20, No. 10). 1971. Presents the movement toward, the inherent hazards of, achieving an international rule of law. hs.

Ethics and Foreign Policy. Council on Religion and International Affairs. 170 E. 64th St. New York, NY 10021. A series dealing with the application of ethics to the world's political, economic, and social problems. $1.00 each. Sample titles are:

An Alternative to War (#107). 32 pp. Considers a course of nonviolent action against the background of threatened nuclear war. hs-ad.

Ethics and National Purpose (#101). 29 pp. Explores tensions existing today in the area of ethics and foreign policy. hs-ad.

Moral Tensions in International Affairs (#108). 28 pp. Suggests ways in which moral principles, properly employed, help us to explore some of our present political dilemmas. hs-ad.

Foreign Policy. The Foreign Policy Assoc., Inc. 205 Lexington Ave. New York, NY 10016. Catalog of publications available free upon request. Sample titles are:

American Foreign Policy for the 80's. 1980. 96 pp. $2.95. A digest of 13 foreign policy issues of great concern for the coming decade. Each section provides background, pros and cons of alternative policies, and references. hs-ad.

►**El Salvador and the U.S.** 1981. 8 pp. $1.00. Details the background of the conflict in El Salvador and the role and policy options of the U.S. hs.-ad.

►**Israel and the United States.** 1982. 12 pp. $1.00. Discusses some alternatives offered to the issue of Palestinian autonomy. hs-ad.

Mexico: The Quest for a U.S. Policy. 1980. 32 pp. $2.00. Surveys the history of U.S.-Mexican relations with text, photographs, cartoons, and charts. hs-ad.

Headline Series. Yearly subscription available. Analyses by experts of major foreign policy problems and world areas. Contains maps, charts, photographs, discussion guide, and bibliography. hs-ad. Titles include:

►**The ABC's of Defense: America's Military in the 1980s** (#254). 1981. 80 pp. $2.00.

►**The Caribbean: Its Implications for the United States** (#253). 1981. 86 pp. $2.00.

►**China's Four Modernizations and the United States** (#255). 1981. 72 pp. $2.00.

Foreign Investment in the U.S.: Costs and Benefits (#249). 1980. 80 pp. $2.00.

►**Nigeria: Power and Democracy in Africa** (#257). 1982. 72 pp. $3.00.

►**Polish Paradox: Communism and National Renewal** (#256). 1981. 72 pp. $2.00.

►**Politics and Religion in the Muslim World** (#258). 1982. 64 pp. $3.00.

►**The Third World: Exploring U.S. Interests** (#259). 1982. 64 pp. $3.00.

World Population: The Present and Future Crisis (#251). 1980. 80 pp. $2.00.

U.S.-Soviet Relations. American Committee on East-West Accord. 227 Massachusetts Ave., N.E.—Suite 300. Washington, DC 20002. Titles include:

Common Sense in U.S.-Soviet Relations. 1978. 84 pp. $3.95. Articles on how improved relations between the U.S. and Soviet Union can be achieved. hs-ad.

Common Sense in U.S.-Soviet Trade. 1979. 112 pp. $3.50. Potential benefits of increased trade between the U.S. and the U.S.S.R. are described. hs-ad.

►**World Trade at a Crossroads** (#643). League of Women Voters Education Fund. 1730 M St., N.W. Washington, DC 20036. 1981. 4-page tabloid. $1.25 (members 75 cents). Examines two issues challenging all countries: export expansion and the impact of imports. Features assorted articles on the role of developing and developed countries in the world economic scene. hs-ad.

GOVERNMENT AND POLITICS

American Freedom: The Next 200 Years. America's Future. 514 Main St. New Rochelle, NY 10801. 1976. 21 pp. Free to students and teachers; 50 cents to others. Discusses the conditions for the preservation of America's way of life. hs.

►**Budget Cuts and Block Grants: Social Needs and the New Federalism** (#103). League of Women Voters Education Fund. 1730 M. St., N.W. Washington, DC 20036. 1982. 8 pp. 75 cents. Details the historical development of federalism, outlines the new block grant programs, and explores how states and localities will cope with budget cuts and block grants. hs-ad.

Customs Service. U.S. Customs Service. Dept. of the Treasury. Washington, DC 20229. Free. Booklet and pamphlet materials on the history of the U.S. Customs Service and its responsibilities, uniforms, and equipment. el.

Elections. Center for Information on America. Washington, CT 06793. Recent booklets in the Grass Roots Guides series. Quantity rates available. Titles are:

> **PACs: What They Are; How They Are Changing Political Campaign Financing Patterns** (#62). 1979. 14 pp. $1.00. Discusses what the legal provisions are and how their results have come about. hs.
>
> **Presidential Nominating Conventions of 1980: What Goes on There!?!** (#63). 1980. 14 pp. $1.00. Describes and analyzes the changes in the 1980 national conventions, and points out convention operations. hs.
>
> **Presidential Primaries of 1980: Where? When? What? Why?** (#61). 1979. 22 pp. $1.00. Explains the role of the primaries in choosing the President in 1980. hs.

Freedom Studies. Freedom House. 20 West 40th St. New York, NY 10018. Publications on world peace and freedom emphasizing current world affairs. Orders must be prepaid. Sample titles:

> ►**El Salvador: Peaceful Revolution or Armed Struggle?** 1982. 48 pp. $2.00. Charges that U.S. news coverage of the conflict in El Salvador was simplistic and misleading, and calls upon journalists to inform the public on the complex issues involved. Includes a chronology of events. hs-ad.
>
> ►**The Map of Freedom.** 1982. 8½″ x 11″. 10 cents. A world map showing current civil and political liberty in every country. el-ms-hs.

Government Intervention. Foundation for Economic Education, Inc. 30 South Broadway. Irvington-on-Hudson, NY 10533. Treatises on alternatives to state intervention in human affairs. Sample titles:

►**The Law.** 1st ed. 1950. Many reprints. 76 pp. $1.00. Presents Federic Bastiat's argument for limited government. hs-ad.

►**The Mainspring of Human Progress.** 1st ed. 1947. Many reprints. 279 pp. 95 cents. Paperback. Henry Grady Weaver's work on the history of human freedom. hs-ad.

►**The Tariff Idea.** 1st ed. 1953. Many reprints. 80 pp. $1.00. W.M. Curtiss' case for free trade. hs-ad.

Grass Roots Guides. Center for Information on America. Washington, CT 06793. Published irregularly. A continuous series of study guide booklets of topical interest designed for high school students. Material is presented in a clear and stimulating fashion and includes references. 50 cents each. Quantity rates and subscriptions available. Sample titles are:

The Electoral College (#21). 1973. 14 pp. Explains how the system works and makes suggestions for reform. hs.

Foundations: Their Role in Our American Pluralistic System (#52). 1974. 14 pp. Describes the history of American foundations, their significance in our society, and why they have come under public accountability. hs.

Impeachment (#51). 1973. 14 pp. Explains the history and the process, and discusses pros and cons of impeaching a president. hs.

Special Districts in American Local Government. (#58). 1977. 15 pp. A detailed account of the various types of special districts and their powers and functions. hs.

NAL Books. New American Library. 1633 Broadway. New York, NY 10019. Paperbacks. Titles include:

The Age of Capital: 1848-1875 (ME1763). 1975. 426 pp. $2.95. The story of the conquest of Europe and America by new economic masters and of their subsequent conquest of the rest of the globe. hs.

To Set the Record Straight: The Break-in, the Tapes, the Conspirators, the Pardon (E9156). 1979. 368 pp. $3.50. Judge John J. Sirica's account of Watergate and the five-year struggle to preserve rule of law in this country. hs.

Political Education. League of Women Voters Education Fund. 1730 M St., N.W. Washington, DC 20036. Offers publications to promote knowledge and thought on timely political questions in such areas as election processes, government spending, international relations, and domestic, social and economic problems.

Write for complete list of available materials. Add 50 cents per order for postage. Sample titles are:

The Balanced Budget: A Closer Look (#632). 1979. 6 pp. 40 cents. Discusses issues related to a constitutional requirement to balance the federal budget. Includes a public budgeting primer. hs-ad.

Choosing the President (#420). 1980. 106 pp. $1.05. Details the process of nominating and electing an American president. hs-ad.

Tell It to Washington (#394). 1979. 24 pp. 35 cents. A guide for citizen action including a congressional directory. hs-ad.

Troubled Cities: Roots, Realities, Remedies (#394). 1980. 20 pp. 90 cents. Discusses causes of today's urban problems and how to make our cities more livable. hs-ad.

Public Affairs Pamphlets. Public Affairs Committee, Inc. 381 Park Ave. S. New York, NY 10016. 50 cents each; quantity rate available. Sample titles are:

The Bill of Rights Today (#489A). 1980. 28 pp. Examines the need for affirmative support of our system of individual rights. hs-ad.

The Great Tax Debate (#582). 1980. 28 pp. Explains terms used in economic debate and discusses pros and cons of various taxes, tax cuts, expenditures, and other issues. hs-ad.

Public Information. Freedom of Information Clearinghouse. P.O. Box 19367. Washington, DC 20036. Provides publications related to the Freedom of Information and the Privacy Act. Write for a listing. Sample title is:

►**The Freedom of Information Act: What It Is and How to Use It.** 8-page folder. 10 cents. Explains major provisions of citizen access to government documents and records. hs-ad.

The Secret Service Story. Dept. of the Treasury. U.S. Secret Service. Office of Public Affairs. Washington, DC 20223. Undated. Free. Provides a brief account of the history and functions of the secret service. Illustrated. hs.

Social Security. U.S. Dept. of Health and Human Services. Social Security Administration. Baltimore, MD 21235; or request from the Social Security Administration office nearest you as listed in local telephone directory. Numerous pamphlets on the various benefits of social security and who is eligible. Free. hs-ad. Titles include:

►**A Brief Explanation of Medicare.** 1982. 14 pp.

►**For the Young Worker . . . Social Security.** 1982. Fold-out leaflet.

►**If You Become Disabled.** 1982. 24 pp.

►**SSI for Aged, Disabled, and Blind People.** 1982. 10 pp.

►**A Woman's Guide to Social Security.** 1982. 16 pp.

►**Your Social Security.** 1982. 32 pp.

Supreme Court. Supreme Court Historical Society. Suite 612. 1511 K St., N.W. Washington, DC 20005. Titles are:

►**Equal Justice Under Law: The Supreme Court in American Life.** 1982. 159 pp. $4.95 plus $1.00 shipping. Provides a political history of the development and actions of our Supreme Court. Includes pictures and terms of all Justices, a section on the Court and federal court system, and many color photographs. hs-ad.

The Supreme Court of the United States. 1982. 32 pp. 50 cents; 30% off on 10 or more copies. Discusses the Court as an institution, its traditions and procedures, constitutional interpretation, and the Court building. hs.

Taxes. Tax Foundation, Inc. Public Information Dept. 1875 Connecticut Ave., N.W. Washington, DC 20009. Offers periodicals, research, briefs, conference proceedings, special reports, and bibliographies related to taxes. Write for free publication listing. Sample titles are:

►**The Congressional Budget Process at the Crossroads.** Special Report. 1981. 14 pp. $1.00 prepaid. Reviews budget procedures and the operations of the agencies established by the 1974 Congressional Budget Act.

►**Reducing Government Expenditures: Overcoming the Obstacles** (Brief #30). 1980. 14 pp. $1.00 prepaid. Suggests ways that modern management techniques can deal with organizational roadblocks to spending reduction. References. hs-ad.

►**The Tax Expenditure Budget: An Exercise in Fiscal Impressionism** (Brief #29). 1979. 21 pp. $2.50, prepaid. Examines pros and cons of the "tax expenditures" concept which is now a part of the official Federal budget. hs-ad.

►**Unemployment Insurance: Trends and Issues.** 1982. 8 pp. Free. Summarizes a research report on major developments in the unemployment insurance system, including benefit determination, cyclical fluctuations, and state and Federal financing policies and problems. hs.

►**Taxes and Taxation** (SB-195). U.S. Gov't. Printing Office. Washington, DC 20402. 1982. 19 pp. Free. A list of many low-cost government publications which may be used in the classroom.

►**Understanding Taxes 1983** (#19, 21). Internal Revenue Service. Washington, DC 20224. 48 pp. Free. IRS student text and teacher's guide to teach about Federal tax system, preparation of the 1040A and 1040 forms, and information about students' rights and tax responsibilities. Three 16 mm color films, "The Subject Was Taxes," "Money Talks," and "What Happened to My Paycheck," may be borrowed free from local IRS offices. ms-hs.

►**Using the Freedom of Information Act: A Step-by-Step Guide** (#013-1). Center for National Security Studies. 122 Maryland Ave., N.E. Washington, DC 20002. 1981. 20 pp. $1.50 plus $1.00 postage. Gives guidelines for dealing with public agency responses to requests and appeals. Includes sample letters. Cross-referenced and indexed. hs-ad.

Vital Issues Series. Center for Information on America. Washington, CT 06793. A continuous series of discussion guides on current public and social topics designed for high school students. Quantity rates and subscriptions available. 4 pp each. 45 cents each. Sample titles are:

Illegal Immigration: What Can Be Done About It? (Vol. 28, No. 4). 1978. Presents arguments about the impact of rising numbers of illegal aliens on the U.S. population and labor market. hs.

Restitution by the Criminal (Vol. 27, No. 2). 1977. Is restitution a "better" way of paying for crimes? Discusses various restitution programs and the prospects for their expansion. hs.

Senior Citizens and Political Power: What's the Situation? (Vol. 28, No. 1). 1978. 6 pp. Explains how older citizens have used their political power to get legislation passed for their benefit. hs.

The Social Security System (Vol. 26, No. 3). 1976. Details the system's evolution and examines its flaws and chances for reform. hs.

GUIDANCE

Barron Guides. Barron's Educational Series, Inc. 113 Crossways Park Dr. Woodbury, NY 11797. Titles are:

►**How to Beat Test Anxiety.** 1979. 134 pp. $2.50. A guide to improve test-taking skills, control test anxiety, and build self-confidence. hs.

►**You Can Succeed.** 1979. 158 pp. $2.25. A guide to improve motivation, reading, note taking, memory, word power, and writing skills. hs.

Career Guidance. Prudential Insurance Co. of America. Box 36. Newark, NJ 07101. Free. Titles include:

Facing Facts About Planning for Your Career. 1980. 28 pp. A guide for high school students who plan to work after graduation.

Facing Facts About Vocational Education for Your Career. 1976. 36 pp. A guide for high school students, counselors, and parents to help in making decisions about vocational preparation.

►**Choosing Your Career.** Administrative Research Associates. Irvine Tower. Box 4211. Irvine, CA 92716. 1979. 45 pp. $2.00 plus 10% for shipping. An aid for appraising one's personal traits and interests and career fields to help one select an appropriate occupation. hs.

Cliffs Test Preparation Guides. Cliffs Notes, Inc. Box 80728. Attn: Faculty Coordinator. Lincoln, NE 68501. Request free brochure on guides available to help students prepare for examinations such as ACT, SAT, GRE, and GED. Free teacher's manual, "Prepare Your Students to Take the SAT and PSAT," also available by request. ad.

Guidance Aids. American Guidance Service. Publishers' Building. Circle Pines, MN 55014. Write for free catalog. Titles include:

> **How to Study.** 1959. 64 pp. $1.95. A high school edition with instructor's guide. hs-ad.
>
> **Programmed Study Technique (How to Study Workbook).** 1964. 57 pp. $1.95. Includes instructor's guide. hs-ad.

Math Graduate Study. American Mathematical Society. P.O. Box 6248. Providence, RI 02940. Titles are:

> **Assistantships and Fellowships in the Mathematical Sciences.** Notices of the AMS published every December in a special issue. $3.00. ad.
>
> **Professional Training in Mathematics.** 1960. Rev. 1976. 16 pp. $2.00. Advice for those considering advanced study in mathematics. ad.

Need a Lift? American Legion. Attn: Need a Lift? Box 1055. Indianapolis, IN 46206. Rev. annually. 136 pp. $1.00 prepaid. Handbook for students, parents, and counselors of current information on careers, loans, and scholarships.

Studies. Natural Resource Professions. Human Environment Center. 810 18th St., N.W. Washington, DC 20006. Titles are:

> ►**Before College.** 1980. 54 pp. Free. Typewritten report describing minority preparation for natural resource professions. Covers pre-requisite skills, career exploration, and environmental awareness. References. hs-ad.
>
> ►**Higher Education.** 1981. 40 pp. Free. Discusses experience of colleges and universities in recruiting and training minority persons for careers in environmental and natural resource professions, and recommends new initiatives. References. hs-ad.

Testing. Guidance Awareness Publications. Box 106. Rancocas, NJ 08073. Titles are:

> **The Implications and Application of Assessment Instruments for Counselors and Teachers.** 1977. $3.00. A synopsis of testing areas, discussion of non-test procedures, and a glossary of testing terms.

What You Always Wanted to Know About Tests but Were Afraid to Ask! 1973. 10 pp. 50 cents. Used by schools to explain to parents and students and teachers the important aspects of testing. Question-answer format.

Testing. The Psychological Corp. 757 3rd Ave. New York, NY 10017. Free annual catalog listing psychological and educational tests for sale. Also lists three series of free bulletins dealing with a variety of topics in measurement. Sample titles are:

►**Assessing School Ability** (TSN 35). 1979. 4 pp. Free.

►**Criterion-Referenced Testing** (TSN 37). 1980. 6 pp. Free.

Don't Be Nervous—It's Only a Test. 1978. 2 pp. Free.

Early Childhood Screening Under Public Law 94-142. 1980. 6 pp. Free.

A Glossary of Measurement Terms (TSN 13). 8 pp. Free.

On Telling Parents About Test Results (TSN 154). 1980. 6 pp. Free.

►**Some Things Parents Should Know About Testing** (TSN 34). 4 pp. Free.

Trade-Technical Schools. National Association of Trade and Technical Schools. 2021 K St., N.W. Washington, DC 20006. Titles include:

►**Career Shortcut: Take a Skill into Your Future.** Leaflet. Free. Tells about training available at private vocational schools. Lists careers.

►**Getting Skilled.** 2nd ed. 1980. 145 pp. $1.50; enclose payment with order. A guide to private trade and technical schools based on field investigations and research. Lists state and national accrediting agencies. References.

►**Handbook of Trade and Technical Careers and Training.** 1981-82. 48 pp. Free. Gives information on dozens of careers and tells where training may be obtained.

►**How to Choose a Career and a Career School.** Leaflet. Free. A practical approach to two important decisions.

University of Rochester Bulletins. University of Rochester. Office of University Communications. Dept. GP. Rochester, NY 14627. Free. Send a self-addressed stamped envelope (#10) for each request. Bulletins give concise information on selecting a college and preparing for college life. hs. Titles include:

►**How to Make the Most of Your Campus Visit: A Guide for Prospective College Students.** 1979. 3 pp.

►**"I Wish I'd Known That Before I Came to College": Some Tips for Tomorrow's College Students . . . from Freshmen at the University of Rochester. 1982. 3 pp.**

►**Is Medicine the Career for Me?** 3 pp.

►**Maybe There's a Career for You in Engineering: Some Tips for High School Students From the University of Rochester's College of Engineering and Applied Science.** 1982. 3 pp.

►**Starting the Job Hunt: How to Write an Effective Resume.** 1981. 3 pp.

►**Staying Fit in College: Tips for Students.** 1982. 2 pp.

►**Surviving Academic Pressures in College. How to Study Better and Fight Pre-Exam Panic.** 1982. 3 pp.

Thinking About a Career in Law? 1979. 3 pp.

Writing an Application That Makes You Look Your Best. 1979. 3 pp.

What to Look for in a Truck Driver Training School. American Trucking Associations. Educational Services Dept. 1616 P St., N.W. Washington, DC 20036. Undated. Leaflet. Free. Pointers for evaluating the minimum quality of a driving school. hs-ad.

HEALTH

►***AAHPERD Materials.*** American Association for Health, Physical Education, Recreation and Dance. 1900 Association Dr. Reston, VA 22091. 1983. 32 pp. Free. Send for catalog of publications and audiovisuals. ad.

AMA Publications. American Medical Assoc. Order Dept. P.O. Box 821. Monroe, WI 53566. Request free annotated catalog of booklets, pamphlets, and posters available at nominal prices.

American Red Cross. Available from local Red Cross chapters. Materials include information on Red Cross services for blood, disaster, nursing, health, safety, and youth. hs.

Appetite Annie's Action-Packed, Fun-Filled Guide to a Healthy Pregnancy. Ralston Purina Co. Corporate Consumer Services. Public Relations. Checkerboard Square. St. Louis, MO 63164. 1977. 27 pp. Up to 50 copies free. A comicbook-like pamphlet for teenagers about nutrition during pregnancy. hs-ad.

Basic Posture Patterns and Distortions With Adapted Exercise Programs. Reedco Research. P.O. Box 345. 51 N. Fulton St. Auburn, NY 13021. 1967. 4 pp. Free. Describes six typical postures and procedures for correcting deficiencies. Pads of related materials are available at modest prices. pr-el-ms.

The Cold Mystique. Beecham Products. Consumer and Public Affairs. Dept. E-1. P.O. Box 1467. Pittsburgh, PA 15230. 1980. 5 pp. Free. A history of the common cold with suggestions for treatment and prevention. ms.

Does Everything Cause Cancer? A Food Safety Primer. Center for Science in the Public Interest. 1755 S St., N.W. Washington, DC 20009. 1979. 11 pp. $1.50. Covers questions asked most about saccarin, nitrite, animal studies, and food safety laws. hs.

Everything Doesn't Cause Cancer (NIH 80-2039). Office of Cancer Communications. Publication Order. National Cancer Institute. Bldg. 31-Room 10A18. Bethesda, MD 20205. 1980. 12 pp. Free. Answers common questions about chemicals which cause cancer and about laboratory animal tests to identify cancer-causing substances. ms-hs.

Eyes and Vision. National Society to Prevent Blindness. 79 Madison Ave. New York, NY 10016. Catalog of publications sent on request. Materials include:

> **The Eye and How We See** (V7). 1978. Leaflet. Single copy free; send self-addressed stamped envelope (#10). $5.00 per 100. Enlarged cross section of the eye defining various parts and describing how the eye works. el.
>
> **How We See** (V8). Wall chart. 22″ x 28″. 50 cents; 10 for $4.00. Depicts a cross section of the eye and diagrams of how we see. pr-el.
>
> **Teaching About Vision** (P619). 1972. 72 pp. $2.00. A teaching aid and reference for teachers and health service personnel who promote the eye health of school children. Includes illustrations, glossary, and bibliography.
>
> **Understanding Eye Language** (P607). 1977. 13 pp. 30 cents; 10 for $2.50. Defines medical terminology related to the eye; includes a labeled cross section of the eye. el.

General Health. Direct requests to the Dairy Council office in your area. If not served by area Council, send to: National Dairy Council. 6300 N. River Rd. Rosemont, IL 60018. Request a free annotated catalog of a variety of materials for grades K-12, consumers, and health professionals dealing with healthy growth and health maintenance. ad.

GPO Materials. U.S. Gov't. Printing Office. Washington, DC 20402. Lists of many low-cost government publications which may be used in the classroom. Sample titles are:

- ►**Heart and Circulatory System** (SB-104). 1981. 4 pp. Free.
- ►**Medicine and Medical Science** (SB-154). 1981. 22 pp. Free.
- ►**Physical Fitness** (SB-239). 1982. 3 pp. Free.
- ►**Publications Relating to the 1982-83 National High School Debate Topic** (SB-043). 1982. 6 pp. Free.

Health and Safety Educational Materials Catalog. Metropolitan Life Insurance Co. Health and Safety Education Div. 1 Madison Ave. New York, NY 10010. Free. Catalog describes inexpensive leaflets, posters, films, and other teaching aids for health and safety subjects. Many are free in single copies. ad.

►**Health Style: A Self Test** (PHS 81-50155). U.S. Public Health Service. Nat'l Health Information Clearinghouse. P.O. Box 1133. Washington, DC 20013. 1981. 10 pp. Free. A brief test that identifies aspects of one's lifestyle that are health risks. ms-hs-ad.

►**Heart Risk Book: A Practical Guide to Preventing Heart Disease** (#20669-9). Bantam Books. 666 5th Ave. New York, NY 10103. 1982. 116 pp. $2.50. Gives practical advice on reducing the risk factors that bring on heart attacks and strokes. Based on research at the Boston University Medical Center. ms-hs-ad.

►**How to Get Unstressed: The Bare Facts** (#175). Wisconsin Clearinghouse. 1954 E. Washington Ave. Madison, WI 53704-5291. 1981. 14 pp. 75 cents postpaid; 60 cents plus self-addressed stamped envelope (#10). Explains stress, what it does to people, and specific pointers for avoiding and coping with stress. hs-ad.

Insurance Learning Materials. American Council of Life Insurance. Education Services. 1850 K St., N.W. Washington, DC 20006. Sample titles are:

> ►**The Life Insurance Teaching Kit.** 1982. Single copy free. A set of materials for teaching about buying and using life insurance. Kit includes lesson plans for five modules, student worksheets, policy sample sheets, and a guide and materials for the teacher. hs-ad.
>
> **A List of Worthwhile Life and Health Insurance Books.** 1979. 80 pp. Reference copy free to librarians and teachers. A list of books of interest to the general public, students, and those in the insurance business. ad.
>
> **Policies for Protection: How Life Insurance and Health Insurance Work.** Rev. 1980. 31 pp. Up to 100 copies free to teachers. Explains the methods and procedures by which life and health insurance function. For business courses; includes exercises and references. hs.

►**Keeping on Schedule With Your Medicine.** Health Information Services. Merck Sharp and Dohme. West Point, PA 19486. 8″ x 11″. 4 pp. 25 cents. Contains a four-week chart on which to record medication data and gives advice on understanding the use and storage of prescription drugs. hs-ad.

►***Natural Hygiene.*** The American Natural Hygiene Society, Inc. 698 Brooklawn Ave. Bridgeport, CT 06604. Send for free list of books and other materials on natural hygiene, natural living, self care, and the dangers of vaccinations.

NIH Materials. National Institutes of Health. U.S. Public Health Service. PIRB-NHLBI. Bldg. 31—Rm. 4A21. Bethesda, MD 20205. Request catalogs and listings of publications available free from various NIH agencies. ad.

Periodicals. Curriculum Innovations, Inc. 3500 Western Ave. Highland Park, IL 60035. Magazine. 9 issues yearly. Sample issue free to teachers. Sample titles are:

> ►**Current Health 1.** Each issue contains the latest health education information for students in grades 4-7.

►**Current Health 2.** Each issue contains the latest health education information for students in grades 7-12.

Public Affairs Pamphlets. Public Affairs Committee, Inc. 381 Park Ave. S. New York, NY 10016. 50 cents each; quantity rates available. Titles include:

Health Hazard Appraisal: Clues for a Healthier Lifestyle (#558). 1978. 28 pp. Helps people realize the risks of smoking, overeating, excessive drinking, and other common practices. Includes a "do-it-yourself" test. hs-ad.

Immunization—Protection Against Childhood Diseases (#565). 1978. 28 pp. Discusses potential for renewed outbreaks and epidemics of childhood diseases because millions of children are not fully immunized. hs-ad.

Know Your Medication (#570). 1979. 28 pp. Guide for consumers on the safe use of common prescription and over-the-counter drugs. Dangers and possible side effects. Uses both generic and brand names. hs-ad.

►**Listen to Your Body: Exercise and Physical Fitness** (#599). 1981. 28 pp. Gives advice on starting an exercise program of jogging or other activities and tells what to expect and to avoid. hs-ad.

Pregnancy and You (#482). 1972. 28 pp. Discusses the three major stages of pregnancy, its physiological and psychological effects, and routines to be followed at each stage. hs-ad.

Stroke: New Approaches to Prevention and Treatment (#576). 1976. 20 pp. 50 cents. Explains causes, prevention, and treatment of stroke—the third leading cause of death. hs-ad.

Understand Your Heart (#514). 1974. 28 pp. Summarizes heart functions, types of heart troubles, risk factors and what can be done to prevent them, and also offers help for heart patients. hs-ad.

Watch Your Blood Pressure! (#483B). 1980. 28 pp. A look at a sometimes subtle and potentially dangerous physical condition. hs-ad.

Prudential Health Series. Prudential Insurance Co. P.O. Box 36. Newark, NJ 07101. Pamphlet. Free. Titles are:

►**Child Safety Is No Accident.** Rev. 1982. 16 pp. On teaching young children about risks. ad.

Childhood Diseases. Rev. 1980. 17 pp. Discusses the common contagious childhood diseases and their treatment. el-ms.

Rabies. American Veterinary Medical Assoc. 930 N. Meacham Rd. Schaumburg, IL 60196. Undated. 5 pp. Single copy free for a self-addressed stamped envelope (#10). Explains rabies and what to do if bitten by an animal. hs.

►**Resources for Healthful Living.** Center for Science in the Public Interest. 1755 S St., N.W. Washington, DC 20009. 8 pp. Free. Publications catalog covering such areas as dieting, nutrition, cancer, and exercise. el-ms-hs.

►**Skin Care.** Johnson Wax. Consumer Services Center. P.O. Box 567—Dept. FI-SC. Racine, WI 53401. 1982. 24 pp. Free; request on post card. Booklet on the nature of skin, personal and environmental factors affecting skin, and cleansers and lotions for the care of skin. ms-hs-ad.

Smoking. American Lung Assoc. of Tennessee. P.O. Box 399. 1717 West End Ave. Nashville, TN 37202. Free. Booklet, sign, buttons, and puzzles to educate children on the dangers of smoking. pr-el.

Vision. American Optometric Assoc. Communications Div. 243 N. Lindbergh Blvd. St. Louis, MO 63141. 1979. Leaflets. hs-ad. Single copy free for a self-addressed stamped envelope (#10). Titles are:

Answers to Your Questions About Bifocals for Children

Answers to Your Questions About Crossed-Eyes

Answers to Your Questions About Eye Coordination

Answers to Your Questions About Farsightedness

Answers to Your Questions About Lazy Eye

Answers to Your Questions About Nearsightedness

Answers to Your Questions About Vision Therapy

Vision Pamphlets. American Optometric Assoc. Communications Div. 243 N. Lindbergh Blvd. St. Louis, MO 63141. Single copy free for a self-addressed stamped envelope (#10), except as indicated. Various pamphlets concerning eye care and proper treatment of visual defects. hs-ad. Titles include:

A Closer Look at Reading and Vision

Facts You Should Know About Vision and School Achievement

Gaining the Extra Edge in Sports Through Vision

Seymour Safely Activity Book. 1974. 31 pp. $2.00. A teacher's guide to a complete health education program on vision for preschoolers through second grade.

►**Seymour Safely's Library Book.** 1979. 8 pp. $1.25. A vision education program for libraries. Each unit in the series includes songs, story, game, library project, and book list. el.

Teacher's Guide to Vision Problems With Checklist

HISTORY: AMERICAN

American Revolution. University Prints. 21 East St. Winchester, MA 01890. 20 prints (black-and-white). 5½" x 8". $1.00. A set of historical prints which depict events and figures of the American Revolution. el-ms-hs.

Anthologies. Curriculum Bulletin. Oceanside, OR 97134. Companion volumes. $2.50 each, postpaid; payment must accompany orders. Titles are:

> **Great Issues in American History** (#333). 1976. 144 pp. Contain primary sources relating to great American issues from Colonial times to the present; includes "literary" selections. A multicultural approach. ad.
>
> **The Heritage of America's Youth: A Source Book for Teachers and Students** (#326). 1975. 124 pp. Includes historic calendar, our nation's documents, national symbols, flag history and etiquette, patriotic songs, heritage poetry, quotations, and materials on moral values. ad.

Black Dimensions in American History. Carnation Co. Public Relations. 5045 Wilshire Blvd. Los Angeles, CA 90036. Free. Slide chart which lists noteworthy achievements of 43 black Americans. ms-hs.

Colonial Settlement. Jamestown Foundation. Drawer JF. Williamsburg, VA 23187. List of publications available on request. To all prices add 4% Virginia sales tax and 63 cents postage per item. Titles include:

> **America's First Legislature.** 12 pp. 20 cents. The meeting of the First Assembly in the New World at Jamestown in 1619. el-ms.
>
> **This Was Green Spring.** 12 pp. 20 cents. Describes one of the first plantations in Virginia. el-ms.
>
> **Virginia Indians: Before and After Jamestown.** 12 pp. 20 cents. A brief history of the Virginia Indians from prehistoric times. el-ms.
>
> **Virginia's Three Capitals: Jamestown, Williamsburg, Richmond.** 10 pp. 20 cents. Pictures of these three historic cities. el-ms.
>
> **The Voyage to Jamestown: A Saga of Seamanship.** 12 pp. 20 cents. The ships and voyage that brought the first settlers in 1607. el-ms.

Documentary Film Classics. National Audiovisual Center. General Services Adm. Information Services Section/JL. Washington, DC 20409. 1980. 48 pp. Free. Lists 40 films produced by the U.S. government since the 1930s which are available at low rental. Most deal with the World War II period, the Depression, and Cold War eras. ad.

Exhibit Guides. The Library of Congress. Information Office. Washington, DC 20540. Two catalogs of former exhibits each containing over 200 vignettes on Lincoln and the Civil War era. Titles are:

Abraham Lincoln. 1959. 94 pp. Free. ms-hs.

The American Civil War. 1961. 88 pp. Free. ms-hs.

The Famous Voyage of Sir Francis Drake, 1577-1580. Museum of Our National Heritage. P.O. Box 519. Lexington, MA 02173. 1979. 30 pp. $3.00 for postage and handling. Multilevel interdisciplinary learning packet focussed on a period of exploration and discovery. Contains reproducible activity sheets. Illustrated. Bibliography. ms-hs.

Federal Documents. The National Archives. National Archives and Records Service (NEPS). General Services Administration. Washington, DC 20408. Titles include:

►**A More Perfect Union: The Creation of the United States Constitution.** 1978. 35 pp. $2.00. Tells the story of the writing of the Constitution at Philadelphia in 1787. Contains the complete text of the Constitution and its amendments. Illustrated. ms-hs.

The Story of the Bill of Rights. 26 pp. $3.50. Documents, rare imprints, and portraits to commemorate the 175th anniversary of the ratification of the *Bill of Rights.* ms-hs.

Facsimiles.

Bill of Rights. 31″ x 33″. $2.00.

Constitution. 31″ x 38″. $2.00.

Declaration of Independence. 29″ x 35″. $2.00.

The Emancipation Proclamation. 11″ x 16½″. 6 pp. $3.00.

Washington's Inaugural Address of 1789. 11″ x 16½″. 13 pp. $3.00.

Films. The Travelers Film Library. 1 Tower Square. Hartford, CT 06115. 16 mm. Color. Sound. Free loan; borrower must pay return postage. Titles are:

Last King of America. 58 min; 2 reels. An imaginative interview of King George III (played by Peter Ustinov) by CBS News commentator Eric Sevareid. Comes with teacher's guide and colorful wall chart. ms-hs.

Suddenly an Eagle. 54 min; 2 reels. Re-creates the events immediately preceding the American Revolution as seen from British and American viewpoints. Comes with teacher's guide and map depicting battlefields. ms-hs.

Franklin D. Roosevelt and Hyde Park. Hyde Park Historical Assoc. P.O. Box 235. Hyde Park, NY 12538. 1977. 18 pp. $1.35. Eleanor Roosevelt's personal recollections about the life of her husband. el-ms-hs.

GPO Materials. U.S. Gov't. Printing Office. Washington, DC 20402. Lists of many low-cost government publications. Sample titles are:

►**Historical Handbook Series** (SB-016). 1982. 6 pp. Free.

►**Presidents of the United States** (SB-106). 1981. 6 pp. Free.

Warren Gamaliel Harding. President Harding's Home. 308 Mount Vernon Ave. Marion, OH 43302. Undated. Pamphlet. Free; include a self-addressed stamped envelope (#10). Harding's life, presidency, and home, and the Harding Memorial and Harding Museum are presented. hs.

Historic Pennsylvania. Pennsylvania Historical and Museum Commission. William Penn Memorial Museum and Archives Bldg. Box 1026. Harrisburg, PA 17120. Send for free publications list of booklets, reprints, leaflets, picture packets and more. ms-hs. Sample titles are:

> **Discovering Pennsylvania's Archeological Heritage.** 1980. 43 pp. $2.75. Treats the evolution of Indian cultures in what is now Pennsylvania.
>
> **Epic on the Schuylkill: The Valley Forge Encampment, 1777-1778.** 1974. 46 pp. $2.50. Portrays life for the men who were encamped at Valley Forge.
>
> **Pennsylvania History in Outline.** 1976. 58 pp. $1.75. A reference work of historical highlights and facts for organizing a series of subjects.

Leaflets. 4 pp. 1-49 copies 15 cents each; 50 or more copies 10 cents each. Forty topics and personalities in the Commonwealth's history; designed for use by students and teachers. Illustrated. Sample titles are:

> **The Amish in American Culture**
>
> **The Pennsylvania Rifle**
>
> **The Conestoga Wagon**
>
> **The Underground Railroad**

Herbert Hoover, the Uncommon Man. Hoover Presidential Library Assoc., Inc. P.O. Box 696. West Branch, IA 52358. 1974. 58 pp. Free. Traces Hoover's accomplishments from early years to post-presidential years. Contains information on the Hoover Presidential Library and the Hoover National Historic Site. Color photographs and illustrations. hs.

Koster: Americans in Search of Their Prehistoric Past (E9198). New American Library. 1633 Broadway. New York, NY 10019. 1979. 249 pp. $2.95. An account of the discovery and excavation of the most important archaeological site in North America, the Lower Illinois Valley. hs-ad.

Lincoln's Gettysburg Address. The Barre Granite Assoc. P.O. Box 481. 51 Church St. Barre, VT 05641. 1 p. Free. President Lincoln's momentous speech on a Civil War battlefield. el-ms.

Minnesota History. Minnesota Historical Society. 1500 Mississippi Street. St. Paul, MN 55101. Titles include:

> **Roots.** 3 themes a year. 32 pp. each. Subscriptions, $5.00; single issues, $2.00. 30 subjects, including: Fur Trade, Lumbering, Mining, Agriculture, Railroads, Rivers, Boundaries, Energy, Education, Immigration, Inventions, Folklife.

The Story of Minnesota. 1977. 75 pp. $3.50. Colorful cartoon history of the state from the Ice Age to the present. el-ms.

Study Guide to the Story of Minnesota. 1978. 16 pp. $1.50. Designed for teachers.

Gopher Historian Leaflet Series. 15 pp. each. 75 cents each. el-ms. Titles include:

►**The Dakota or Sioux**

►**The Ojibway People**

Picture Packets. 8 packets in series. $1.00 each. el-ms. Titles include:

►**Dakota and Ojibway Indian Peoples of Minnesota**

►**Minnesota Exploration—French**

Pilgrim Series. Plimoth Plantation, Inc. Box 1620. Plymouth, MA 02362. Sample titles are:

Arms and Armor of the Pilgrims. 1957. 28 pp. $1.75. Shows the armor, firearms, ammunition, and cannons used by pilgrims. ms-hs.

Captain John Smith's Map of New England. 9″ x 12″. 50 cents. A reproduction of a 1614 map. el-ms.

The Pilgrim Coloring Book. 25 pp. $1.50. A picture coloring book for children telling the story of the Pilgrims. pr-el.

Prelude to Revolution. Smithsonian Magazine. 900 Jefferson Dr., S.W. Washington, DC 20560. 1976. 63 pp. $1.25 postpaid. Historical events in the American colonies from October of 1773 to April of 1775 are related as if they were currently happening. hs-ad.

The Price They Paid. National Federation of Independent Business. Education Dept. 150 W. 20th Ave. San Mateo, CA 94402. Undated. 1 p. Free. Tells what happened to the signers of the Declaration of Independence. el-ms-hs.

The Roosevelts. Sales Shop. Franklin D. Roosevelt Library. Hyde Park, NY 12538. Books, documents, photographs, posters, and slides relating to the life and times of Franklin and Eleanor Roosevelt; send for catalogue. Titles are:

►**Franklin D. Roosevelt in Pictures.** 1975. 17 pp. $1.25. Black and white photos with brief text present some highlights of FDR's life. ms-hs.

►**Eleanor Roosevelt in Pictures.** 1975. 17 pp. $1.25. Black and white photos with text. A companion booklet on Mrs. Roosevelt's life. ms-hs.

Siteline. Smithsonian Institution. Traveling Exhibition Service. Publications Section. Washington, DC 20560. Quarterly newsletter. Free. Contains information about exhibition services and new publications on art, history, and science. Publications list also available. hs-ad.

►**SITES Publications.** Smithsonian Institution. Traveling Exhibition Service. Publication Section. Washington, DC 20560. Free. Annual catalog. Contains descriptions and photographs of books, catalogs, educational materials, and posters published for SITES exhibitions.

The Thomas Jefferson Murals. The Library of Congress. Information Office. Washington, DC 20540. 1970. 26″ x 10″ foldout. Free. Black-and-white print of mural paintings based on themes from Jefferson's writings on freedom, labor, education, and government. Gives brief interpretation of each mural. el-ms.

►**G. Washington: A Figure Upon the Stage Resource Kit.** National Museum of American History. Office of Public and Academic Programs. Room B 1016. Smithsonian Institution. Washington, DC 20560. Free. Teacher's kit designed for classroom use. Each kit contains an audiovisual slide program based on the exhibition and supplementary activities and worksheets. May be used either as preparation for a museum visit or as supplements to historical studies. el-ms.

►**George Washington: American Superhero.** Museum of Our National Heritage. P.O. Box 519. Lexington, MA 02173. 1982. 24 pp. $3.00 postpaid. Packet of 12 duplicatable sheets of visual material, descriptive text, and suggested activities. Each sheet explores an aspect of Washington's life or the theme of hero-worship that may be used in units on the American Revolution, heroes in history, and 18th century life. el-ms.

George Washington: The Life and Legend. Washington National Insurance Co. Public Relations Dept. Evanston, IL 60201. 1979. Packet. Single copy free. Contains teacher's guide, lesson plans, and duplicating masters for six activities for a study unit; also two large wall charts of 15 color reproductions of little-known events in Washington's life, each with brief narrative. G5-9.

Roger Williams: A Brief Biography. R.I. Dept. of Economic Development. 7 Jackson Walkway. Providence, RI 02903. 4 pp. Free. Short biography of the founder of Rhode Island with suggested readings. ms-hs.

HISTORY: WORLD

Ancient Sites. UNESCO. Room 2401. U.N. Building. New York, NY 10017. Set of 4. 4 pp. each. Free. Color photographs and text describing historic monuments under destruction—the problem and the solution. Each presents the narrative in English, French, Spanish, and Arabic. el. to hs. Sample titles are:

►**Borobudur: Man-Made Mountains**

►**Carthage: Must Not Be Destroyed**

►**Fez: Symbol of Creative Genius**

►**Symbols in Stone: Three Monuments of Haiti's Liberty**

China. China Books and Periodicals. 2929 24th St. San Francisco, CA 94110. Also branches at: 125 5th Ave. New York, NY 10013; 174 W. Randolph St. Chicago, IL 60601. A variety of books and periodicals in English imported from China are available. Write for free catalog. Sample titles are:

New Archaeological Finds in China (I). 1974. 73 pp. $3.95. History of cultural objects discovered in China during the Cultural Revolution. Color photographs. ms-hs.

New Archaeological Finds in China (II). 1978. 127 pp. $3.95. History of excavations after 1974, including the 6,000 life-size pottery soldiers in the tomb of Qin Shihuang. Color photographs. ms-hs.

►**The Gutenberg Bible: Landmark in Learning.** Huntington Library Publications. 1151 Oxford Road. San Marino, CA 91108. 1975. 24 pp. $2.75 postpaid. Details John Gutenberg's remarkable achievement of using movable type in printing the Bible and the significance of this invention for the intellectual life of mankind. ms-hs.

Mentor and Signet Books. New American Library. 1633 Broadway. New York, NY 10019. Extensive paperback books in the category of world history are available at prices generally ranging from $1.50 to $2.95. Write for complete listing of titles and prices.

►**Pictures From a Living Past.** UNESCO. Room 2401. U.N. Building. New York, NY 10017. 1978. 40 pp. Free. A booklet of photos and descriptions of historical monuments from around the world. ms-hs.

Pre-Columbian America. Organization of American States. Dept. of Publications. Sales and Promotion. OAS General Secretariat. Washington, DC 20006. Brief accounts of civilizations during ancient Latin America. Illustrated. Send for publications list.

Prints. The University Prints. 21 East St. Winchester, MA 01890. Offers a series of Special Topics Study Sets. Black-and-white prints, 5½" x 8". Request free brochure for complete listing. ms-hs-ad. Minimum order $3.00; postage paid on prepaid orders. Sample titles are:

►**Actors and Actresses.** 30 prints. $1.50. Anonymous and named performers shown in art of all ages.

Brief Art History: African. 30 prints. $1.50. A selection of art and architecture of major periods, schools, and styles.

Classical Mythology. 90 prints. $4.50. Depicts the major Greek and Roman mythological figures and stories.

Development of America. 120 prints. $6.00. Depicts scenes and peoples of six periods of American growth.

Napoleon's France. 30 prints. $1.50. Shows important persons, sights, and events of this significant cultural era.

►**Shakespeare's World.** 30 prints. $1.50. Prints of Elizabethan world and worlds of the dramas.

A Visit to Ancient Rome. 66 prints. $3.00. Includes portraits, buildings, and scenes depicting religion, arts, and daily life.

World History Series. Greenhaven Press, Inc. 577 Shoreview Park Rd. St. Paul, MN 55112. A new series of 64 booklets each dealing with a single civilization, person, issue, revolution, or movement of historical significance. Illustrated. G7-9 reading level. Teacher's guide with time chart for any order. 1980. 32 pp. each. $2.25 each; add 7% of total for shipping ($2.00 min.). Request free brochure for complete listing. Sample titles are:

►**Ancient America**

►**The Chinese Revolution**

►**The Communications Revolution**

►**Ghandi**

►**Japan's Modernization**

►**Nyerere and Nkrumah**

HOME ECONOMICS

Barbara Taylor's Book on Quilting. Taylor Bedding Manufacturing Co. P.O. Box 979. Taylor, TX 76574. 30 pp. $1.00. Instructions for making quilts and toys, decorating accessories, and "Quickie Quilting" with the sewing machine. ms-hs.

► **Catalog of Learning Aids 1983.** Sears, Roebuck and Co. Consumer Information Services. Sears Tower, D-703. Chicago, IL 60684. 1983. 10 pp. Free. Describes teacher and student materials offered; includes order form. ad.

Clorox Aids. Clorox Co. Consumer Services. P.O. Box 24305. Oakland, CA 94623. Titles include:

►**Affordable Bathroom Makeovers.** 9 pp. Up to 25 copies free. A folder containing a start-up check list and action steps to find answers to specific remodeling problems. hs.

All About Laundry. 1979. $1.50. A kit containing four laundry lessons covering basic laundering, laundering costs, additives and appliances, and coin-op laundering. Duplicating masters included. ms-hs.

►**Doing It Over and Maintaining Your Investment.** 6 pp. Up to 25 copies free. A folder designed to help you get the most for your money before and after remodeling. It includes tips on caring for various household surfaces. hs.

►**Household Helps.** Wall chart, 16″ x 11″. Up to 25 copies free. A color chart describing many non-laundry uses for liquid bleach in the home. ms-hs.

Guide to Cleaner Washes. Chart, 9″ x 10″. Up to 25 free. One side gives directions for using liquid bleach in the family wash. The other side gives procedures for dealing with common stains. hs.

The Kingsford Barbecue Guide. Undated. $1.50. A kit of lesson plans and duplicating masters for teaching five units on outdoor cooking. hs.

Kitchen Remodeling. 1979. 25 pp. 50 cents. Step-by-step handbook for planning an efficient kitchen design. hs.

Clorox Bulletins. Clorox Co. Consumer Services. P.O. Box 24305. Oakland, CA 94623. 1977. A series of 14 Clorox Service Bulletins. 1 pp. each, 8½″ x 11″. Up to 25 copies free. Explains specific uses of liquid bleach for purification, disinfection, and sanitation. hs.

Cooking. EKCO Housewares Co. Educational Dept. 9234 W. Belmont Ave. Franklin Park, IL 60131. 50 cents for each order of four pamphlets. hs. Titles are:

All About Cookware. 1967. 6 pp.

All About Garnishes. 1971. 8 pp.

All About Knives and Carving. 1965. 6 pp.

The Names in the Cooking Game. 1969. 6 pp.

Detergents. The Soap and Detergent Assoc. Consumer Affairs Dept. 475 Park Ave. S. New York, NY 10016. Pamphlets and leaflets. Free in limited quantities except as priced. Titles include:

►**Laundry Detergent Package Directions.** Brochure. Illustrates the variables involved in laundering, from water conditions to soil types, and tells why directions and information on a box or bottle of laundry detergent are important. el-ms.

►**Measuring Your Way to a Better Wash.** 1982. 7 pp. Explains the proper detergent usage to give best cleaning and total performance. ms-hs.

►**Soaps and Detergents.** 1981. 32 pp. A booklet about cleaning products covering historical and environmental aspects, their ingredients, how they are made, how they work, and the various kinds available to consumers. Illustrated in color. hs.

►**Understanding Automatic Dishwashing.** 1982. 10 pp. Why only a specially formulated product can be used in automatic dishwashers. ms-hs.

Films. 16 mm. Color. 15 min. Available on free loan basis; return postage paid by user. Request brochures and order forms. Titles are:

Commitment to Safety. Answers safety and environmental questions about soaps and detergents. ms-hs.

Pursuit of Cleanliness. Shows how modern-day detergents work. ms-hs.

Dyeing. Dye-Craft. Dept. FILM—82. P.O. Box 307. Coventry, CT 06238. Several brochures are available giving instructions and procedures for different types and techniques of dyeing fabric and other materials. Write for literature list and order form. Sample titles are:

Dye-Craft. Poster 29″ x 22″. 15 cents. ms-hs.

►**Rit Tint & Dye Color Chart**

Wonderful Art of Color Dyeing. 6 pp. 15 cents. ms-hs.

Education Catalog. General Mills Inc. Publications & Editorial. Box 1113. Minneapolis, MN 55440. 11 pp. Free. An annotated listing of free-loan filmstrips with tape cassette narrations, books, and pamphlets related to home economics and nutrition.

Facts About Man-Made Fibers (CU-26). Celanese Fibers Marketing Co. Information Services. 1211 Avenue of the Americas. New York, NY 10036. 1974. 8 pp. Free. Describes ten generic man-made fiber groups most widely used for consumer goods. hs.

Food Cost Saver Calculator. EKCO Housewares Co. Educational Dept. 9234 W. Belmont Ave. Franklin, IL 60131. 50 cents. A dial chart which gives the true cost per ounce, pound, pint, or quart for packaged foods. hs.

Food Preservation. Ball Corp. Joan Randle, Manager of Consumer Affairs. 345 S. High St. Muncie, IN 47302. Titles include:

Ball Blue Book. 30th ed. 1977. 96 pp. Single copy $2.00; additional copies $1.50 plus postage. A guide to home canning and freezing. hs.

Ball Freezer Book. 1976. 48 pp. Single copy 75 cents; for additional copies add postage. A complete guide to home freezing. hs.

Science of Food Preservation. 8 pp. Single copy 5 cents; for additional copies add postage. Tells how micro-organisms cause foods to spoil. hs.

Floor and Furniture Care. Johnson Wax. Consumer Services Center. P.O. Box 567. Dept. FI-83-HDM. Racine, WI 53401. Free booklets; request on postcard. Titles include:

Floor Care. 38 pp. How to choose the correct floor care product. hs-ad.

Furniture Care. 23 pp. A guide to furniture care and care products. hs-ad.

Home Care. 33 pp. Booklet on cleaning and maintenance jobs stresses that thought and organization are as important as muscle and stamina. hs-ad.

HEEA Publications. Home Economics Education Assoc. 1201 16th St., N.W. Rm. 232. Washington, DC 20036. Request listing of current materials for students and teachers priced from $1.00 to $4.00. ms-hs.

Helps. American Home Economics Assoc. 2010 Massachusetts Ave., N. W. Washington, DC 20036. $3.75. Home Economics Learning Programs that include a variety of low-cost printed instructional materials. Send for list. ad.

Home Appliances. Association of Home Appliance Manufacturers. 20 N. Wacker Dr. Chicago, Il 60606. Offers several materials on the purchase and use of ordinary appliances. Send for listing. Sample titles are:

►**Choosing and Using Your Automatic Dishwasher.** 9 pp. 40 cents. ms-hs.

►**Consumer Recommendations on the Safe Use of Appliances.** 9 pp. Single copy free. ms-hs.

►**MACAP's Handbook for the Informed Consumer.** 1974. 57 pp. $1.10. Covers the purchase, use, and care of major appliances. ms-hs.

►**Use and Care Tips for Your Clothes Dryer.** 16 pp. 50 cents. ms-hs.

►**Home Economics** (SB-276). U.S. Gov't. Printing Office. Washington, DC 20402. 1981. 14 pp. Free. A listing of many low-cost government publications.

Homemaking Aids. Beecham Products. Consumer and Public Affairs. Dept. E-1. Box 1467. Pittsburgh, PA 15230. Free. Distribution limited in some cases because of phosphate restrictions. Sample title is:

The Dishwashing Book. 29 pp. Ways to wash different types of tableware and utensils efficiently by hand or automatic washer; presents solutions to common dishwashing problems in chart form. hs.

Kerr Home Canning and Freezing Book. Kerr Glass Manufacturing Corp. Consumer Products Div. Box 97. Sand Springs, OK 74063. 1980. 72 pp. Single copy free to instructors (give school name); $2.00 each to others. Available only in the U.S., Canada, and Puerto Rico. Home canning and freezing instructions and recipes. Illustrated. hs.

Kitchen Clean-Up. The Maytag Co. Consumer Education Dept. Newton, IA 50208. Free in reasonable quantities. Titles include:

A Dishwasher: You'll Welcome the Difference (125YG). 8 pp. Highlights the benefits of dishwasher ownership, the models available, and tips for using the appliance to its fullest advantage. ms-hs-ad.

A Food Waste Disposer—the First Step for Easy Kitchen Cleanup (167YG). 8 pp. Complete information concerning use, operation, installation, and selection of food waste disposers. ms-hs-ad.

Laundering. The Maytag Co. Consumer Education Dept. Newton, IA 50208. Free in reasonable quantities. Titles include:

The Facts of Laundry for Teenagers and Young Adults (181YG). 10 pp. Gives laundry tips for anyone doing laundry for the first time. ms-hs-ad.

What You Need to Know to Choose a Laundry Detergent (184YG). 6 pp. Provides concise information about the different types of laundry detergent available, amounts to use, and tips to achieve the best results. ms-hs-ad.

A Young People's Guide to Clean Jeans (and Other Fine Washables). A teaching kit. $1.00. Kit consists of a four-page teacher's guide and four activity-oriented spirit duplicating masters; instructions for using the masters and suggestions for activities. May be used as a supplement to the free-loan film "It All Comes Out in the Wash." ms-hs-ad.

►**Laundry Facts: Products & Special Methods** (#31). Gold Seal Co. Bismark, ND 58501. 1982. 4 pp. Available free to teachers in reasonable quantities. Prepunched, notebook-size leaflet which explains the use of various laundry products and the care of special laundry. hs.

New Room in Your Kitchen. Rubbermaid, Inc. Home Service Center. Dept. FI. 1147 Akron Rd. Wooster, OH 44691. 4 pp. Free; send self-addressed stamped envelope (#10). Kitchen storage tips for your home, including the refrigerator and freezer, and kitchen cut-out arrangement schemes. ms-hs.

Only Silk Is Silk. International Silk Assoc. (U.S.A.), Inc. c/o Rudolph-Desco Co., Inc. 580 Sylvan Ave. P.O. Box 907. Englewood Cliffs, NJ 07632. Educational kit available to teachers free of charge except as indicated. Kit consists of: Teacher's Guide to the Study of Silk; Student Study Aid to Silk; Cocoon Box ($1.00) containing a cocoon, raw silk, silk sewing thread, swatches of silk fabrics; and a pamphlet, *The Story of Silk*. ms-hs.

►**Packaging—Understanding Its Real Value.** Ralston Purina. Corporate Consumer Services. Public Relations. Checkerboard Square. St. Louis, MO 63164. Free. Explains the material selection, testing, and quality assurance procedures involved in package design. ms-hs.

Sewing and Needlework. Coats & Clark. Dept FILM. P.O. Box 1010. Toccoa, GA 30577. Free catalogs. Titles are:

Educational Materials From Coats & Clark (XE 2175). Describes inexpensive educational leaflets and teaching aids for sewing and art needlework students. ms-hs.

Coats & Clark Products Catalog (XE 2275). Describes sewing and art needlework products available at special prices for educational use. ad.

Sewing Guides. Pellon Corp. Education Dept. 119 W. 40th St. New York, NY 10018. Several leaflets on interfacing techniques are offered 75 cents to $1.00 per package of 25 copies. Request "Pellon Educational Order Form" for complete listing. hs.

Sew On and Sew Forth. Celanese Fibers Marketing Co. Information Services. 1211 Avenue of the Americas. New York, NY 10036. 1972. 12 pp. Free. Suggestions on sewing with newer types of fabric. Includes a fabric conversion chart to determine correct yardage for patterns. hs.

►**Space Organizers.** Rubbermaid Inc. Home Service Center. Dept. FI. 1147 Akron Road. Wooster, OH 44691. Brochure. 16 pp. 25 cents and self-addressed stamped envelope (#10). Presents ways to use space more efficiently all over the house. Illustrated. hs.

Step-by-Step Pictorial Cookbook. Ralston Purina Co. Corporate Consumer Services. Public Relations. Checkerboard Square. St. Louis, MO 63164. 1979. 50 pp. $2.00. A graphically illustrated cookbook for those with mental or physical handicaps which gives sequential steps for preparing recipes at three skill levels—no cook, minimal cook, and full cook. ms-ad.

Synthetic Textile Fibers. E.I. Du Pont de Nemours & Co. Textile Fibers Dept. Wilmington, DE 19898. Titles are:

> **Du Pont Fiber Facts** (E-02092). 4 pp. Fold-out chart. 34″ x 11″. Free. Describes Du Pont textile products, their manufacture, uses, and care. hs.
>
> **Facts About Fabrics** (E-29102). 5 pp. Free. Describes yarn and fabric construction, dyeing and finishing, and care suggestions. hs.
>
> **Home Cleaning Guide for Articles Containing Du Pont Textile Fibers** (E-06770). 10 pp. Free. Covers washing instructions for articles such as knit wear, insulated apparel, curtains, upholstery, and carpets. hs.
>
> **Home Sewing Techniques for Fabrics Containing Du Pont Fibers** (E-20518). 5 pp. Free. A booklet on selection of fabric, pattern, and findings, on preparation for sewing, and on pressing. hs.

Taylor Materials. Taylor Instrument. Consumer Products Div. Sybron Corp. Arden, NC 28704. Free in classroom quantities; request on school stationery. Titles are:

> **All You Want to Know About Humidity.** 1960. Pamphlet answers 30 questions about humidity and its regulation in the home. hs.
>
> **Cooking With Taylor Thermometers.** 1971. Brochure. Recommends the best temperatures for 11 cooking operations. hs.

Washing and Cleaning. Lever Brothers Co. Consumer Education Dept. 390 Park Ave. New York, NY 10022. Free. Tips and hints for using cleansing products. Titles are:

> ►**How to Get the Best Out of Your Automatic Dishwasher.** Leaflet. Gives solutions to some common dishwashing problems. ms-hs.
>
> ►**It's Washday, What Do I Do About . . . ?** Pamphlet. Contains helpful facts about laundry procedures and tips on energy efficiency and stain removal. ms-hs.

►**Stain Removal Chart.** 9″ x 11″. 2 pp. Tells how to remove 27 common stains from washable fabrics. ms-hs.

Wood Floor Care Guide. Oak Flooring Institute. 804 Sterick Bldg. Memphis, TN 38103. Undated. 14 pp. 25 cents. Comprehensive maintenance manual for hardwood flooring, types of finishes, and how to preserve them, including stain removal. hs.

Wool. Pendleton Woolen Mills. Home Economics Dept. 218 S.W. Jefferson St. Portland, OR 97201. Single copies free to teachers, librarians, and administrators in the continental United States. Titles include:

Wool . . . a Natural. 20 pp. General information on the selection, use, and care of woolens. ms-hs.

Wool Fiber in the Making. 1966. A chart exhibit on wool manufacturing. Includes samples of wool, lanolin, yarn, and finished fabric. ms-hs.

The Wool Story From Fleece to Fashion. Rev. 1980. 35 pp. An account of the history and economic importance of wool—"the living fiber." ms-hs.

INDUSTRIAL TECHNOLOGY

Asphalt. The Asphalt Institute. Asphalt Institute Bldg. College Park, MD 20740. Titles are:

Asphalt—a Pictorial Overview. 1977. 16 pp. $1.25 payable in advance. A pictorial survey of the many uses of our oldest engineering material. ms-hs.

Magic Carpet—the Story of Asphalt. 1973. 16 pp. Free in reasonable quantities. Describes history and major roles of asphalt. Color illustrations. el.

►**Basic Machines and How They Work** (#217095). Dover Publications, Inc. 180 Varick St. New York, NY 10014. 1971. 161 pp. $4.00. Presents details on 15 machines such as levers, wheel and axle, internal combustion engine, and basic computer mechanisms. hs-ad.

►**The Bright Choice.** The International Nickel Co., Inc. Inco-Sterling Forest. P.O. Box 200. Suffern, NY 10901. Free. Two filmstrips, cassette tape, and narration guide to present the history and daily uses of nickel. ms-hs-ad.

Cotton. National Cotton Council of America. P.O. Box 12285. Memphis, TN 38112. Titles are:

►**The Story of Cotton.** 20 pp. Free. Tells the story of cotton in simple terms, including where and how it is grown, processed, and woven into cloth. el.

►**Cotton Wall Chart.** Four-color. 22″ x 29″. One free per class; additional copies 50 cents each. Shows steps in cotton production, processing, and manufacturing, plus uses of fiber and seed. pr-el.

Fiberglas Educational Kit. Owens-Corning Fiberglas Corp. Inquiry Dept. Attn: L.H.G. Meeks. Fiberglas Tower. Toledo, OH 43659. Single copy free to librarians and teachers. An assortment of pamphlets, leaflets, and charts on the uses and properties of Fiberglas. hs-ad.

Glass—the Miracle Worker. Libbey-Owens-Ford Co. Advertising Dept. LOF Glass. P.O. Box 799. 811 Madison Ave. Toledo, OH 43695. Undated. 15 pp. Up to 35 copies free. A brochure describing the history of glass manufacturing and the different types of glass. ms-hs.

Man-Made Fibers. Man-Made Fiber Producers Assoc., Inc. 1150 17th St., N. W. Washington, DC 20036. Titles include:

> **Flow Chart.** 1 p. Free. Shows the various steps of man-made fiber production from raw materials to finished products. hs.
>
> **Man-Made Fibers—A New Guide.** 1977. 16 pp. Free. Covers basic principles of production, uses, characteristics, care, trademarks, and other information about fibers used in textile and industrial products. hs.

Papermaking. American Paper Institute. 260 Madison Ave. New York, NY 10016. Single copy free. Various materials on paper products and their manufacture. Titles include:

> **How Paper Came to America.** Rev. 1975. Large wall chart. Gives brief history of paper's invention and machinery for making paper. el.
>
> **How You Can Make Paper.** 1977. 3 pp. Directions for making paper in the classroom. A glossary of paper types is also included. pr-el.
>
> **Paper and Paper Manufacture.** Undated. 8 pp. Presents general background of papermaking, paper's many uses today, and its emerging future uses. ms-hs.

Papermaking. Hammermill Paper Group. P. O. Box 1440. Erie, PA 16533. Titles include:

> **From Forest Tree to Fine Papers.** 1977. Leaflet. Free. Illustrates the process of paper manufacturing. el-ms.
>
> **How to Make Paper by Hand.** 25 cents. A kit containing full instructions for making paper by hand. el-ms.
>
> ►**Seeds of Wonder—Papermaking at Hammermill.** 16 mm film (or ¾″ TV cassette). Sound. Color. 27 min. Free loan, except for cost of return postage; give alternate dates when ordering. Takes viewers on a trip from forest to paper mill to finished product.

Plastics. Plastics Education Foundation. Education Director. Box 12443. Albany, NY 12212. Various materials are available about plastics, their increasing applications, the industry and its technology, and career opportunities. Single copy free. Sample titles are:

Injection Molding. 1967. 27 pp. Free. Explains materials and methods used in the injection molding process. hs-ad.

The Need for Plastics Education. 1976. 24 pp. Free. Results of a survey on future manpower needs in the plastics industry. hs-ad.

Recycling Scrap Metal. Institute of Scrap Iron and Steel, Inc. 1627 K St., N.W. Washington, DC 20006. Materials are available on the use of scrap iron and steel. Sample titles are:

Background Kit for Educators. Free. Materials emphasize the environmental and energy savings realized when scrap iron is used instead of iron ore to make new steel and the issues confronting the ferrous scrap industry. ad.

Mines Above Ground. Free in classroom quantities. How iron and steel are recycled into new products. el-ms.

Recycling Iron and Steel Scrap Saves Energy. 16 pp. Free. General information on the scrap processing industry. el-ms.

Rubber. Firestone Tire and Rubber Co. Educational Aids Div. 1200 Firestone Pkwy. Akron, OH 44317. Rev. 1977. 31 pp. Free. History of rubber, development of the rubber industry, and present and future uses of rubber. Teacher's manual available. A filmstrip, *A Class Studies Rubber,* also is available; one to each school building. el-ms.

Steel. American Iron and Steel Institute. 1000 16th St., N.W. Washington, DC 20036. Request list of available teaching aids including films and filmstrips. Single copies free to teachers. Sample titles are:

A Flowline of Steelmaking. Wall chart, 25″ x 15″. An illustrated diagram depicting the major steps and processes in converting iron ore to steel. In color. ms-hs.

►**Science of Steelmaking.** Sound cassette, filmstrip, and teachers guide. A unit on steel ranging from mining ore to producing finished steel. ms.

Steelmaking Flowlines. 1980. 20 pp. Illustrations and text present the treatment of raw materials, the basic processes, and environmental controls in making steel. ms-hs.

Stretching Your Mind. Firestone Tire & Rubber Co. Dept. of Public Relations. 1200 Firestone Pkwy. Akron, OH 44317. 1979. Packet. Free to G4-7 teachers only. Teacher's guide, a 22″ x 34″ wall chart, and four activity masters for teaching about the production and uses of rubber. el-ms.

Tapping the Treasure in Corn. Corn Refiners Assoc., Inc. 1001 Connecticut Ave., N. W. Washington, DC 20036. 1976. Leaflet. Free. Illustrates the process of corn refining and many of the products derived. hs.

Textile Industry. American Textile Manufacturers Institute. 1101 Connecticut Ave., N.W. Washington, D.C. 20036. Newer items may be substituted; all items subject to discontinuance at any time. Single copy free. Titles include:

Mankind's Magic Carpet. 1974. 21 pp. Tells how textiles have contributed to civilization and industrial progress. el-ms.

►**Textiles.** 1981. 16 pp. Illustrated booklet provides basic economic and social primer on textiles. ms.

Textiles From Start to Finish. 1974. 21 pp. Tells about fibers, yarns, and fabrics. el-ms.

Textiles—Our First Great Industry. 1975. A resource unit covering the history of textile manufacturing and present day technologies and products; includes student activities. One for el-ms; one for hs.

Textile Manufacturing. WestPoint Pepperell. Public Relations. Attn: Joy Story. Box 71. West Point, GA 31833. Up to 10 copies free. Titles are:

►**Textiles.** 16 pp. Describes the people, products, processes, and the economic impact of the textile industry. Includes facts, figures, charts, color photos, and bibliography of sources. ms-hs.

Textiles From Start to Finish. Undated. 20 pp. Discusses fibers, yarn manufacture, fabric construction, weaving, knitting, and finishing. Illustrated. ms-hs.

LANGUAGE ARTS

ACEI Publications. Assoc. for Childhood Education International. 3615 Wisconsin Ave., N. W. Washington, DC 20016. Add 10% for postage and handling. Send payment with orders under $10.00; no Canadian currency. Publications concerned with children from birth to preadolesence. Sample titles are:

Creative Dramatics for All Children. 1973. 64 pp. $4.00. Suggestions for using the senses, pantomine, and dramatic activities with special groups of children for presenting a story. Includes a source list.

Literature, Creativity, and Imagination. 1973. 20 pp. 75 cents. Three children's authors present some of their ideas.

On Reading. 1979. 8 pp. 50 cents; 10 copies $4.00. ACEI Position Paper on what reading is, how it should be taught and its progress measured, and what the schools can do to improve the teaching of reading. ad.

►***Activity Books.*** Milliken Publishing Co. 1100 Research Blvd. St. Louis, MO 63132. Offers a wide assortment of books of duplicating masters for basic curriculum areas. Most sell for $4.95. Send for catalog for grades K-3, K-6, 4-6, or 7-12.

All About Letters (#01135). National Council of Teachers of English. 1111 Kenyon Rd. Urbana, IL 61801. 1979. 64 pp. $2.50; 20 or more copies $1.50 each. A guide to teaching letter writing skills that includes examples of construction and style. ms-hs.

►**Anywhere Workbooks** (IB110-119). Instructor Publications, Inc. 757 3rd Ave. New York, NY 10017. 1982. 32 pp. each. A series of student workbooks that use high interest games, puzzles, and other devices for review and practice in common problem areas. Send for free catalog for descriptions. el.

►***Bilingual Education.*** National Clearinghouse for Bilingual Education. 1555 Wilson Blvd., Suite 600. Rosslyn, VA 22209. Write or call toll free (800-336-4560) to obtain information on bilingual education and related areas. Brochures, articles, *Forum* (monthly newsletter), and other items are available free or for less than $5.00.

Card Aids. Teacher's Exchange of San Francisco. 28 Dawnview. San Francisco, CA 94131. Add 75 cents to prices for shipping. Titles include:

Face Maker. 1974. $1.25. By turning the wheels students can make 1000 possible faces. Useful for art lessons, creative writing, and the like. ms.

"Spelling 24" Task Cards. 1974. $2.50. 24 plastic-coated 6 1/2″ x 6 1/2″ cards. Students complete tactile projects (visual, auditory, etc.) using their own spelling words. G2-4.

Survival Reading. Set of 34 cards. 4 1/2″ x 6 1/2″. $3.50. Activities include phone directory, newspapers, fill-out forms, labels, signs, and following directions for learning to function successfully in today's world. G4-6.

Word-Detecto Cards. 1975. $1.00. 16 hidden word puzzle cards. From a group of letters the student finds words of three letters or more. G3-6.

Classical Language. American Classical League. Miami University. Oxford, OH 45056. Offers a variety of materials in Latin, Greek, and English translations for teachers and students of the classical languages. Write for a free listing and prices. Sample title is:

►**Latin Words in Current English.** 54 pp. $1.60. Lists over 7,000 English words from the Latin language with minor or no changes. hs-ad.

Diagramming Sentences Made Easy. Rex Barks. P.O. Box 703. McLean, VA 22101. 1976. 158 pp. $3.95; quantity rates available. A step-by-step guide to diagramming sentences. ms-hs.

►**Films and Filmstrips for Language Arts: An Annotated Bibliography** (#17260). National Council of Teachers of English. 1111 Kenyon Road. Urbana, IL 61801. 1981. 103 pp. $5.75 (members $5.00). Describes nearly 300 films and filmstrips issued during the 1970s and assesses each film's appropriateness to the elementary school curriculum, including its potential for generating classroom activities and emotional and intellectual impact. el.

French and Spanish. Emporia State University. Director of the Service Bureau for Modern Language Teachers. Dept. of Foreign Languages. Emporia, KS 66801. A variety of mimeographed bulletins for French and Spanish teachers. List available upon request (small charge for duplicating and postage on each bulletin). Sample titles are:

American Sources of French Realia

Lingua Games

Series for Spanish Conversation

Suggestions for Modern Language Laboratory

Tests and Test Building

How to Be a Word Detective. Academic Therapy Publications. 20 Commercial Blvd. Novato, CA 94947. 1975. 48 pp. $3.00. Payment should accompany all orders and include 10% handling charge (minimum $1.50). Official purchase orders over $15 may be billed. U.S. currency only; California residents must include sales tax. Gives methods for teaching decoding or word attack skills for deducing the pronunciation of an unfamiliar word. el-ms.

►**How to Do Research** (SC-5966). World Book, Inc. Merchandise Plaza. Chicago, IL 60654. 1983. 26 pp. 20 cents. Gives step-by-step instructions on how to plan, prepare, and present a research report. G7-12.

►**Instant Speaking Course** (#2176-4). The Interstate Printers & Publishers, Inc. 19-27 N. Jackson St. Danville, IL 61832. 1981. 32 pp. $1.50; quantity rates available. Provides pointers for speech-makers from gaining credibility with an audience to judging acoustics and handling interruptions. ms-hs.

►**Learning to Spell** (#27894). National Council of Teachers of English. 1111 Kenyon Road. Urbana, IL 61801. 1981. 38 pp. $2.50 (members $2.00). Tells how to help children become better spellers and describes 41 word games that can be played with simple materials. pr-el.

Let's See. American Optometric Assoc. Vision Education Service. 243 North Lindbergh Blvd. St. Louis, MO 63141. 1970. 28 pp. $1.00. An activity book to promote vision skills and make young children aware of the world around them. pr.

Mind Benders. Midwest Publications. P.O. Box 448. Pacific Grove, CA 93950. Series. 30 pp. each. $3.95 each. Twelve books containing mental games to develop deductive thinking skills useful for cognitive learnings. Volumes vary in difficulty and may be used at various grade levels.

Modern Language. Modern Language Assoc. of America. 62 5th Ave. New York, NY 10011. Send for catalog of MLA publications which include selected bibliographies for instruction in several foreign languages. ad.

New Horizon Ladder Dictionary of the English Language for Young Readers (AE1332). New American Library. 1633 Broadway. New York, NY 10019. 1970. 686 pp. $2.50. Dictionary based on the 5,000 most frequently used words in the English language. el-ms.

Original Writing. Bantam Books. 666 5th Ave. New York, NY 10019. Titles include:

> **Short Story Writing** (#20645-1). 1976. 179 pp. $2.25. Guide to what the student needs to know for planning, writing, and revising the successful short story. hs-ad.
>
> **30 Ways to Help You Write** (#20793-8). 1980. 170 pp. $2.75. A series of writing experiments for learning to write, edit, and rewrite with ease, skill, and confidence. hs-ad.

Pamphlet Series. The Thrift Press. P. O. Box 85. Ithaca, NY 14850. A series of pamphlets dealing with composition, grammar, literature, cultural background, and customs in German, French, Italian, Portuguese, Russian, Spanish, Greek, and Latin. Most sell for under $1.00. Send for listing. ad.

Paragraph Development (#2-37438). Houghton Mifflin Co. 1 Beacon St. Boston, MA 02108. 1979. 92 pp. $3.84. Workbook for student practice in writing topic sentences, supporting sentences, and whole paragraphs. ms-hs.

Penguin Books. Viking Penguin, Inc. 625 Madison Ave. New York, NY 10022. Sample titles are:

> **The Great American Writing Block.** 1979. 187 pp. $3.95. Examines the decline in writing ability among students and proposes approaches and techniques for treating the problem.
>
> ►**The Read-Aloud Handbook.** 1982. 223 pp. $5.95. Delineates a commonsense approach to help parents, teachers, and children rediscover the joy of reading aloud. Includes a guide to 300 selected books. ad.

Quickie Ideas: The Newspaper in Your Classroom. Joy Lindner. P. O. Box 274. Tualatin, OR 97062. 1980. 23 pp. $3.00; payment must accompany order. Gives 99 creative ideas for using the newspaper in writing and reading and for fun. el-ms.

Reading and Spelling Crossword Puzzles (RRB1). Hayes School Publishing Co. 321 Pennwood Ave. Wilkinsburg, PA 15221. 1975. 28 pp. $1.95. Exercises the students' basic reading and spelling skills through phonetic puzzles. pr.

Resource Handbooks. Instructor Publications, Inc. P.O. Box 6177. Duluth, MN 55806. 48 pp. each. $2.95 each. Several booklets are available which provide content and instructions for classroom activities in the language arts curriculum in grades 1-8. Send for free catalog for descriptions.

Short Course in Remedial English Composition. The Interstate Printers and Publishers, Inc. 19-27 Jackson St. Danville, IL 61832. 1977. 104 pp. $3.95. Designed for college freshmen who need special practice in English composition to successfully continue their college careers. ad.

Sound Drills. The Interstate Printers and Publishers, Inc. 19-27 N. Jackson St. Danville, IL 61832. Sample titles are:

> **A Book of Modern Tongue Twisters.** 1970. 58 pp. $3.25. Drills for children to practice particular sounds and improve fluency and rhythm in speech. pr-el.
>
> **The Road to the Land of "R."** 1970. 48 pp. $1.00. A drillbook of games and picture stories for the child learning to make the "r" sound. pr-el.
>
> **The Road to the Land of "S."** 1969. 47 pp. $1.00. A drillbook of games and picture stories to sustain the interest of a child who is learning the "s" and "z" sounds. pr-el.
>
> **The Road to the Land of "TH."** 1971. 48 pp. $1.00. A drillbook of games and picture stories to motivate and sustain the interest of a child who is learning the "th" sound. pr-el.
>
> **Switch (R Sound)** (#2005). 1978. 53 playing cards, 2 1/4" x 3 1/2". $3.50. An auditory discrimination card game designed to help children learn where the "r" sound is located in a word. Includes instruction booklet. el.
>
> **Switch (S Sound)** (#1790). 1976. 53 playing cards and 8 page instruction booklet. $3.50. Games designed to help children learn where the "s" is located in a word. el.

Student Materials. Instructional Fair, Inc. P.O. Box 1650. Grand Rapids, MI 49501. Publisher offers a line of duplicating or wipe-clean cards for student use in drills and exercises to strengthen grammar, spelling, vocabulary, word analysis, phonics, and reading. Available for different ability levels. $4.50 per set. Request free catalog for detailed descriptions.

Teacher Aid Book Series. Pitman Learning, Inc. 6 Davis Drive. Belmont, CA 94002. Orders must be accompanied by check or money order for payment in full plus 8% (min. $2.00) for shipping. Titles are:

> **Creative Writing in the Classroom** (#1680-Z090). 1968. 64 pp. $4.50. Aimed towards developing a creative atmosphere in the classroom; includes sections on writing stories and poems. ms.

Games Make Spelling Fun (#3255-Z090). Rev. 1973. 32 pp. $3.95. Fun activities to stimulate student interest in spelling and to improve oral and written facility with the language. el.

Hands-on Grammar: An Instant Resource (#3072-Z090). 1977. 46 pp. $3.95. A logical, concise primer of basic grammatical forms and usage. hs.

One-Minute Game Guide: Chalkboard Learning Games for the Elementary Grades (#5070-Z090). 1968. 40 pp. $3.95. A book for teaching language arts and mathematics through simple classroom games. el.

Tips and Bright Ideas! Carolyn Hammer. Route 27. Luttrell Rd. Knoxville, TN 37918. 1978. 9 pp. $1.00 and self-addressed, stamped, business-size envelope; postage paid on 10 or more copies. Suggestions for encouraging daily creative writing and 200 topic titles. ms.

►**200 Tips to Students on How to Study.** (#1232). The Interstate Printers and Publishers, Inc. 19-27 N. Jackson St. Danville, IL 61832. 45 pp. $1.00 prepaid; quantity rates available. A handbook of techniques to help students improve study habits and skills. Includes hints for specific subjects.

A Very Important Person's Workbook. C.J. Frompovich Publications. R.D. 1, Chestnut Rd. Coopersburg, PA 18036. 1980. 16 pp. $2.50; quantity rates available. Writing activities intended to strengthen self-concept. pr-el.

►**Words and What They Do to You.** Institute of General Semantics. R.R. 1, Box 215. Lakeville, CT 06039. 1965. 128 pp. $4.00. Gives beginning lessons in general semantics for junior and senior high school. Includes suggestions for 16 lessons and an extensive resource listing. hs-ad.

►**Writing!** Curriculum Innovations, Inc. 3500 Western Ave. Highland Park, IL 60035. Magazine. 9 issues yearly. Sample issue free to teachers. Each issue is dedicated to helping students improve their writing skills. hs.

Writing Instruments. Corporate Relations Dept. The Parker Pen Co. P.O. Box 5100. Janesville, WI 53547. Undated. Free. 8½" x 11", typewritten. Materials on the history of writing and writing instruments. el-ms. Titles include:

►**A Chronology: Parker Writing Instruments.** 4 pp.

Development of the Ball Pen. 3 pp.

Development of the Fountain Pen. 3 pp.

The History of Writing. 5 pp.

Yellow Pages for Students and Teachers (#88-9). Incentive Publications, Inc. 2400 Crestmoor Rd. Nashville, TN 37215. 1980. 96 pp. $5.95. Contains word lists and other special resources for teaching reading, writing, and thinking skills. pr-el.

LANGUAGE ARTS: READING

About 100 Books. The American Jewish Committee. Institute of Human Relations. 165 E. 56th St. New York, NY 10022. 1977. 40 pp. $1.00. An annotated list of 100 books for children and young adults; includes publisher, date, number of pages, price and recommended age level.

Adapted Classics. Globe Book Co. 50 W. 23rd St. New York, NY 10010. Offers shortened and simplified versions of 12 classics. Each contains study questions emphasizing higher-level reading skills. Accompanying teacher's guides free upon request. Discounts on 10 or more copies. Sample titles are:

The Adventures of Sherlock Holmes. 192 pp. $4.76. Reading level 6-7.

Moby Dick. 272 pp. $5.04. Reading level 5-6.

Tom Sawyer. 224 pp. $4.76. Reading level 3-4.

The War of the Worlds. 288 pp. $5.04. Reading level 7-8.

Bantam Series. Bantam Books. 666 5th Ave. New York, NY 10103. Many titles in each series. Send for listing. Most priced from $1.50 to $1.95. Series are:

►**Choose Your Own Adventure.** Features books in which the reader becomes the main character and selects plot choices for the story's evolution. For ages 7-9 and 10-14.

►**HI/LO Books.** Novels, fiction, and non-fiction books written to appeal to the interests of teenagers who read at the fourth grade level or below.

►**Sweet Dreams Books.** Features stories with a romantic focus that deal with real situations many youth face. For ages 11 and older.

A Better Reading Workshop. Globe Book Co. 50 W. 23rd St. New York, NY 10010. Series of four text-workbooks with teaching guide. 1978. 64 pp. each. $2.34 each; 10 or more copies, $1.95 each. G4-6 reading level. Each book presents a variety of high-interest reading material and skill exercises to teach different reading methods. Titles are:

Reading for Speed and Accuracy (Book 1).

Reading With Care (Book 2).

Making Inferences (Book 3).

Special Study Skills (Book 4).

►**Bibliography of Books for Children.** ACEI. 3615 Wisconsin Ave., N.W. Washington, DC 20016. 1980 ed. 112 pp. $5.95 plus 10% postage/handling; 10% discount to members. No billed orders under $10.00. An annotated listing of fiction, nonfiction, and reference books for children under 15 years old. Includes reference collections for an elementary school library and a list of publishers. pr-el-ms.

Black Is—. Enoch Pratt Free Library. Publications Dept. 400 Cathedral St. Baltimore, MD 21201. 1972. 60 pp. 85 cents. An annotated list of children's books by and about black Americans.

Booklists. American Library Assoc. Young Adult Services Div. 50 E. Huron St. Chicago, IL 60611. Single copy for 25 cents each and a self-addressed mailing label. Prepay orders less than $10.00. Pamphlet series. Titles include:

►**Best Books for Young Adults.** 1982. Rev. annually. An annotated reading list for teenagers.

►**High-Interest, Low-Reading Level Booklist.** 1980. 9 pp. 50 cents. Annotated list of books for reading levels 1-3 and 4-5 published durng 1977-1979. Levels determined by the revised Fry formula.

►**Libros a tu Gusto.** 1982. Annotated list of young adult books available in Spanish.

►**Outstanding Biographies for the College Bound.** 1982. Annotated list of noted biographies.

►**Outstanding Books on the Performing Arts for the College Bound.** 1982. Annotated list of books on dance, film, television, music, and related arts.

►**Outstanding Non-Fiction for the College Bound.** 1982. Annotated reading list.

►**Outstanding Fiction for the College Bound.** 1982. Annotated list of fiction with which every student should be familiar.

►**Selected Films for Young Adults.** 1982. Revised annually. An annotated filmography.

►**Books for the Teen Age.** Office of Young Adult Services. Branch Libraries. 455 5th Ave. New York, NY 10016. Published yearly. 1982. 67 pp. $3.00 plus handling charges of $1.00 for 1 to 5 copies. An up-to-date booklist with a wide range of subjects having special appeal for youth.

Children's Book & Music Center Catalog. Children's Book & Music Center. 2500 Santa Monica Blvd. Santa Monica, CA 90404. Revised bi-annually. 96 pp. $1.00. Contains recordings, books, multi-media, and rhythm instruments for all curriculum areas and all grade levels. Several items less than $5.00. Titles are arranged under 10 headings and indexed. ad.

Choosing a Child's Book. The Children's Book Council. 67 Irving Place. New York, NY 10003. Leaflet. For free copy send self-addressed envelope with first-class postage (1 ounce). Gives guidelines for selecting books for children. ad.

The Enoch Prattler. Enoch Pratt Free Library. Publications Dept. 400 Cathedral St. Baltimore, MD 21201. 1981. 4 pp. 50 cents. A reading list for young adults produced in a lively newspaper format. hs.

►**Exploring Many Worlds Through Books** (SC-4303). World Book, Inc. Merchandise Mart Plaza. Chicago, IL 60654. Rev. 1983. 8 page foldout. 1-19 copies 20 cents each. An independent study guide designed for use with *World Book* to help intermediate grade and junior high readers realize that fun and learning wait for them in libraries. ms.

►**Guinness Book of Daring Deeds and Fascinating Facts** (#14918-0). Bantam Books. 666 5th Ave. New York, NY 10103. 1979. 96 pp. $1.50. Brief accounts of unusual exploits and events written for the young reader. el-ms.

Hooked on Books: Program and Proof. Berkley Publishing Co. 200 Madison Ave. New York, NY 10016. 1966. 236 pp. $2.75. Explains ways to get reluctant readers to read. ad.

Learning Guides. World Book, Inc. Merchandise Plaza. Chicago, IL 60654. Titles are:

►**Through the Year With Childcraft** (SC-3088). 1981. 48 pp. $1.00. Contains references to *Childcraft* volumes to answer questions that interest young children. For use by adults with children or independently. ps-pr.

►**Through the Year With World Book** (SC-104). 1981. 48 pp. $1.00. Contains games, puzzles, quizzes, and other activities designed for use with *World Book* to develop skills in finding, reading, and interpreting information. el-ms.

Parent Brochures. International Reading Assoc. 800 Barksdale Road. P.O. Box 8139. Newark, DE 19711. Single copy free; send a self-addressed stamped envelope (#10); for more than three brochures, include First Class postage for two ounces. Six brochures on ways parents can promote reading in the home. ad. Titles are:

Good Books Make Reading Fun for Your Child

Summer Reading Is Important

You Can Encourage Your Child to Read

►**You Can Help Your Child in Reading by Using the Newspaper**

You Can Use Television to Stimulate Your Child's Reading Habits

Your Home Is Your Child's First School

Parent Guides. International Reading Assoc. 800 Barksdale Road. P.O. Box 8139. Newark, DE 19711. 50 cents (members 35 cents). Sample titles are:

How Can I Encourage My Primary Grade Child to Read? (#875). 1972. 12 pp. Helps parents understand and develop a child's reading interest. ad.

How Can I Help My Child Build Positive Attitudes Toward Reading? (#879). 1980. 12 pp. Offers practical suggestions for parents to help stimulate reading interests in children of all ages. ad.

How Can I Help My Child Get Ready to Read? (#876). 1972. 24 pp. Urges parents to use routine home experiences to develop skills that will help children learn to read. ad.

Why Read Aloud to Children? (#877). 1974. 12 pp. Offers suggestions for a home environment and reading-related activities to stimulate a desire to learn to read. ad.

►**A Parent's Guide to Children's Reading** (#22705). Bantam Books. 666 5th Ave. New York, NY 10103. Rev. 5th ed. 1982. 271 pp. $3.50. An update of the 1975 version of a handbook on reading development and books that appeal to various age levels. Written by the founder of the International Reading Association.

►**Reading** (SB-164). U.S. Gov't. Printing Office. Washington, DC 20402. 1981. 2 pp. Free. A listing of many low-cost government publications.

Reading Development. Houghton Mifflin Co. 1 Beacon St. Boston, MA 02108. Sample titles are:

Primer for Parents: How Your Child Learns to Read (1-28134). 1982. 29 pp. 1-49 copies, 54 cents each. A story for parents to decode—to remind them of the difficulties of learning to read. ad.

Your Child and Reading: How You Can Help (1-26711). 1973. 15 pp. 1-49 copies, 45 cents each. Suggestions for parents; includes a bibliography. ad. Spanish version (1-26710).

Reading for Living Series. New Readers Press. Box 131. Syracuse, NY 13210. 1971. 16 to 32 pp. each. 75 cents each; prepay orders under $10.00. Each book contains illustrations, samples, and exercises. Titles include:

How to Read and Write Business Letters

How to Read and Write Personal Letters

How to Read Maps

How to Read Newspapers

How to Read Signs

How to Use Telephones

How to Use the Dictionary and Other Reference Books

Reading Ideas. Scholastic Inc. 50 W. 44th St. New York, NY 10036. Three booklets of projects and activities contributed by teachers that emphasize the fun of reading. Titles are:

►**Fifty Creative Ways to Use Paperbacks in the Primary Grades.** 1980. 61 pp. $2.25. pr.

►**Fifty Creative Ways to Use Paperbacks in the Middle Grades.** 1980. 64 pp. $2.25. el.

►**The Great Paperback Contest Book.** 1980. 91 pp. $2.25. ms-hs.

Reading Instruction. International Reading Assoc. 800 Barksdale Road. P.O. Box 8139. Newark, DE 19711. Many pamphlets and booklets on reading are available from IRA. Titles include:

How to Read a Book (#209). 1970. 44 pp. $2.00 (members $1.75). Suggests ways teachers can help students learn to study textbook material and to read narrative material proficiently. ad.

Reading and the Bilingual Child. 1976. 48 pp. $3.00 (members $2.00). Provides practical ideas for teachers of bilingual and bidialectal students. ad.

Reading and the Black English Speaking Child. 1978. 48 pp. $2.50 (members $1.75). A report on recent work exploring the differences between standard English and Black English in reading. ad.

Television and the Classroom Reading Program (#214). 1973. 32 pp. $2.00 (members $1.75). Presents practical ways teachers can use the home television habits of students to improve reading/language arts instruction. ad.

Thinking Thursdays: Language Arts in the Reading Lab. 1978. 92 pp. $3.00 (members $2.50). Gives practical suggestions for secondary school teachers of students reading below grade level. ad.

Reading Resources. National Council of Teachers of English. 1111 Kenyon Road. Urbana, IL 61801. Free annotated catalog of over 400 books and cassettes entitled *Professional Publications for the Teacher of English and the Language Arts* is available.

Storybooks. The Dial Press. Books for Young Readers. Dept. PP-22. P.O. Box 2000. Pine Brook, NJ 07058. Offers paperback books for children in the Pied Piper Picturebooks series and the Easy-to-Read Books series. Prices range from $1.95 to $3.75. Write for complete catalog of current titles.

Survival Reading. New Readers Press. Box 131. Syracuse, NY 13210. Eight individual self-contained workbooks (with answer keys) to develop reading comprehension in three skill areas: locating facts, interpreting facts, and applying knowledge. Prepay orders under $10.00. Titles include:

Caution: Fine Print Ahead. Book 8. 1978. 64 pp. $2.10. Practice in reading and understanding common legal documents and regulations. G6.

It's on the Map. Book 6. 1977. 64 pp. $2.10. Practice in reading many kinds of maps using basic map skills—road maps, bus and train routes, weather maps, and others. G5.

Label Talk. Book 3. 1976. 64 pp. $2.10. Reading labels correctly is important for our health and convenience. Some lessons are clothing-care, aspirin, cereal, and anti-freeze labels. G4.

Let's Look It Up. Book 7. 1977. 64 pp. $2.10. Practice in using reference materials found in daily life includes a book index, charts and graphs, an interstate bus schedule, and dictionary and encyclopedia entries. G6.

Read Instructions First. Book 4. 1976. 64 pp. $2.10. Lessons include instructions for using frozen foods, a copy machine, a traffic citation, and cold capsules. G4.

Signs Around Town. Book 2. 1976. 64 pp. $2.10. Each lesson is a sign taken from one of the many places around us—grocery store, airport, campground, and others. G4.

Your Daily Paper. Book 5. 1977. 64 pp. $2.10. Provides practice in reading the newspaper for information and entertainment. G5.

Teacher's Exchange Materials. Teacher's Exchange of San Francisco. 28 Dawnview. San Francisco, CA 94131. Add 75 cents to prices for shipping. Sample titles are:

Grope 'n Group. 1972. Set of 30 cards for G1, $3.00; set of 15 cards for G1-6, $1.50. Word classification cards using words found in basic texts and standard word lists; helps to learn synonyms. pr-el.

Reading Reel. 1972. $1.25. Student follow-up projects for a reading selection of his own choice in ten categories. el.

Tangram Tasks. 1973. $1.75. Set of 15 cards. Puzzles which require use of from two to seven tangram pieces for forming a variety of shapes and pictures. el.

Title Twister. G3-6, $1.00; G4-8, $1.00. A dial chart giving 400 possible titles for creative writing.

Teaching Aids. Alpha Kappa Alpha Sorority. 5211 S. Greenwood Ave. Chicago, IL 60615. A series of monographs designed to help students achieve good reading ability. ad. $1.00 each. Titles include:

Reading and the Black Child. 9 pp.

Study Skills: Aids in Locating Information. 14 pp.

Teenage Reading: Some Problems and Some Solutions. 8 pp.

Toward a Better Start in Reading. 9 pp.

When Is Reading Reading? 21 pp.

►**Television and the Classroom: A Special Relationship.** CBS Television Reading Program. CBS Broadcast Group. 51 West 52 St. New York, NY 10019. 1979. 23 pp. Free, A report on a nationwide television script-reading program begun in 1977 telling how it works and how teachers, students, and parents feel about it. ad.

Workbooks. Skyview Publishing. Drawer L. Bellmore, NY 11710. Classroom workbooks using DRP format tasks to help students with comprehension difficulties. Each includes answer key and suggestions for teachers. Titles include:

►**Class Trips.** 1979. 64 pp. $3.50. Workbook with 30 stories about various places students might visit on a class field trip. Reading level 3.5-4.5.

Money Matters. 1982. 64 pp. $4.00. Workbook with 15 articles about important concepts in banking, borrowing, and consumer rights. Writing skills follow each article. Reading level 5.9-6.9.

Popular Careers. 1980. 64 pp. $3.50. Workbook with 30 articles that provide information about preparing for a career in many occupations. Reading level 5.0-5.9.

►**Popular Stars.** Rev. 1981. 64 pp. $3.50. Workbook with 30 articles and interviews with popular show business personalities. Reading level 4.0-4.9.

World Traveler. A. G. Bell Assoc. for the Deaf. Publications Sales. 3417 Volta Place, N.W. Washington, DC 20007. 1974-1976. Two packets of 9 booklets each. 16 pp. each. $2.50 per packet. High-interest, low-vocabulary booklets on subjects in history, social studies, science, and geography. G3 reading level. Sample titles:

The Human Body

►**Island Life**

Jungles of the World

Our Changing World

►**Shapes in Nature**

The Sun

LATIN AMERICA

Brasil. Brasilian Consulate General. 1306 ITM Bldg. New Orleans, LA 70130. Free. Brochures on the various regions of Brasil and tourist maps. ms-hs.

Colombia. Colombia Information Service. Colombian Center. 140 E. 57th St. New York, NY 10022. Titles are:

Colombia: Land of Contrasts. Updated. 14 pp. Free. A brief look at the geography, history, and culture of this country. el-ms.

Colombia Today. Published periodically. 6 pp. Free. A newsletter on current developments and life in Colombia, South America. ms.

Sketch of Colombia. 1980. 48 pp. Free. General information on Colombia, including history, principal cities and regions, national government, economy, education, and arts. hs.

Chile. Embassy of Chile. Office of the Cultural Attache. 1732 Massachusetts Ave., N.W. Washington, DC 20036. Titles are:

Chilean Antarctica, Easter Island, and Juan Fernandez Archipelago (#3). 1978. 27 pp. Free. Gives basic data on Chile in addition to the title topics. hs.

Mistral, Neruda, Huidobro, Three Figures in Chilean Literature (#4). 1979. 30 pp. Free. Gives basic data on Chile in addition to the title topics. hs.

Honduras. Embassy of Honduras. 4301 Connecticut Ave., N.W. Washington, DC 20008. Send for materials currently available.

OAS Material. General Secretariat. Organization of American States. Dept. of Publications. Sales and Promotion. 17th St. and Constitution Ave., N.W. Washington, DC 20006. Send for catalog of pamphlets and booklets covering all countries in Central and South America and the Caribbean. Some materials available in Spanish. ms-hs.

Panama Canal. Panama Canal Commission Information Office. APO Miami. 34011. Titles include:

Basic Information on the Panama Canal. Rev. 1980. 2 pp. Free. el-ms.

The Panama Canal. Free. A full-color brochure in several languages. ms.

Peru. Embassy of Peru. Cultural Dept. 1700 Massachusetts Ave., N.W. Washington, DC 20036. Send for information currently available.

Venezuela. Embassy of Venezuela. Office of Information and Cultural Affairs. 2437 California St., N.W. Washington, DC 20008. Free. Several materials on Venezuelean history and geography, industry and commerce, culture and current events. el-ms-hs.

Visual Geography Series. Sterling Publishing Co. 2 Park Ave. New York, NY 10016. 64 pp. each. $2.95 each. Orders must be prepaid and include postage. Booklets discuss the land, history, people, government, and economy of each country. Illustrated with photographs and maps. ms. Sample titles are:

El Salvador Pictures

Guyana in Pictures

Honduras in Pictures

Venezuela in Pictures

LAW AND ORDER

ABA Materials. The American Bar Assoc. 1155 E. 60th St. Chicago, IL 60637. Titles are:

The American Lawyer: How to Choose and Use One. 1978. 40 pp. $1.00. A guide on when and how to use legal counsel to avoid problems and costs. hs-ad.

Law and the Courts. 1980. 36 pp. 50 cents. A layman's handbook of court procedures with a glossary of legal terms. hs-ad.

►**Analyzing Crime and Crime Control: A Resource Guide** (#267). Joint Council on Economic Education. 1212 Avenue of the Americas. New York, NY 10036. 1981. 61 pp. $4.50. Presents an economics-political science approach to the causes of crime and to its prevention. Contains instructional activities and materials for classroom use. hs.

Citizen Initiative in Crime Prevention: What Can Your Local Community Do to Help Reduce Crime? (Vol. 30, No. 1). Center for Information on America. Washington, CT 06793. 1980. 4 pp. 60 cents. A Vital Issues discussion guide that explains what community crime prevention is, how it developed, and how it works. hs.

Civil Liberties. American Civil Liberties Union. 132 W. 43rd St. New York, NY 10036. Offers pamphlets, handbooks, and reports dealing with individual rights and liberties. Write for listing. hs-ad.

FBI Materials. U.S. Dept. of Justice. Federal Bureau of Investigation. Washington, DC 20535. Free in limited quantities. Titles include:

►**The FBI Laboratory.** Rev. 1982. 39 pp. A brief history, the services, and the operating techniques of the scientific crime laboratory. ms-hs.

►**Fingerprint Identification.** 1977. 25 pp. A history of the development of the science of fingerprint identification. ms-hs.

►**99 Facts About the FBI.** 7th ed. 31 pp. Answers 99 questions about the nature and operation of the FBI; includes job descriptions, job qualifications, and training of FBI Special Agents. ms-hs.

►**The Story of the Federal Bureau of Investigation.** Rev. 1982. 19 pp. A booklet to acquaint youth with the FBI. ms-hs.

The Freedom of Information Act: What It Is and How to Use It. Freedom of Information Clearinghouse. P.O. Box 19367. Washington, DC 20036. 8 pp. 10 cents. Explains how the federal law on public information works, the exemptions to it, and how to make a request to the government. hs-ad.

►**Juvenile Delinquency** (SB-074). U.S. Gov't. Printing Office. Washington, DC 20402. 1981. 9 pp. Free. A listing of many low-cost government publications which may be used in the classroom.

►*Legal Services.* National Resource Center for Consumers of Legal Services. 3254 Jones Ct. Washington, DC 20007. Free listing of consumer-oriented articles on legal services is available. Most items are $1.00 or less.

The Living Will. Concern for Dying. 250 W. 57th St. New York, NY 10107. Rev. 1978. Free. Document enabling individuals to express in writing their wishes regarding care during terminal illness. Other materials available. hs-ad.

Public Affairs Pamphlets. Public Affairs Committee, Inc. 381 Park Ave. S. New York, NY 10016. 50 cents each; quantity rates available. Titles include:

►**Dispute Resolution: Settling Conflicts Without Legal Action** (#597). 1981. 28 pp. Presents the advantages of dispute resolution over traditional litigation for many contested matters. hs-ad.

The Legal Rights of Retarded Persons (#583). 1980. 28 pp. Reviews developments in the legal protection of the mentally retarded. hs-ad.

The Promise of Justice—Legal Services for the Poor (#561). 1978. 28 pp. Traces legal help for poor people in criminal and civil cases as a result of the historic Gideon decision and describes several new directions. hs-ad.

Proposals for Prison Reform (#510A). 1980. 28 pp. Recommends some approaches for prison reform, such as smaller prisons, more humane conditions, voluntary rehabilitation, and better staff training. hs-ad.

Protecting Yourself Against Crime (#564). 1978. 28 pp. Offers guidance on how individuals can reduce the risks of becoming victims of crime. hs-ad.

The Public Interest Law Firm: New Voices for New Constituencies. Ford Foundation. Office of Reports. 320 E. 43rd St. New York, NY 10017. 1973. 40 pp. Single copy free. Examines the rationale for and development of public interest law and illustrates its advocacy practice with typical case histories. hs-ad.

Reducing Crime and Assuring Justice. Committee for Economic Development. 477 Madison Ave. New York, NY 10022. 1972. 86 pp. $2.15. Specific proposals for overhauling the administration of criminal justice, especially police, corrections agencies, and courts and attorneys. hs-ad.

LIBRARIES AND MEDIA CENTERS

ALA Materials. American Library Association. Order Dept. 50 East Huron St. Chicago, IL 60611. Titles include:

Directions for Library Service to Young Adults. 1977. 24 pp. $3.00. Presents a rationale and a model for serving the education, personal growth, and well-being of persons in their teens—the majority of library users.

Notable Children's Books 1940-1970. 1977. 84 pp. $3.00. An annotated bibliography of books for children—preschool through 14—cited as notable during a thirty year period.

Storytelling: Readings/Bibliographies/Resources. 1978. 16 pp. $1.00. Annotated bibliography for students and practitioners of storytelling. ad.

Be Informed on Using the Library. New Readers Press. P.O. Box 131. Syracuse, NY 13210. 1971. 40 pp. $1.20; prepay orders under $10.00. Topics include what a library is, using the card catalog, finding and borrowing a book, periodicals and reference books, and special services. Includes teacher's guide. el-ms.

Book Lists. Dept. of Cultural Resources. Div. of State Library. 1811 N. Boulevard. Raleigh, NC 27635. Two resources to facilitate library use by visually handicapped children. Titles are:

Books for Visually Impaired Young Children: An Annotated Bibliography. 1978. 48 pp. $1.00.

Books for Visually Impaired Young Children: An Annotated Bibliography. 1980 Supplement. 1980. 17 pp. 50 cents.

Books and Films for Children. Assoc. for Library Service to Children. A Div. of the American Library Assoc. 50 E. Huron St. Chicago, IL 60611. Write for a current checklist of materials available. Single copies of several bibliographies sent free for a self-addressed mailing label and 28 cents in stamps. Sample titles:

►**Caldecott Medal Books.** 1982. Rev. annually. Annotated list of medal winners including current honor books.

►**Newbery Medal Books.** 1982. Rev. annually. List of medal winners.

Notable Children's Books. 1981. Rev. annually. Annotated list.

►**Notable Children's Films.** 1982. Rev. annually. Annotated list.

►**Notable Children's Filmstrips.** 1982. Rev. annually. Annotated list.

►***Books From EMC.*** EMC Publishing. 300 York Ave. St. Paul, MN 55101. 1982. 14 pp. Free catalog of high-interest, low-vocabulary book selections tailored to elementary reading levels. Other catalogs available for foreign languages, special education, and instructional kits.

Children's Book & Music Center Catalog. Children's Book & Music Center. 2500 Santa Monica Blvd. Santa Monica, CA 90404. Revised bi-annually. 96 pp. $1.00. Contains recordings, books, multi-media, and rhythm instruments for all curriculum areas and all grade levels. Several items less than $5.00. Titles are arranged under 10 headings and indexed.

►**Children's Books for Holiday Giving and Year-Round Enjoyment.** Cleveland Public Library. Community Services Dept. 325 Superior Ave. Cleveland, OH 44114-1271. 1981. 15 pp. Free for a 6″ x 9″ self-addressed envelope bearing 20 cents postage and marked Third Class. An annotated book list.

Elementary School Kids' Book of Lists (#47-X). Incentive Publications, Inc. 2400 Crestmoor Rd. Nashville, TN 37215. 1981. 156 pp. $4.95. Contains lists of notable people, places, and things and study helps. A child's resource for home or classroom. pr-el.

ERIC Bibliographies. Informational Resources Publications. 130 Huntington Hall. Syracuse University. Syracuse, NY 13210. Titles are:

►**Media and Mainstreaming: An Annotated Bibliography and Related Resources** (IR-45). 1979. 35 pp. $4.00 postpaid. Contains a description of literature and other materials to help media specialists learn about methods, techniques, services, and materials to use with handicapped students. ad.

►**Microcomputers and the Media Specialist: An Annotated Bibliography** (IR-57). 1981. 70 pp. $5.25 postpaid. A selective listings of 250 recent books, articles and materials on microcomputers in education; arranged in nine categories, such as hardware, software, computer literacy, and library applications. ad.

►**How to Find What You Want in the Library.** Barron's Educational Series, Inc. 113 Crossways Park Dr. Woodbury, NY 11797. 1978. 123 pp. $4.95. Manual to aid in locating books and documents and in compiling research papers. Contains checking exercises and search questions and clues. For group instruction or self-instruction. hs-ad.

►**How to Use the Readers' Guide to Periodical Literature.** H. W. Wilson Co. 950 University Ave. Bronx, NY 10452. Rev. 1981. 16 pp. Free up to 50 copies. Defines, illustrates, and describes the use of the *Readers' Guide to Periodical Literature.*

►**I & R: A Training Manual.** Enoch Pratt Free Library. Publication Dept. 400 Cathedral St. Baltimore, MD 21201. 1979. 63 pp. $2.00. A step-by-step guide for librarians and others interested in teaching themselves how to offer information and referral service.

►**Indexing and Cataloging Services of the H. W. Wilson Company.** H. W. Wilson Co. 950 University Ave. Bronx, NY 10452. Rev. 1978. 33 pp. Free up to 50 copies. Designed to introduce the reader to the Wilson catalogs and indexes. Explains and illustrates each publication.

Library of Congress Publications. Library of Congress. Washington, DC 20540. Free. Sample titles are:

Folk Recordings Selected From the Archive of Folk Song. Rev. 1976. 29 pp. Lists 53 recordings of folk songs, sea shanties, spirituals, tales, and ballads available from the Library's Recorded Sound Section. ad.

Library of Congress Publications in Print. Rev. biannually. 60 pp. Includes some items of interest to teachers of grades 4-12.

►**Library of Congress Selected Publications.** 1982. Annual. 26 pp. Summary of 23 publications.

The Library of Congress: Services to the Nation. 1979. 9 pp. Brief history, collections, facilities, and services of the Library. (Available in English, French, German, Japanese, and Spanish.) el-ms.

►**Libraries and Library Collections** (SB-150). U.S. Gov't. Printing Office. Washington, DC 20402. 1982. 14 pp. Free. A listing of many low-cost government publications which may be used in the classroom. ad.

The Library: What's in It for You? The Interstate Printers and Publishers, Inc. Danville, IL 61832. 1973. 18 pp. 40 cents; quantity rates available. A simplified booklet of basic information about how to use a library's facilities. el-ms.

Professional Aids. Ohio Educational Library/Media Assoc. 40 S. 3rd St., Suite 409. Columbus, OH 43215. Make checks payable to OELMA. Sample titles are:

►**Cable TV, Now What?** 1982. 22 pp. $2.00. Offers basic information designed for those planning to use cable TV for educational purposes. ad.

Practical Public Relations. 1979. 51 pp. $3.00. Lists techniques for media specialists/librarians to use with students, faculty, administrators, and community groups. ad.

►**School Libraries and Intellectual Freedom.** 1982. 32 pp. $3.00. Presents guidelines for policies and procedures regarding the selection and circulation of library materials. ad.

References. Enoch Pratt Free Library. Publications. 400 Cathedral St. Baltimore, MD 21201. Orders from individuals should be prepaid. Titles include:

►**Literacy Resources: An Annotated Check List for Tutors and Librarians.** 1982. 144 pp. $5.00. A guide to materials useful for anyone engaged in tutoring functionally illiterate adults. Subjects covered include basic English, reading, English as a second language, life coping skills, and mathematics. Includes list of publishers and an index. ad.

Reference Books: A Brief Guide. 8th ed. 1978. 179 pp. $3.00; 10 or more copies $2.50 each. Completely revised and greatly expanded guide to popular reference materials for those who want to use libraries expeditiously.

Reference Book Guides. World Book Inc. Merchandise Mart Plaza. Chicago, IL 60654. Titles include:

Look-It-Up Book 1—How to Use the Encyclopedia (SC-4246). 1976. 8 pp. 10 cents. Workbook of easy exercises on alphabetical order, guide words, using an index, and so forth. G3-5.

Look-It-Up Book 2—Developing Skills for Independent Investigation. (SC-4220). 1975. 12 pp. 10 cents. Workbook to help children in intermediate grades learn reference skills through the use of the encyclopedia. ms.

Resources for Librarians. D. Shaffer. Library Consultant. 437 Jennings Ave. Salem, OH 44460. Titles include:

►**The Educator's Source Book of Posters—Mostly Free: For Teachers and Librarians.** 1981. 36 pp. $3.95. Contains descriptions of over 1000 items available from 255 sources that can be used for display, including posters, charts, maps, and pictures. Arranged by subject. pr. to ad.

►**A Handbook of Library Ideas: 150 Innovative Practices for the Creative Librarian.** 1977. 33 pp. $3.50. Contains over 150 suggestions for applying new techniques in library services. ad.

►**Management Concepts for Improving Libraries: A Guide for the Professional Librarian.** 1979. 40 pp. $3.95. Contains a collection of management concepts and principles for library administrators interested in developing an effective management philosophy. Arranged by key management area. ad.

Selection Guides. Assoc. for Childhood Education International. 3615 Wisconsin Ave., N.W. Washington, DC 20016. Add 10% to prices for shipping. No billed orders under $10.00; prepay in U.S. currency. Titles include:

Excellent Paperbacks for Children. 1979. 56 pp. $3.50. Gives a selective bibliography of relatively inexpensive books for teachers, librarians, parents; includes special resource guide. Co-published with the American Association of School Librarians.

Guide to Children's Magazines, Newspapers, Reference Books. 1977. 11 pp. 75 cents; 5 copies for $3.00. Contains descriptions and ordering information for 135 magazines and newspapers and 40 reference books.

Serving the Handicapped. National Library Service for the Blind and Physically Handicapped. The Library of Congress. Washington, DC 20542. Request information on materials distributed free to blind and physically handicapped persons who participate in the LC's free reading program.

Student Learning Guides. World Book, Inc. Merchandise Mart Plaza. Chicago, IL 60654. 1976. 8 page foldout. 1-19 copies 20 cents each; 20 or more copies 15 cents each. Guides designed for use with *World Book* for the student's independent investigation in the library. el-ms. Titles include:

►**The Earth: Our Restless Blue Planet** (SC-4304). 1983.

Earth's People: The Four Billion (SC-4305). 1977.

►**The Energy Problem** (SC-4300). 1982.

►**Exploring Many Worlds . . . Through Books** (SC-4303). 1983.

►**Exploring the World of Animals** (SC-4302). 1983.

Exploring the World of the Arts (SC-4306). 1978.

Exploring the World of Work (SC-4307). 1978.

►**Indians of the Americas** (SC-4301). 1982.

LITERATURE AND PLAYS

Black Literature for High School Students (#03308R). National Council of Teachers of English. 1111 Kenyon Road. Urbana, IL 61801. 1978. 370 pp. $5.95 (members $4.25). A guide for teachers who want to introduce black literature into the curriculum. The authors discuss issues and problems in teaching black literature and appropriate goals for studying it. ad.

►**Catalog of Plays and Musicals.** Dramatic Publishing Co. 4150 N. Milwaukee Ave. Chicago, IL 60641. Rev. 1982. 288 pp. Single copy free. A descriptive catalog of royalty and nonroyalty plays available for amateur productions. Includes prices and royalty costs. ad.

Children's Authors and Illustrators. The Scribner Book Cos. Library Services Dept. 597 5th Ave. New York, NY 10017. Free. Send a 7″ x 10″ envelope, self-addressed, with 41 cents (first class) postage. Eight biographical brochures of currently published writers and/or illustrators. el.

Classic Scenes (ME1779). New American Library. 1633 Broadway. New York, NY 10019. 311 pp. $2.75. A collection of 48 outstanding examples of playwrighting genius, each accompanied by explanatory commentary. hs-ad.

Dell Drama Editions. Dell Publishing Co., Inc. 1 Dag Hammarskjold Plaza. New York, NY 10017. Extensive paperback books in the category of plays are available at moderate prices Write for complete listing of titles and prices. ad.

Dell Laurel Editions. Dell Publishing Co. Educational Sales Dept. 1 Dag Hammarskjold Plaza. New York, NY 10017. Extensive paperback books in the category of English literature are available at moderate prices Write for complete listing of titles and prices. hs-ad.

An Educator's Guide to Literary Study Aids. Cliffs Notes, Inc. Attn: Faculty Coordinator. Box 80728. Lincoln, NE 68501. Free. A brochure listing available titles in the Cliffs Notes and Cliffs Complete Study Edition series priced from $1.75 to $3.95. Study aids contain reference material including synopsis, commentary, and character analysis of plays and novels most frequently assigned in school. hs-ad.

Fawcett Books. Fawcett Books. Educational Marketing Dept. 1515 Broadway. New York, NY 10036. Write for complete list of books in the category of literature and leisure reading.

A Geography of Poets (#20171-9). Bantam Books. 666 5th Ave. New York, NY 10103. 1979. 608 pp. $3.95. A selection of grass roots writings presenting the different regions, peoples, and concerns of the U.S. which reflect American language and culture. hs-ad.

Historic Literature. Huntington Library Publications. 1151 Oxford Road. San Marino, CA 91108. Facsimiles of notable works of literature. Listing available. Includes 75 cents postage for 1-5 copies. Titles include:

►**The American Pictorial Primer: Or the First Book for Children.** 1970. 48 pp. $1.00. First published about 1845. pr.

►**Casey at the Bat.** 1977. 16 pp. $1.00. First published in 1901. Illustrated. pr-el.

►**The Lady's Guide to Perfect Gentility.** 1973. 40 pp. $1.50. First published in 1856. hs.

►**Old Mother Hubbard and Her Dog.** 1973. 17 pp. $1.00. 1805 edition. Illustrated. ps-pr.

Literary Figures. Huntington Library Publications. 1151 Oxford Road. San Marino, CA 91108. Include 75 cents postage for 1-5 copies. Titles are:

►**Frontiersman of the Spirit: Four Masters of Twentieth-Century Literature.** 1980. 24 pp. $2.00. Discusses the literary originality of William Yeats, James Joyce, Wallace Stevens, and Conrad Aiken. hs-ad.

Thoreau's Walden. 1978. 24 pp. $2.00. A short history of David Thoreau's life and writings. Illustrated. hs.

►**William Blake and the Power of Imagination.** 1979. 32 pp. $2.00. A discussion of the creative talents of a distinguished poet and painter. hs-ad.

William Shakespeare at the Huntington. 1978. 23 pp. $2.00. A short history of Shakespeare's well-known works. Illustrated. hs.

Literary Landmarks. Literary Sketches. Box 711. Williamsburg, VA. 23185. 1974. 170 pp. $2.95 plus 50 cents postage. A listing by states of 80 homes of American writers open to the public; includes a thumbnail sketch of each author. hs-ad.

Literary Prints Catalog. Yorke Studio. 62 Kramer St. Hicksville, NY 11801. Free to English teachers and librarians when requested on school stationery. A catalog of sets of literary prints, mostly related to English literature, suitable for displays and posters. ad.

The Mentor Book of Short Plays (ME1985). New American Library. 1633 Broadway. New York, NY 10019. 1969. 348 pp. $2.95. A selection of one-act plays by modern writers with biographical and critical prefaces. hs.

Mentor-Signet Editions. New American Library. 1633 Broadway. New York, NY 10019. Extensive paperback books in the category of American literature are available at prices generally ranging from $1.50 to $2.95. Write for complete listing of titles and prices.

Modern American Scenes for Student Actors (#22640-1). Bantam Books. 666 5th Ave. New York, NY 10103. 1978. 319 pp. $3.95. Contains fifty selections from plays which can be presented before an audience as monologues and dialogues. hs.

A New Way: Handbook on Participation Plays. Dramatic Publishing Co. 4150 N. Milwaukee Ave. Chicago, IL 60641. 32 pp. Single copy free. Practical advice on children's participation plays in which the audience participates with the actors. Includes descriptions, prices, and royalty costs for eight plays. ad.

Plays for Children. Abingdon. Customer Service Dept. 201 8th Ave. S. Nashville, TN 37202. Payment should accompany all orders; schools and libraries entitled to 25% discount. Titles are:

> **Funny-Bone Dramatics.** 1974. 96 pp. $4.95. A collection of plays, riddles, and skits for children aged 4-8. ps-pr.
>
> **The Right Play for You.** 1960. 160 pp. each. $3.75. Emphasizes using your own imagination for the right play for the occasion. el.

►**Poetry and Literature** (SB-142). U.S. Gov't. Printing Office. Washington, DC 20402. 1981. 5 pp. Free. A listing of many low-cost government publications which may be used in the classroom.

Songs of Innocence and Experience. Huntington Library Publications. 1151 Oxford Road. San Marino, CA 91108. 1975. 32 pp. $2.50 plus 75 cents postage for 1-5 copies. A booklet containing 16 colored plates with poems by William Blake. ms-hs.

The Signet Classic Shakespeare Series. New American Library. 1633 Broadway. New York, NY 10019. Sample titles are:

> **The Two Gentlemen of Verona** (CE 1649). 1964. 200 pp. $2.50. hs-ad.
>
> **The Winter's Tale** (CE1700). 1963. 223 pp. $2.50. hs-ad.

MAPS

Atlas Materials. Hammond, Inc. 515 Valley St. Maplewood, NJ 07040. Usable at el. to ad. levels except where otherwise noted. Titles include:

> ►**Atlas Moderno Universal.** 1981. 48 pp. $2.99. Many regional maps in Spanish. ms-hs-ad.

Comparative World Atlas. 1979. 48 pp. $2.99. Maps show religion, agriculture, and physical features.

►**Headline World Atlas.** 1981. 52 pp. $2.95. Many regional maps.

Historical Atlas. 1979. 48 pp. $2.99. Growth of civilization to the present.

►**History Atlas of Our Country.** 1981. 48 pp. $2.50. Elementary maps of America from its discovery to the present day with text. pr-el.

Intermediate World Atlas. 1979. 80 pp. $2.99. All maps in the *Map Transparency Series.*

Map Skills Readiness Book. 1980. 64 pp. $2.25. Activity book introducing basic map study skills in the primary grades.

My First Atlas. 1980. 64 pp. $2.50. Complete introduction to all map skills. Detailed guide to accompany: *My First Atlas—Teacher's Manual.* 1980. $1.32. G3-5.

My First World History Atlas. 1979. 64 pp. $2.50. Maps showing growth of civilization to the present with text.

United States History Atlas. 1979. 64 pp. $3.65. Maps of America from its discovery to the present day.

The World. 50″ x 33″. $1.95. A map in the *Superior Wall Map* series.

World Atlas for Students. 1980. 56 pp. $2.50. Maps of plants, regions, population distribution, and many other aspects.

Historic Maps. National Ocean Survey NOAA. Physical Science Services Branch. Rockville, MD 20852. Facsimiles of early maps of the nation's capital. Titles include:

Ellicott Map of Washington, D.C.—1792. 23″ x 30″. $2.15.

L'Enfant Plan of Washington, D.C.—1791. 30″ x 48″. $2.15.

How to Teach Map and Compass Skills (#471-14704). National Science Teachers Assoc. 1742 Connecticut Ave., N.W. Washington, DC 20009. 1976. 12 pp. $1.50. Contains several exercises and games for teaching. ms-hs.

►**Maps and Atlases (United States and Foreign)** (SB-102). U.S. Gov't. Printing Office. Washington, DC 20402. 1981. 22 pp. Free. A listing of many low-cost government publications which may be used in the classroom.

Topographic Maps. U.S. Dept. of the Interior. Geological Survey. Mail Stop 580. Reston, VA 22092. 1978. 27 pp. Free. Explains what topographical maps are, how they are made, how they are used, and symbols which appear on maps. Includes several map examples. hs.

MATHEMATICS AND METRICS

Be Informed on Using Measurements. New Readers Press. Box 131. Syracuse, NY 13210. 1970. 40 pp. $1.20; prepay orders under $10.00. Topics include time, distance, weight, liquid and dry measures, and temperature. Includes teacher's guide with resource list. el-ms.

►**Bonus Points** (#174-2). Ann Arbor Publishers, Inc. P.O. Box 7249. Naples, FL 33940. Undated. 55 pp. $3.50. Provides an auditory program of math skills building for students with learning disabilities. ms-hs.

Cheat Sheet for Stat. Samuel W. Cochran. P.O. Box 309. Commerce, TX 75428. 1975. 37 pp. $1.50. An aid to learning or relearning basic statistical manipulations. hs.

Drafting Experiences in Metrics. (#241-7). Goodheart-Willcox Co. 123 W. Taft Dr. S. Holland, IL 60473. 1977. 78 pp. $5.28; school price, $3.96. Gives plans for drawing insignia patches (armed forces, scouts, civil defense) to provide experiences in metric measurement and geometric construction. ms-hs.

Drill Materials. Hayes School Publishing Co. 321 Penwood Ave. Wilkinsburg, PA 15221. Titles include:

> **Fun and Easy Steps to Metric Measurement Mastery** (Book I). 1975. 104 pp. $1.95. A workbook of 18 lessons of drill and practice pages using the common metric units, without reference to the traditional American units. el.
>
> **Hayes Mastery Arithmetic Drills and Tests.** 1969. 28 pp. $3.95. Contains 28 duplicating masters for exercise lessons in arithmetic. G1.
>
> **Know the Essentials of Metric Measurement** (Book I). 1974. 18 pp. $3.95. Contains 18 duplicating masters for lessons to teach basic metric units in the primary grades. Book II is available for the upper grades.

Duodecimal System. Dozenal Society of America. Math Dept. Nassau Community College. Garden City, NY 11530. Titles include:

> **Duodecimal Reciprocals 4/6 Places.** 1969. 66 pp. $1.00. A table of dozenal reciprocals produced by computer. hs.
>
> **An Excursion in Numbers.** 14 pp. Single copy free; additional copies 20 cents each. Presents a system of counting based on twelve. hs.
>
> **Manual of the Dozen System.** 1960. 33 pp. $1.00. Current practices for using the twelve-base system most conveniently. hs.

Glossary of Metric Conversions. Henry Lavin Associates, Inc. 12 Promontory Dr. Cheshire, CT 06410. 1974. 18 pp. $1.00. Useful alphabetical listing of measures and means of metric conversion. hs-ad.

GPO Materials. U.S. Gov't. Printing Office. Washington, DC 20402. Lists of many low-cost government publications. Titles are:

►**Mathematics** (SB-024). 1981. 5 pp. Free.

►**Weights and Measures** (SB-109). 1981. 5 pp. Free.

Math Puzzles. Dover Publications, Inc. 180 Varick St. New York, NY 10014. Titles are:

Mathematical Diversions (#23110-0). 1975. 183 pp. $2.75; $2.60 in Canada. Contains creative math problems for recreation and learning. hs-ad.

Mathematical Puzzles for Beginners and Enthusiasts. Rev. 1954. 248 pp. $2.95. An entertaining book of mathematical puzzles to challenge one's logic, ingenuity, and knowledge; arranged from simple arithmetic solutions to permutations, combinations, and probability. hs-ad.

Measure Metric. Harcourt, Brace, Jovanovich. 1372 Peachtree St., N.E. Atlanta, GA 30367. Four books (A,B,C,D). 1974. 32 pp. each. $2.40 each; Teacher's edition $2.40. A sequential study of the metric system in four workbooks which emphasize measuring in metric units. pr-el.

Metric Handbook. LaPine Scientific Co. 6001 S. Knox Ave. Chicago, IL 60629-5496. 1978. 105 pp. $1.95. Features activities, exercises, problems, and puzzles for a complete course which stresses measuring, evaluating, and estimating and terms likely to be in everyday use. ad.

Metric Slides. Slide Chart Corp. P.O. Box 527. Westchester, PA 19380. Slide charts for converting U.S. weights and measurements to their metric equivalents and other math applications. $1.00 each. Titles are:

Fundamental Metric Converter. 1975. Features liquid volume, weight, area, temperature, and distance. ms-hs.

Instant U.S. to Metric Conversions. 1971. Features length, area, volume, weight, speed, energy, pressure, and temperature. ms-hs.

Rotary Slide Rule. 5″ diameter.

Trigonometric Function Calculator. 1975. A slide for calculating various functions of right and oblique triangles. hs.

Metric Measurement: Activities and Bulletin Boards (#319). The Instructor Publications, Inc. 757 3rd Ave. New York, NY 10017. 1973. 48 pp. $2.95. Provides 50 activities or displays emphasizing concepts of measurement for length, area, weight, and volume in a natural manner. el-ms.

Metric Units of Measure and Style Guide (USMA #8). U.S. Metric Assoc., Inc. 10245 Andasol Ave. Northridge, CA 91325. Rev. 1979. 12 pp. $1.00; quantity rates available. Orders under $10.00 must be accompanied by remittance. Summarizes the basic rules for the use of metric units, prefixes, and their symbols. Consistent with the International System of Units.

Metrics. Barron's Educational Series, Inc. 113 Crossways Park Dr. Woodbury, NY 11797. Titles are:

►**Metrics Made Easy.** 1977. 32 pp. 95 cents.

►**Metric Converter.** 1976. $1.25. Slide chart. Conversions for mass, area, length, and volume based on International Systems of Units (SI). ms-hs.

Metrics Handouts. U.S. Metric Assoc., Inc. 10245 Andasol Ave. Northridge, CA 91325. Five sheets for teaching basic metric measurements. Free when requested with a self-addressed envelope (#10) with 37 cents postage affixed. Titles are:

►**Antoine Frame-of-Reference Method of Remembering the Everyday Metric Units and Questions and Answers About Metric Conversion.** 2 pp.

►**Comparison of U.S. Customary and Metric System Measurements.** 1 p.

►**Easier Comparison Shopping With Decimalized Metric System.** 1 p.

►**Quick Reference Table for Metric Units.** 1 p.

►**Some Technically Correct SI Training Materials.** 2 pp. A bibliography.

NCTM Publications. National Council of Teachers of Mathematics. 1906 Association Drive. Reston, VA 22091. Titles include:

Activities for the Maintenance of Computational Skills and the Discovery of Patterns. 1980. 96 pp. $4.50. Provides practice exercises for students in nonroutine activities; pages can be removed for duplicating. Includes answer keys. G6-9.

Classroom Ideas From Research on Computational Skills. 1976. 58 pp. $3.40. How to teach better computational skills. el.

How to Study Mathematics. 1977. 32 pp. $1.70. Tips on studying math to aid secondary students.

Mathematics and Humor. 1978. 58 pp. $4.00. A collection of jokes, riddles, and cartoons to add levity to bulletin boards and test papers and pique the interest of students. ms-hs.

Mathematics Through Paper Folding. 1975. 64 pp. $2.25. Offers active experiences in discovering and demonstrating mathematical relationships. hs.

Metric Measurement Activity Cards. 1974. 70 pp. $2.50. An introduction to metric concepts of length, area, and volume. el.

Secret Codes, Remainder Arithmetic, and Matrices. 1961. 54 pp. $2.00. Problems for excelling math students. ms-hs.

Sets, Probability, and Statistics. American Council of Life Insurance. Education Services. 1850 K St., N.W. Washington, DC 20006. Rev. 1978. 36 pp. Free up to 100 copies. Discusses mathematics in relation to applications in life insurance. Includes problems. hs.

Student Materials. Instructional Fair, Inc. P.O. Box 1650. Grand Rapids, MI 49501. Publisher offers a line of duplicating or wipe-clean cards for student use in drills and exercises to strengthen calculation and word problem skills. Available for different levels. $4.50 per set. Request free catalog for detailed descriptions.

Task Cards. Teacher's Exchange of San Francisco. 28 Dawnview. San Francisco, CA 94131. Add 75 cents to prices for shipping. Titles include:

Geoboard Tasks. 1972. $1.75. 19 task cards (printed on both sides), 5″ x 7″, designed for standard 25 nail geoboard to teach perimeters, area, and coordinates. el-ms.

Math Breakthrough. 1976. $2.95. Set of 36 multi-purpose task cards involving addition, subtraction, multiplication, and division of whole numbers, fractions, and decimals. Contains directions, Sample Big Test, and Sample Chart. el.

Open-Ended Task Cards. 1972. $2.00. Set of 18 cards with activities involving measuring, counting, and graphing. el-ms.

Teacher's Aids. National Council of Teachers of Mathematics. 1906 Association Dr. Reston, VA 22091. Current reference lists to printed, visual, and audio materials and kits, games, and objects for teaching mathematics. Single copies free. Titles include:

Free Materials for the Teaching of Mathematics

Sources of Materials Available on Careers in Mathematics

A World of Numbers to Know. Sportshelf. P.O. Box 634. New Rochelle, NY 10802. 1971. 15 pp. $1.00 postpaid. A handy reference guide for measurements, time, and currency. ms-hs.

MENTAL HEALTH

APA Publications. American Psychological Assoc. Clearinghouse on Precollege Psychology. 1200 17th St., N.W. Washington, DC 20036. Books, guides, articles, bibliographies, and bimonthly newsletter on teaching psychology in secondary schools. Some free to teachers and APA affiliates. Write for information.

►**Adolescent Suicide.** The Boys Town Center. Boys Town, NE 68010. 1981. 6 pp. Free. Presents some clues for identifying potential victims and for helping to prevent suicide among young people. ms-hs-ad.

Children. Child Welfare League of America, Inc. 67 Irving Place. New York, NY 10003. Titles include:

Problems in Recognizing Emotional Disturbances in Children (CW-21). 1963. 15 pp. $1.50. Reprint from *Child Welfare* which stresses the need for those who work with children to recognize feelings and problems. ad.

Safeguarding the Emotional Health of Our Children (CD-10). Rev. 1973. 16 pp. $1.50. An inquiry into the concept of the rejecting mother. ad.

The "Coping With" Series. American Guidance Service. Publishers' Bldg. Circle Pines, MN 55014. $1.95 each. Titles include:

Do I Know the "Me" Others See? 1973. 55 pp. Coping with seeing ourselves as others see us. ms.

Easing the Scene. 1970. 49 pp. Discusses attitudes responsible for pleasant human relations. ms.

Living With Differences. 1973. 59 pp. Coping with accepting our many differences as assets. ms.

My Life—What Shall I Do With It? 1973. 50 pp. Coping with one's entire future. ms.

You Always Communicate Something. 1973. 58 pp. Presents the things we tell each other unintentionally. ms.

Hogg Foundation Materials. The Hogg Foundation for Mental Health. University of Texas. Univ. Station Box 7998. Austin, TX 78712. Materials on mental health and social psychology, ranging from newsletters to small books to cassette recordings. Send for free publications and price list. Titles include:

Becoming a Person. 1969. 23 pp. 90 cents. What it means to find oneself and fulfill a basic search for identity. hs-ad.

Can an Adult Change? Rev. 1980. 16 pp. 45 cents. Discusses why an adult may need to change and ways to approach change. hs-ad.

The Human Condition. Leaflet. Free. Describes audiomaterials on mental health available on loan from the Foundation library. hs-ad.

►**Mental Health: An Interdisciplinary and International Perspective.** 1981. 18 pp. 80 cents. Presents a concise view of the continuing issues in the mental health movement. hs-ad.

The Nature of Mental Health. 1975. 8 pp. Single copy free. Discusses the subjects of self-acceptance, security, maturity, love, and others relative to the healthy adult personality. hs-ad.

Leaflets. 7 pp. each. Up to a total of 25 copies free, single or mixed titles; additional copies 5 cents each. Series of pamphlets which present some of the causes of unhappiness in children, adults, and families and suggest some preventive measures. Titles in the "Human Condition" series include:

►**Caring: Building Children's Self-Esteem**

►**On Adolescence**

►**On Stress**

►**On the Gifted Handicapped**

►**Romantic Love**

►**Seeking Love Through Exchange**

►**Teenage Pregnancy**

Journey to Self-Discovery. Winston Press. 430 Oak Grove, Suite 203. Minneapolis, MN 55403. 1977. 95 pp. $3.50. A valuable workbook of various exercises for people who want to learn more about themselves. hs-ad.

Mental Retardation. Association for Retarded Citizens. 2501 Ave. J. P.O. Box 6109. Arlington, TX 76011; or, contact your local ARC unit. Numerous publications related to mental retardation, education, legislation, and family responsibilities. Most sell for under $1.00; quantity rates available. Write for a free list. Sample titles are:

►**It Can Happen to Anyone.** 16 pp. 30 cents. Designed to provide prospective parents with information on simple procedures to help birth a healthy baby. hs-ad.

►**Your Down's Syndrome Child.** 32 pp. 50 cents. Describes what parents can expect in their Down's Syndrome child at each age level from infancy through adulthood. ad.

Mental Retardation. U.S. Dept. of Health and Human Services. President's Committee on Mental Retardation. Washington, DC 20201. Titles are:

Hello World. 1978. 24 pp. Free. Explains the degrees of mental retardation, causes, prevention, and avenues of action, hs.

The Problem of Mental Retardation. 1979. 20 pp. Free. An introduction to testing, classifying, services, and prevention measures. hs.

NIMH Publications. National Institute of Mental Health. Public Inquiries Sec. 5600 Fishers Lane. Rockville, MD 20857. Single copies free. A listing of various publications on aspects of mental health.

Public Affairs Pamphlets. Public Affairs Committee, Inc. 381 Park Ave. S. New York, NY 10016. 50 cents each; quantity rates available. Titles include:

Adolescent Suicide: Mental Health Challenge (#569). 1979. 20 pp. Explores the psychological and social causes of adolescent suicide. Describes the warning signs and explains ways of helping. hs-ad.

Help for Emotional and Mental Problems (#567). 1979. 28 pp. Describes kinds of disturbances, their symptoms, various therapies, and how community agencies can help. hs-ad.

Mental Retardation—a Changing World (#577). 1979. 28 pp. Explains the causes and manifestations of mental retardation, services available, and the rights of retarded persons. Includes resource list. hs-ad.

Partners in Coping: Groups for Self and Mutual Help (#559). 1978. 28 pp. How groups operate to meet members' needs in a common concern such as alcoholism, living with chronic illness, and parenting. hs-ad.

►**Phobias: The Ailments and the Treatments** (#590). 1980. 28 pp. Describes a variety of phobias, possible causes, forms of therapy used to treat phobias, and agencies that help. hs-ad.

►**The Psychotherapies Today** (#596). 1981. 28 pp. Discusses why psychotherapy is often needed, several therapeutic approaches, what patients can expect, approximate costs of treatment, and how to choose a therapist. hs-ad.

Self-Improvement. Administrative Research Associates. Irvine Tower Center. Box 4211. Irvine, CA 92716. Quantity rates available. Titles include:

Living With Yourself. 1970. 64 pp. $1.50. Designed to help people know and understand themselves better and control tension, anxiety, and frustration. hs-ad.

Understanding People and Getting Along With Them. 1970. 64 pp. $1.50. Presents ideas on controlling one's own attitude and behavior to promote a favorable regard by others and harmonious relations with them. hs-ad.

Suicide Prevention. Health Information Services. Merck Sharp and Dohme. West Point, PA 19486. Five pamphlets on the phenomenon of suicide, recognizing the danger signs, and helping to prevent suicides. 25 cents each; send payment with orders. ms-hs-ad. Titles include:

►**Before It's Too Late.** 10 pp.

►**Suicide in Young People.** 9 pp. Includes selected bibliography.

►**Suicide in Youth and What You Can Do About It—a Guide for School Personnel.** 9 pp.

►**Suicide—It Doesn't Have to Happen.** 13 pp. Includes "facts and fables on suicide" and further references.

Understanding Mental Disorders in Childhood. Interstate Printers and Publishers, Inc. 19-27 N. Jackson St. Danville, IL 61832. 1971. 68 pp. $2.50. Presents ways in which mental disorders develop in the first decade of life and through adolescence. Helps those working with children to observe and understand mental illnesses. ad.

MIDDLE EAST

AMEU Materials. Americans for Middle East Understanding, Inc. 475 Riverside Dr. Room 771. New York, NY 10115. Payment must accompany order. Sample titles are:

►**The Arab World: A Handbook for Teachers.** 1978. 128 pp. 8½″ x 11″. $3.50. Provides a critique of misinformation about life and events in the Arab regions and presents essays and articles to counter inaccuracies and misconceptions. el-ms.

The Arabian Peninsula. 1977. 30″ x 21″. Free for 50 cents postage and handling. A color wall map showing mountain ranges, deserts, and cultivated areas. el.

The Link. Newsletter. 5 issues yearly. Free subscription by request. Features articles dealing with the culture, history, and values of the Middle East. Back issues available in bulk for classroom use. hs-ad.

►**The Middle East and South Asia, 1981.** 1981. 106 pp. $3.50. Reviews the historical backgrounds and present political situations of the countries of Southwest Asia. Maps, photographs, and illustrations. hs-ad.

Arab Publications. Arab Information Center. 747 Third Ave. New York, NY 10017. Inquire about free materials available.

Israel. Consulate General of Israel. Dept. of Information. 800 2nd Ave. New York, NY 10017; 805 Peachtree St., Suite 656. Atlanta, GA 30308; 450 Park Square Bldg. 31 St. James Ave. Boston, MA 02116; 111 E. Wacker Dr., Suite 1308. Chicago, IL 60611; 1 Greenway Plaza East, Suite 722. Houston, TX 77046; 1720 Lewis Tower Bldg. 225 South 15th St. Philadelphia, PA 19102; 693 Sutter St. San Francisco, CA 94102; 6380 Wilshire Blvd., Suite 1700. Los Angeles, CA 90048; 330 Biscayne Blvd., Suite 510. Miami, FL 33132; Embassy of Israel. 3514 International Dr., N.W. Washington, DC 20008. Requests should be directed to the nearest Israeli Representation. Send for listing of free materials.

Lebanon. Lebanon Tourist and Information Office. 405 Park Ave. New York, NY 10022. Free. Several brochures giving highlights of the country and its major cities. Photographs.

Middle East Publications. The American Jewish Committee. Institute of Human Relations. 165 E. 56th St. New York, NY 10022. Titles include:

Israel and America's National Interest. 1975. 11 pp. 25 cents. Discusses questions people ask about the U. S. role and interest in Israel. ms-hs.

►**The Palestinians in Perspective.** 1982. 109 pp. $3.50. Contains six essays written by noted American and Israeli analysts that examine the complex Palestinian issue and its importance to peace in the Middle East. hs-ad.

Writings on Jewish History: A Selected Annotated Bibliography. 1974. 27 pp. 75 cents. Listings include history, biography, and fiction. ms-hs.

►**Politics and Religion in the Muslim World** (#258). Foreign Policy Assoc. 205 Lexington Ave. New York, NY 10016. 1982. 72 pp. $3.00. An introduction to Islam in its historical and contemporary setting which stresses the West's need to understand the faith and culture of one-fifth the world's population. hs-ad.

Teaching Guide. Middle East Institute. 1761 N St., N.W. Washington, DC 20036. Titles are:

►**The Middle East Content Priority Teaching Guide.** 1979. 38 pp. Free to teachers. Outlines units of study of three, six, nine, and eighteen weeks duration such as history, geography, politics, economics, and culture. Suggests readings and other materials. hs.

►**The Middle East Institute Resource Guide for Teachers.** 1979. 55 pp. Free to teachers. Companion guide to filmstrips, films, books, and supplements for units and courses. hs.

Turkey. The Turkish Tourism and Information Office. 821 United Nations Plaza. New York, NY 10017. Free. Booklets, pamphlets, and maps of information on Turkey and its principal cities. el-ms.

Visual Geography Series. Sterling Publishing Co. 2 Park Ave. New York, NY 10016. 64 pp. each. $2.95 each; payment must accompany order. Illustrated studies of the history, government, people, and geography of countries and regions. ms. Sample titles are:

Lebanon in Pictures

Kuwait in Pictures

MONEY AND BANKING

►**Banking School Kit** (881400). American Bankers Assoc. Order Processing Dept. 1120 Connecticut Ave., N.W. Washington, DC 20036. 1980. Single copy free; additional copies $3.00. Kit includes booklets on the history of banking, bank services, bank careers, and credit and money management. ms-hs.

Be Informed on Banking. New Readers Press. Box 131. Syracuse, NY 13210. 1977. 40 pp. $1.20; prepay orders under $10.00. Topics include how to shop for a bank and to get higher paying savings, important checking skills, reconciling the bank statement, and machine banking. Includes teacher's guide with resource list. el-ms.

Counterfeiting and Forgery. Dept. of the Treasury. U. S. Secret Service. Office of Public Affairs. Washington, DC 20223. Undated. Pamphlet. Free. Gives facts about paper and coin currency, ways of recognizing counterfeit currency and forged money instruments, and tells what to do about it. hs.

Federal Reserve Materials. Federal Reserve Bank of New York. Public Information Dept. New York, NY 10045. Offers a variety of publications and teaching units dealing with money, checks, banking, foreign exchange, economics, and the Federal Reserve System. Quantities available free to schools and several others. Request free descriptive listing. el-ms-hs.

Federal Reserve System. Federal Reserve Bank of Minneapolis. Office of Public Information. Minneapolis, MN 55480. Sample titles are:

Genuine or Counterfeit. 1974. Leaflet. Free. Describes differences between a counterfeit and genuine currency. ms-hs.

►**Money, Banking, and the Federal Reserve System.** Rev. 1982. Free. An instructional unit of six separate sections covering money and banking, the Federal Reserve System, money creation, and monetary policy. Background information and activity sheets are provided for each section. Includes an instructor's guide. ms-hs.

►**Your Money and the Federal Reserve System.** Rev. 1982. 16 pp. Free. Emphasizes how currency and coin are supplied and how Federal Reserve actions influence the supply of money and bank reserves. ms-hs.

Foreign Currency. Deak-Perera L.A., Inc. Attn: Money Converter/R-1. 677 S. Figueroa St. Los Angeles, CA 90017. 1980. Free for a stamped self-addressed envelope. Titles include:

►**Foreign Money Converter.** Pamphlet. Gives currency tables for more than 60 countries. ms-hs.

►**What You Should Know About Foreign Currency.** Leaflet. Answers common questions about exchanging monies and exchange banks. el-ms-hs.

►**Fundamental Facts About United States Money.** Federal Reserve Bank of Atlanta. Research Department. Atlanta, GA 30301. 1982. 16 pp. Free. Booklet describing the sizes and types of currency in the history of the U.S. el-ms.

Monetary Policy. Federal Reserve Bank of Minneapolis. Office of Public Information. 250 Marquette Ave. Minneapolis, MN 55480. Free. Titles are:

Eliminating Policy Surprises: An Inexpensive Way to Beat Inflation. 1979. 14 pp. Discusses how a gradual and steady reduction of the rate of money growth and government debt can reduce or eliminate inflation without high costs in terms of output and unemployment. hs-ad.

►**Meeting the Challenges of a New Banking Era.** 1982. 20 pp. Discusses changes in the banking system as unregulated and nonfinancial institutions engage in activities that traditionally have been the domain of depository institutions. hs-ad.

►**A New Law, A New Era.** 1981. 14 pp. Discusses the 1980 Depository Institutions Deregulation and Monetary Control Act's effects on monetary policy and financial services. hs-ad.

Rational Expectations—Fresh Ideas That Challenge Some Established Views of Policy Making. 1978. 17 pp. Examines a theory of economic policy which says that policymakers' actions are anticipated by a public that acts to offset policy effects. Compares the rational expectations view with the traditional view of how the economy works. hs-ad.

The Tax-Cut Illusion. 1980. 15 pp. An explanation of why proposed tax cuts without accompanying reductions in government spending and deficits would only replace direct taxes with an "inflation" tax. hs-ad.

Money and Debt. Public Information Center. Federal Reserve Bank of Chicago. Box 834. Chicago, IL 60690. Single copy free. Titles include:

ABCs of Figuring Interest. Rev. 1979. 9 pp. Describes some of the more common methods of calculating interest and their effects on total interest charges. hs-ad.

Counterfeit. 1979. A pamphlet describing differences between a counterfeit and a genuine bill and what to do if a counterfeit is found. el-ms.

►**Modern Money Mechanics.** Rev. 1983. A workbook on deposits, currency, and bank reserves. hs-ad.

Two Faces of Debt. Rev. 1979. 34 pp. A discussion of debt in both public and private sectors and its functions in the U.S. economy. hs-ad.

Production of Government Securities. Bureau of Engraving and Printing. 14th & C Sts., S.W. Washington, DC 20228. 8 pp. Free. A pamphlet describing how currency and postage stamps are manufactured. el-ms.

The World Bank. World Bank. 1818 H St., N.W. Washington, DC 20433. Rev. 1977. 11 pp. Free. Leaflet summarizing the work of the World Bank and International Development Association, such as technical assistance and aid coordination. ms-hs.

Your Insured Deposit. Federal Deposit Insurance Corp. Office of Information. 550 17th St., N.W. Washington, DC 20429. 1970. 13 pp. Free. Explains how the FDIC protects deposits. ms.

MONEY MANAGEMENT

Consumer Affairs Pamphlets. Federal Reserve of Philadelphia. Consumer Affairs Dept. P.O. Box 66. Philadelphia, PA 19105. A series of pamphlets to inform consumers about credit, saving, borrowing, debts, and other aspects of personal financing. hs-ad. Free in quantities. Titles include:

Electronic Fund Transfer (Regulation E). 1980.

The Fair Debt Collection Practices Act. 1978.

How the New Equal Credit Opportunity Act Affects You. 1978.

How to Establish and Use Credit

Options for Savings. 1980.

►**The Rule of 78's.** 1981. How unpaid interest is figured.

►**Your Credit Rating.** 1982.

Consumer's Primer on Money (#31). Center for Information on America. Washington, CT 06793. Rev. 1972. 15 pp. 50 cents. A Grass Roots Guide which explains how the financial system works and what consumers should know about using financial services. hs.

Credit. National Foundation for Consumer Credit. 8701 Georgia Ave., Suite 601. Silver Springs, MD 20910. Several pamphlets explaining various aspects of consumer credit are offered. Titles include:

Consumer Credit. 1970. 12 pp. 25 cents. ms-hs.

Establishing Good Credit. 1970. 25 cents. ms-hs.

The Forms of Credit We Use. 1970. 10 pp. 25 cents. ms-hs.

Getting a Hold on Credit. 1980. 8 pp. 15 cents.

►**Credit Guide.** Public Information Center. Federal Reserve Bank of Chicago. Box 834. Chicago, IL 60690. 1982. Free in quantities. A pamphlet which leads the reader along the road to credit-ability, providing basic guidelines for obtaining and using consumer credit. hs-ad.

Financial Planning and Insurance. American Council of Life Insurance. Education Services. 1850 K St., N.W. Washington, DC 20006. Request free *Catalog of Educational Materials* describing free and low-cost booklets, filmstrips, and teacher resource materials for the study of life and health insurance and financial plannings. Materials include:

The Booklet You Have in Your Hand Is Not Designed to Sell You Life Insurance. 1974. 24 pp. Up to 50 copies free to teachers or community leaders. Offers basic information in question-and-answer format about life insurance and how it applies to individuals and families. ms-hs.

A Date With Your Future. Rev. 1979. 36 pp. Free in quantities up to 100. Examines personal and family financial decisions. Workbook format. hs.

►**Financial Planning, Employee Benefits and You.** 35 pp. Up to 35 copies free to teachers. A workbook designed for adults in basic education programs to explain the elements of financial planning and how to incorporate various employee benefits into personal financial plans. ad.

A Guide to Life Insurance for Women Only. 1978. 12 pp. Up to 50 copies free to teachers or community leaders. Describes the purposes of life insurance and annuities and the types of coverages for single and married women. hs-ad.

►**The Life Insurance Teaching Kit.** 1982. Single copy free. A set of materials for teaching about buying and using life insurance. Kit includes lesson plans for five modules, student worksheets, policy sample sheets, and a guide and materials for the teacher. hs-ad.

Planning With Your Beneficiaries. 1980. 19 pp. Up to 50 copies free to teachers or community leaders. Discusses wills, trusts, investments, and life insurance and how they help in planning for financial security. hs-ad.

Teaching Topics. 8 pp. Single copy free. Published semi-annually. Contains topics of interest to teachers of family finance and money management. ad.

Investing. Investment Company Institute. 1775 K St., N.W. Washington, DC 20006. Sample titles are:

►**The Age-Old Question: How Can I Have More Money in the Future Than I Have Today?** 1982. 19 pp. Free. Explains various types of mutual funds as potential investments. Illustrated. hs.

►**Invest Today . . . for a Child's Tomorrow.** 1982. 12 pp. Free. Indicates how investing for a minor can be advantageous to all. hs.

►**Plan Tomorrow With Your Own IRA.** 1982. 28 pp. Free. Explains how Individual Retirement Accounts can be set up to supplement other benefit programs. hs-ad.

Investment Cautions. U.S. Securities and Exchange Commission. Office of Consumer Affairs. 500 N. Capitol St. Washington, DC 20549. Two pamphlets to acquaint consumers with the intricacies of investing. Free. hs. Titles are:

Investigate Before You Invest. 1978. 6 pp.

Investing in Oil, Gas & Coal. 1979. 13 pp.

►**What Every Investor Should Know.** 1982. 43 pp.

Life Insurance. Dept. of Consumer Economics and Housing. c/o Dr. Heinz B. Biesdorf. 120H MVR Hall. Cornell University. Ithaca, NY 14853. Set of seven brochures on life insurance for consumer education. 1971. 2-6 pp. each. $2.00 per set; make checks payable to Cornell University. hs-ad. Titles include:

►**Basic Life Insurance Policies.** Discusses the differences between term insurance, straight life, limited payment, and endowment policies.

►**Common Mistakes in Buying Life Insurance.** Tells how sound principles will give families the best insurance program to fit their needs.

►**Policy Variations and Provisions.** Outlines variations among types of life insurance, such as family policy, family income policy, mortgage insurance, credit life insurance, and travel insurance.

►**Programming Life Insurance to Meet Your Needs.** Explains factors in planning life insurance for maximum utility over the family life cycle.

►**Shopping for Life Insurance.** Covers such topics as rating a life insurance company, choosing an agent, and comparing policies.

Mind Your Money Series. Money Management Institute. Household. Dept. FI. 2700 Sanders Rd. Prospect Heights, IL 60070. 1979. 15 pp. each. 50 cents per set. Three leaflets designed for use with those of limited income, reading ability, or experience. Available in Spanish also. Titles are:

When You Shop. Offers simple-to-follow steps for judging quality of products, selecting stores, and shopping wisely. hs.

When You Spend. Presents easy-to-understand charts to make developing a spending plan easier. hs.

When You Use Credit. Presents basic guidelines for knowing when to use credit, the kinds of credit available, and the costs of credit. hs.

Money and Credit Management Education. National Consumer Finance Assoc. 1000 16th St., N.W. Washington, DC 20036. A catalog of educational aids for teachers, including audio-visual aids, is available.

Money Management. Money Management Institute of Household International. Dept. FI. 2700 Sanders Road. Prospect Heights, IL 60070. Sample titles:

Your Guide for Teaching Money Management. Rev. 1981. 75 pp. 50 cents. Presents concepts, learning experiences, resources, and evaluation criteria for teaching personal economics to students of different ages and abilities. A resource list for additional materials attends each major topic. hs.

►**Credit: Handle With Care.** 1981. $5.50. Kit includes filmstrip, 89 frames, 20 minutes, color; cassette; 32 pp. teacher's guide and script text; and 3 spirit masters for student activities. Explains such facets of credit as the application, the costs, consumer rights and responsibilities, and how to establish a favorable credit history. hs.

Booklet Series. 32-44 pp. 75 cents each; $5.00 per set of 12. A series of booklets covering all important areas of personal and family finance. Write for a free folder describing materials. Titles include:

►**Children and Money Management.** Aids adults in teaching their children skills for managing money by using everyday experiences. el-ms-hs.

Managing Your Credit. Presents a comprehensive and objective guide to understanding consumer credit. ms-hs.

Your Automobile Dollar. Discusses buying, maintaining, and operating a car. hs-ad.

Your Clothing Dollar. Gives wardrobe planning, buying, and care information. ms-hs.

Your Equipment Dollar. Suggestions for buying appliances and equipment for the home. hs-ad.

Your Financial Plan. Presents a personalized, easy-to-use plan for managing income. hs-ad.

Your Food Dollar. How to plan and shop for food. Guidelines for all types of food. hs-ad.

Your Home Furnishings Dollar. Guidelines for buying home furnishings and decorating needs. hs-ad.

Your Housing Dollar. Advice on how to buy or rent a home that will fit into your spending and savings plan. hs-ad.

Your Recreation Dollar. Suggests ways to plan recreation expenses and vacation travel. hs-ad.

Your Savings and Investment Dollar. How to set up a program based on present and future needs and goals. hs-ad.

Your Shopping Dollar. Tells how to plan spending, select goods and services, and handle consumer problems.

To the Point Series. New Readers Press. Box 131. Syracuse, NY 13210. $2.20 each; prepay orders under $10.00. A series of units designed to teach the use of money in ways that bring personal satisfaction. Each book contains exercises and questions for discussion and perforated, self-correcting worksheets. Illustrated. G3-4 reading level. Teacher's guide available. Titles are:

Insuring Yourself. 1980. 48 pp.

Making a Budget. 1980. 47 pp.

Saving and Investing. 1980. 48 pp.

Using a Checking Account. 1980. 48 pp.

Using Credit. 1980. 56 pp.

You and Your Money. Federal Reserve Bank of Richmond. Bank & Public Relations Dept. Richmond, VA 23261. 14 pp. Free in quantities. A cartoon booklet dealing with the causes of inflation and deflation and some remedies. hs.

Your Guide to Consumer Credit and Bankruptcy. American Bar Assoc. 1155 E. 60th St. Chicago, IL 60637. 1980. 36 pp. $1.00. Information on types of credit and on how to apply and use credit. hs-ad.

MULTICULTURAL STUDIES

Note: Several entries in this section appear under the subdivision of Indians.

American Jewish Committee. American Jewish Committee. Institute of Human Relations. 165 E. 56th St. New York, NY 10022. Sample titles are:

Better Than You. 1971. 64 pp. $1.25. A study of discrimination against ethnic minorities. hs.

Black-Jewish Relations in the U.S. 26 pp. 75 cents. An annotated listing of writings on relations between Black and Jewish peoples. hs.

The Many Faces of Anti-Semitism. 1978. 39 pp. $1.50. A study of religious, political, and social discrimination in historical and psychological context. hs.

What We Know About Young American Jews. 1970. 19 pp. 35 cents. An annotated bibliography of facts about young Jews. hs.

Black Americana. Public Relations. Detroit Public Library. 5201 Woodward Ave. Detroit, MI 48202. Rev. annually. 28 pp. $2.00. Bibliography of current black literature; separate listing of children's books. Consists of a main volume of books during the 1970's and all annual issues to date, as available. pr. to hs.

Black Culture Quiz (#346). The Sperry and Hutchinson Co. Consumer Services. 2900 W. Seminary Dr. Fort Worth, TX 76133. 1979. 25 pp. 25 cents. Provides answers to questions important to understanding black history and culture in America. References. el-ms-hs.

The Blacklist. Enoch Pratt Free Library. Publications Dept. 400 Cathedral St. Baltimore, MD 21201. 1975. 24 pp. 75 cents. Annotated reading list of literature oriented to black people. hs-ad.

The Chicano (ME2132). New American Library. 1633 Broadway. New York, NY 10019. 1971. 316 pp. $3.50. Collection of short stories tracing the Chicano experience from the stereotyped Mexican to the new economic, political, and cultural life of the Mexican American. hs.

Children and Intercultural Education. Assoc. for Childhood Education International. 3615 Washington Ave., N.W. Washington, DC 20016. 1974. Packet of 3 booklets. $1.50 plus 10% for postage and handling. Prepay orders under $10.00 by check or money order in U.S. currency. Describes the feelings of anxiety and frustration felt by people from different minority groups. Gives background information on research conducted with minority groups and suggests ways of working with people of different origins and backgrounds. hs-ad. Titles are:

Are There Unwelcome Guests in Your Classroom? 38 pp.

Overview and Research. 19 pp.

Some Minorities Speak Out. 12 pp.

GPO Materials. U.S. Gov't. Printing Office. Washington, DC 20402. Lists of many low-cost government publications. Sample titles are:

►**Minorities** (SB-006). 1982. 12 pp. Free.

►**Women** (SB-111). 1981. 21 pp. Free.

Pluralism. American Jewish Committee. Institute on Pluralism and Group Identity. 165 E. 56th St. New York, NY 10022. Titles include:

The Image of Pluralism in American Literature: The American Experience of European Ethnic Groups. 1974. 73 pp. $1.50. A selective annotated bibliography dealing with the white ethnic experience and literature of European ethnic groups in America. hs-ad.

The Schools and Group Identity: Educating for a New Pluralism. 1974. 78 pp. $1.75. Discusses ethnicity and how schools can generate change for the "new pluralism" in information, values, self-concepts, and skills. ad.

►**Understanding You and Them: Tips for Teaching About Ethnicity** (187). Social Science Education Consortium. Publications. 855 Broadway. Boulder, CO 80302. 1976. 66 pp. $3.95. Presents a philosophical basis for the teaching of ethnic studies. Includes several sample lessons and teaching activities, descriptions of materials available. and how to select them. hs-ad.

Indians

American Indian (VA170). Hayes School Pub. Co., Inc. 321. Pennwood Ave. Wilkinsburg, PA 15221. 12 pp. $2.50. Eight 9″ x 12″ posters depicting life styles of different American Indians and brief narratives on their cultures. el.

The American Indian as Hunter. Pennsylvania Historical and Museum Commission. William Penn Memorial Museum and Archives Bldg. Box 1026. Harrisburg, PA 17120. Rev. 1967. 23 pp. $1.00. Tells of the significance of hunting in the life of the Indian. el-ms.

Indian Affairs. U.S. Dept. of the Interior. Bureau of Indian Affairs. 19th and E Sts., N.W. Washington, DC 20240. Free. Brochures and fact sheets about U.S. Indian policy and programs and commonly asked questions about American Indians. Some bibliographies. ad.

Indian Culture. U.S. Department of the Interior. Bureau of Indian Affairs. Washington, DC 20242. Free. Set of 5 pamphlets on the American Indian. Each includes a reading list. el-ad. Titles include:

►**Indians: Languages.** 1978.

►**Indians: Legends and Myths.** 1978.

►**Indians: Origin.** 1963.

►**Indians: Religions and Ceremonials.** 1978.

►**Indians: Wars and Disturbances.** 1979.

Indian Stories. Bellerophon Books. 36 Anacapa St. Santa Barbara, CA 93101. Titles are:

Myths and Legends of the Indians of the Southwest: Navajo, Pima, Apache. Book I. 1978. 50 pp. $2.95. Interesting stories of these tribes for younger readers with illustrations to color. el-ms.

Myths and Legends of the Indians of the Southwest: Hopi, Ocoma, Tewa, Zuni. Book II. 1978. 50 pp. $2.95. Stories of Indian tribes for younger readers with illustrations to color. el-ms.

Indians Today. Indian Rights Assoc. 1505 Race St. Philadelphia, PA 19102. Single copies free with stamped self-addressed envelope (#10); additional copies 10 cents each plus postage. Titles are:

American Indians. 8 pp. A brief discussion of the status of Indians in the United States. hs.

Film Brochure. Describes three rental films on American Indians. Produced between 1975-1978. ad.

Indian Lands and Communities. An 8″ x 11″ map locating the native communities of American Indians. hs.

Indian Truth. Bimonthly newsletter of topical interest. Free sample issue.

Iroquois Culture (Leaflet #5). New York State Library. Gift and Exchange Section. Empire State Plaza. Albany, NY 12230. 1962. 14 pp. $1.00 prepaid.

Mississippi Indians. Dept. of Archives and History. P.O. Box 571. Jackson, MS 39205. Undated. 1 p. Free. Describes the history and culture of the different Mississippi tribes. el-ms-hs.

MUSIC AND MOVEMENT

AMC Materials. American Music Conference. 1000 Skokie Blvd. Wilmette, IL 60091. Titles include:

►**National Music Awards.** 1976. 48 pp. $1.00. Gives biographical sketches of the 121 recipients of the first National Music Awards for their contributions to American music from the Revolutionary War through the late 1950s.

New Zoo Music Revue. 1972. Poster 24″ x 36″. $3.00. AMC's musical alphabet poster. Examples of musical instrument families are depicted with characters from the "New Zoo Revue" children's television show. pr-el.

The Role of Music in the Life of Man. 1978. 22 pp. $1.50. An inquiry into the significance of the educational, therapeutic, recreational, and social aspects of music, with excerpts from research in the field. ad.

Charleston, Anyone? Interstate Printers and Publishers, Inc. 19-27 N. Jackson St. Danville, IL 61832. 1978. 45 pp. $2.95. Designed for use in schools and in dance classes as a fundamental reference for this round dance. ms-hs-ad.

Children's Book & Music Center Catalog. Children's Book & Music Center. 2500 Santa Monica Blvd. Santa Monica, CA 90404. Revised bi-annually. 96 pp. $1.00. Contains recordings, books, multi-media, and rhythm instruments for all curriculum areas and all grade levels. Several items less than $5.00. Titles are arranged under 10 headings and indexed. ad.

Developing Music Abilities in Young Children (C-1071). Cooperative Extension Service. University of Illinois at Urbana-Champaign. Urbana, IL 61801. 1973. 12 pp. 25 cents. Introduces children to the basics of music, musical instruments, and singing. Includes a sound recording. pr-el.

Music (SB-221). U.S. Gov't. Printing Office. Washington, DC 20402. 1980. 3 pp. Free. A listing of many low-cost government publications.

Music Materials. National Federation of Music Clubs. 1336 N. Deleware St. Indianapolis, IN 46202. Send for publication lists. All materials, free or for a fee, require 75 cents for postage and handling. Sample titles are:

> **American Folk Song List** (F4). Mimeographed. 5 pp. 25 cents. Compiled by Music Div., Library of Congress. pr. to hs.
>
> **Approved Course of Study Book List** (B1). 1975-77. Mimeographed. Free. Sr. division. hs-ad.
>
> **Chamber Operas for Grass Roots Production** (#01). 1965. 24 pp. 75 cents. Annotated list of 134 operas with publisher's key. ad.
>
> **Let's Have a Folk Festival** (F3). 1973. 14 pp. 75 cents. Organizing, staging, and publicizing a folk festival. References and bibliographies. hs-ad.
>
> **Modern Dance Syllabus** (D3). 6 pp. 10 cents. Warm-up exercises graded for ages 6-9, 9-12, and 12-18.
>
> **Musicianship Study Outline** (JF28). 3 pp. 10 cents. Basic musicianship requirements. el-ms-hs.

American Music Sample Programs A1-A16. Graded easy to difficult. Mimeographed. Free. Sample titles are:

> **Flute and Piano** (A7).
>
> **Piano Trio** (A11).
>
> **Piano, Violin, Percussion** (A14).
>
> **Piano With String Quartet** (A12).
>
> **Piano With String Quartet and Trio** (A13).
>
> **Piano With Woodwinds** (A8).
>
> **Piano With Woodwinds and Brass** (A9)
>
> **Piano With Woodwinds and Strings** (A10).
>
> **SATB, SSA, SSAA** (A15).

International Music Relations Lists of Music Title for International Music Programs. Includes all types of music except symphony and opera. Each list contains key to publishers. hs-ad. Lists include:

English (I-13). 30 cents.

French (I-14). 30 cents.

German (I-15). 30 cents.

Italian (I-16). 25 cents.

Russian (I-19). 30 cents.

Complete Set (I-111). $2.50.

The Musical All-Americans. McDonald's Corporation. A 16 mm, color, sound film. 28 min. Available for viewing through local McDonald's restaurants; ask for the Community Relations Representative. A film about McDonald's All-American High School Band filmed on tour featuring the band members' voices and music. Ideal for school bands and community groups.

The Royal Ballet of Flanders, 1970-1980. Belgian Consulate General. 50 Rockefeller Plaza. New York, NY 10020. 1980. 68 pp. Free. Contains a short history of the Royal Ballet and synopses and scenes from its major productions. hs-ad.

A Self-Instruction Guitar Book for Children. Scotty MacGregor Publications. 10 Pineacre Dr. Smithtown, NY 11787. 1970. 51 pp. $2.00. Children can teach themselves to play the guitar if they read at fourth grade level. Contains self-testing worksheets. el-ms-hs.

NATIONAL DEFENSE, ARMS CONTROL, AND WORLD PEACE

Arms Control. The Arms Control Assoc. 11 Dupont Cir., N.W. Washington, DC 20036. Free publications list on request. Sample titles are:

- ►**Arms Control Today.** Published monthly. 12 pp. Single issue free; subscriptions available. A compendium of opinion, analysis, and factual information on various aspects of arms control and national security. hs-ad.

- ►**A Glossary of Arms Control Terms.** 1979. 16 pp. Single copy free; quantity rates available. An explanation of terms to aid in understanding weapons technology and arms negogiations. hs-ad.

►**Nuclear Arms Control: Options for the 1980's.** 1982. 58 pp. Single copy free; quantity rates available. Articles by five authors discuss nuclear freeze and the new START program of the Reagan administration. hs-ad.

Demilitarization. Institute for World Order. 777 United Nations Plaza. New York, NY 10017. Sample titles are:

The Disarmament Process: Where to Begin. 1977. 22 pp. 75 cents. Describes thirteen approaches to disarmament, asking of each, "Is it feasible, is it desirable, and can citizens mobilize support for it?" hs-ad.

Toward a Dependable Peace: Proposal for an Appropriate Security System. 1978. 58 pp. $2.00. Security analysis showing why arms control policies will not lead to either increased security or decreased arms. Presents feasible steps for establishing a demilitarized system. hs-ad.

World Military and Social Expenditures, 1982. 1982. 40 pp. $4.00. Color tables and graphs show comparative statistical data on expenditures for military forces, health care and education, international peacekeeping, and foreign aid by 140 nations. ad.

►**Disarmament and Arms Control** (SB-127). U.S. Gov't. Printing Office. Washington, DC 20402. 1981. 8 pp. Free. A listing of many low-cost government publications which may be used in the classroom.

500-Mile Island—the Philippine Nuclear Reactor Deal (Vol. 10, No. 1). The Pacific-Studies Center. 222B View St. Mountain View, CA 94041. 1979. 45 pp. $2.50. Discusses the expansion of the American nuclear industry into the Philippines from several viewpoints. hs-ad.

►**Important Questions and Answers on a Comprehensive Nuclear Test Ban (CTB).** The Committee for National Security. 2000 P St., N.W. Washington, DC 20036. 1982. 14 pp. 25 cents. Responses to eleven questions covering the basic issues of a treaty to ban nuclear tests. hs-ad.

Lockheed World. Lockheed Corp. Corporate Publications, P.O. Box 551. Burbank, CA 91520. Free in quantities up to 25. Text and pictures describing Lockheed's current and earlier aircraft, missiles, spacecraft, and other products, ms-hs.

Military Budgets and Social Needs: Setting World Priorities (#551). Public Affairs Committee, Inc. 381 Park Ave. S. New York, NY 10016, 1977. 24 pp. 50 cents. Compares world expenditures for military and social purposes and discusses some of the socioeconomic consequences. hs-ad.

Nuclear Dangers. American Friends Service Committee. Rocky Flats Disarmament/Conversion Project. 1660 Lafayette St. Denver, CO 80218. Publications and reprints on the dangers of nuclear weapons and power plants and on the need for disarmament and conversion. Write for current listing.

Nuclear Mapping Kit. American Friends Service Committee. 15 Rutherford Pl. New York, NY 10003. 1979. 15 pp. $1.00 plus 50 cents postage. Directions for an exercise using a local map to plot the consequences of a nuclear bomb explosion for one's community. hs-ad.

►**Nuclear Power and Political Surveillance** (Report #6). Center for National Security Studies. 122 Maryland Ave., N.E. Washington, DC 20002. 1981. 119 pp. Typewritten. $3.50. Presents how the government and private interests are involved in spying relative to nuclear and anti-nuclear activities. hs-ad.

Nuclear Warfare. Center for Defense Information. 122 Maryland Ave., N.E. Washington, DC 20002. Many materials are offered on the defense activities of the U.S. and other countries. Write for current listing.

Peace Education. Women's International League for Peace and Freedom. 1213 Race St. Philadelphia, PA 19107. Three resource units for teachers are offered. Titles are:

> **Building Blocks for Peace.** 1973. 18 pp. $2.00. Contains ten lessons for kindergarten classes. Suggests games, things to make and do, songs, books, and filmstrips for each lesson objective. K.
>
> **Learning Peace.** 1972. 50 pp. $1.00. Outlines seven student activities to teach about attitudes and prejudices which underlie war and conflict. Includes bibliography and list of resources. G7-12.
>
> ►**Our Patriotic Duty to Dissent.** Folder. 25 copies for $1.50 postpaid. Gives statement of basic freedoms and basic responsibilities in a democracy and looks at the role of dissenting minorities throughout our history. hs.
>
> **Peace Is in Our Hands.** 1975. 90 pp. $1.00. Outlines eight series of activities designed to help students understand the personal bases for peace. Includes bibliography and audio-visual resources. G1-6.

SANE Materials. Citizens' Organization for a Sane World. 711 G St., S.E. Washington, DC 20003. Offers several free pamphlets and leaflets in opposition to nuclear weapons. Request information on "The Race Nobody Wins," a slideshow/filmstrip available to teachers for rental fee of $10.00. hs-ad.

►**Space: The High Frontier in Perspective** (#50). Worldwatch Institute. 1776 Massachusetts Ave., N.W. Washington, DC 20036. 1982. 72 pp. $2.00. Argues that the increasing militarization of space by the U.S. and U.S.S.R. threatens the benefits of civilian programs and undercuts agreements to limit nuclear weapons. hs-ad.

►**UNESCO Scientists and Disarmament.** UNESCO. Room 2401. U.N. Building. New York, NY 10017. 1982. 4 pp. Free. Summarizes the conclusions and recommendations from the Pugwash Conferences on Science and World Affairs, February 1982. hs-ad.

U.S.-U.S.S.R. America's Future. 514 Main St. New Rochelle, NY 10801. Pamphlets which assess the posture of the U.S. in relation to the Soviet Union. Free to students and teachers for classroom use; 50 cents each to others. hs-ad. Titles are:

From Detente to a Forward Strategy. 1978. 23 pp.

The Fruits of Detente. 1980. 22 pp.

National Defense and the Soviet Threat. 1978. 21 pp.

National Security and the News Media. 1980. 23 pp.

►**What About the Russians?** Student/Teacher Organization to Prevent Nuclear War. c/o Stop Nuclear War. Box 232. Northfield, MA 01360. 1982. 48 pp. $1.75. Deals with the distrust that Soviet behavior arouses among the American public and how that impinges on the peace movement. hs.

World Order. Institute for World Order. 777 United Nations Plaza. New York, NY 10017. Books, pamphlets, working papers, articles, and newsletters promoting world peace. Send for free catalog. Titles include:

Transition. Occasional. Free. Presents discussions of current affairs which affect world security. hs-ad.

A World Order Perspective on Authoritarian Tendencies. 1980. 67 pp. $2.00. Discusses the structure of authoritarian regimes, their impact on world order, and ways to change these systems. hs-ad.

World Peace. Institute for World Order. 777 United Nations Plaza. New York, NY 10017. Provides papers, booklets, articles, books, and visuals about alternatives to war, poverty, racial injustice, and ecological damage. Free listing of publications. Costs range from 25 cents up. Titles include:

►**How to Avoid Death and Taxes.** 1979. 13 pp. 25 cents. Espouses that war is an "institution that has outlived its usefulness." hs-ad.

►**Nuclear Strategy and World Order** (#23). 1982. 52 pp. $2.00. Maintains that current U.S. strategy goes beyond counterforce and deterrence; it fosters preparation for nuclear warfare. An alternative for avoiding nuclear war is proposed. hs-ad.

World Peace Papers. World Peacemakers. 2852 Ontario Rd., N.W. Washington, DC 20009. Offers a series of pamphlets dealing with the issues of security and arms control. hs-ad. 30 cents each postpaid. Sample titles are:

Hope in the American Crisis (#6). 10 pp.

Moving Toward True Security (#4). 14 pp.

►**Peace in the Reagan Era** (#8). Undated. 18 pp. 30 pp.

A Policy in Search of a President (#5). Undated. 14 pp.

A Time to Stop (#1). Undated. 10 pp.

►**Vision of Peace: Redeeming the American Dream** (#7). Undated. 14 pp.

NATURAL RESOURCES

Note: Several entries in this section appear under the subdivision of Forests.

Alaska Land: A National Issue. What Is to Be Done With It? (Vol. 27, No. 6). Center for Information on America. Washington, CT 06793. 1978. 4 pp. 45 cents. Discusses the problem of disposing of public domain lands in Alaska. hs.

A Brief Story of Aluminum and Alcoa. Aluminum Co. of America. 800 Alcoa Bldg. Pittsburgh, PA 15219. Wall chart. Single copy free to students; free to teachers in class quantities. How aluminum was discovered, how it is made today, and its importance to the world. Illustrated. ms.

Borax. United States Borax and Chemical Corp. Public Relations Dept. P.O. Box 75128. Sanford Station. Los Angeles, CA 90005. Free booklets on the production of borax in the United States. el-ms. Titles include:

Borax for a Fact. 1979. 22 pp.

The Story of Borax. 1979. 56 pp.

Coal. National Coal Assoc. 1130 17th St., N.W. Washington, DC 20036. Several publications on various aspects of the coal industry designed for use by teachers, librarians, and counselors. Single copies free to educators only. Titles include:

Coal. 1979. 18 pp. An illustrated reprint of *The World Book Encyclopedia* article on coal. G7-12.

The Power of Coal. Undated. 19 pp. A teacher's guide, text, and student quizzes about the history, production, and uses of bituminous coal. G1-6.

Mineral Resources. Bureau of Mines. Publications Branch. 4800 Forbes Ave. Pittsburgh, PA 15213. Single copy free. Titles include:

Coal Products Tree. 10″ x 12″. Line drawing showing the many and varied products of coal. ms-hs.

The Petroleum Tree. 10″ x 12″. Line drawing showing products obtainable from crude oil. ms-hs.

►**Minerals and Mining** (SB-151). U.S. Gov't. Printing Office. Washington, DC 20402. 1981. 21 pp. Free. A listing of many low-cost government publications.

Mississippi River. Lower Mississippi Valley Div. Attn: LMVPA P.O. Box 80. Vicksburg, MS 39180. Titles include:

Channel Improvement and Stabilization on the Lower Mississippi River. 1979. Pamphlet. Free. Details on channel improvement and stabilization on the Lower Mississippi River through means of cutoffs, revetment, dredging, and dikes. el-ms-hs.

►**Free-Loan Informational Films** (EP 360-1-16). 1982. 13 pp. Free. Lists 16 mm films available on navigation, flood control, emergency operations during natural disasters, environmental enhancement, and other subjects. ad.

Mississippi River & Tributaries Project, Cairo to the Gulf. 1977. Pamphlet. Free. Gives history and description of a project to protect against floods and aid navigation. el-ms-hs.

Mississippi Valley. U.S. Army Engineer Dist. P.O. Box 60. Attn: LMKPA. Vicksburg, MS 39180. Send for catalogue of maps, pamphlets, and books on Corps projects on the Mississippi River (Natchez to Memphis) and surrounding areas. hs-ad.

Oil. Quaker State Oil Refining Corp. P.O. Box 989. Oil City, PA 16301. Free to teachers and prospective teachers. Kit of materials containing information about petroleum, its history, its use, and some of its by-products. ms.

Rubber. Malaysian Rubber Bureau. Suite 204. 1925 K St., N.W. Washington, DC 20006. Pamphlets. Free up to 6 copies. Sample titles are:

►**Map of Malaysia.** 4 pp. Fold-out map with text.

►**Natural Rubber: How Nature and Science Serve Mankind.** 1971. 15 pp. A fact booklet in scriptographic style.

►**Natural Rubber: A Product of Nature Plus Science.** Large wall chart.

►**The Story of Malaysian Natural Rubber.** Fold-out pamphlet. Illustrated.

The TVA. Tennessee Valley Authority. Information Office. 400 W. Summit Hill Dr. Knoxville, TN 37902. Free to teachers and libraries. Brochures containing maps, photos, statistics, and narrative on the TVA system. ms-hs. Sample titles are:

Answers to Questions Most Frequently Asked About TVA

►**TVA: An Agency for Regional Development**

►**TVA Electric Rates**

►**TVA Reservoir Operations**

TVA Tames the River

Forests

►**API Directory of Films.** American Paper Institute, Inc. 260 Madison Ave. New York, NY 10016. 1981. 20 pp. $1.00. An annotated guide to films available from many sources on forestry and paper and related topics in environment, careers, and safety. ad-ms-hs.

Arbor Day News. The National Arbor Day Foundation. Arbor Lodge 100. Nebraska City, NE 68410. Quarterly; back issues available. Free. Articles on tree planting and care in urban areas, Arbor Day, and other and tree-related classroom activities. el-ms.

Forest Institute. American Forest Institute. 1619 Massachusetts Ave. Washington, DC 20036. An annotated listing of available publications, teaching aids, posters, and films on forest management and products sent free by request. Sample titles are:

►**Forests and Trees of the United States.** Rev. 1982. Map. Single copy free; additional copies 30 cents each. Teaching guide included. el-ms-hs.

Green America. Periodical. Back issues available. Single copy free; additional copies 40 cents each. Write for descriptive order sheet. Articles and photos concerning the commercial forestry industry. el-ms.

Growth of a Tree. 1978. Wall chart, 24″ x 34″. Single copy free; additional copies 30 cents. A color chart identifing tree parts and their functions. Accompanying teacher's guide suggests science, language arts, and art activities. el.

Indian Valley. 16 pp. Single copy free; additional copies 30 cents each. An educational gaming technique on environmental management. ms-hs.

Learn to Love Trees. Single copy free; additional copies 20 cents. Forest appreciation for elementary teachers.

Trees Want You. 1973. Single copy free; additional copies 20 cents. Forest appreciation for high school teachers.

Forestry. State University of New York. College of Environmental Science and Forestry. Syracuse, NY 13210. Free to teachers. Write for list of 67 popular and technical forestry publications. Sample titles are:

Recipe for Tree Planting. 1966. 6 pp. Explains how to plant, when to plant, and how to care for trees. el-ms.

The Story of Your Christmas Tree. Rev. 1978. 6 pp. Gives history and characteristics of the Christmas tree. el-ms.

Forestry. Georgia-Pacific. 900 S.W. 5th Ave. Portland, OR 97204. Free. A variety of pamphlets, posters, charts, tree seed samples, and free-loan films are available. Titles include:

How a Log Is Cut Into Lumber. Undated. Wall chart, 26″ x 17″. Diagrams show basic cuts generally made for softwood lumber production. el-ms-hs.

To Grow a Tree. 1979. 15 pp. Describes aspects of the commercial forestry industry and lists types of trees and tree products. el-ms-hs.

Redwoods. California Redwood Assoc. 1 Lombard St. San Francisco, CA 94111. Three pamphlets on the redwood forests and lumbering. Free up to 100 copies; additional copies 10 cents each. Titles include:

The Story of the Redwood Forest. 1976. 7 pp. Describes procedures used with redwood trees, including cutting regulations and replanting. ms.

The Story of the Redwood Lumber Industry. 1976. 77 pp. The processing of redwood lumber from the forest to the consumer. ms.

The Tall Trees. 1976. 11 pp. A guide to redwood parks and their facilities in California. ms.

Redwoods. Rellim Redwood Co. Public Relations Dept. P.O. Box 247. Crescent City, CA 95531. Single copies free. Pamphlets and booklets on redwood and other trees and scientific forest management. Titles are:

Demonstration Forest Tour Guide. 22 pp. Illustrated. ms.

Redwoods Forever. 19 pp. Illustrated. el-ms.

Southern Pine. Southern Forest Products Assoc. P.O. Box 52468. New Orleans, LA 70152. Titles include:

Our Forests. 28 pp. 25 cents. A booklet designed for a unit on trees and forests. Ten-page teacher's guide included. el-ms.

Questions & Answers About Forests. 15 cents. Reveals some surprising facts about forest ownership, products, cultivation, and economics. hs-ad.

The South's Third Forest. 11 pp. 15 cents. Describes an ambitious program of timber resource development and environmental improvement. el-ms.

Tree Charts and Leaflets. Forest Service, USDA. 12th and Independence, S.W. P.O. Box 2417. Washington, DC 20013. el. Titles are:

Forestry (FS-40). 1977. Leaflet. Single copy free.

How a Tree Grows (FS-32). 1970. 8 pp. Free to teachers only.

Suggestions for Incorporating Forestry Into the School Curriculum (FS-62). 1977. Pamphlet. Free to teachers only.

What We Get From a Tree (FS-279). 1963. Large wall chart. Free to teachers only. In color.

Why Leaves Change Color (FS-12). 1975. Leaflet. Single copies free to students; quantities free to teachers.

►**Trees, Forest Products, and Forest Management** (SB-086). U.S. Gov't. Printing Office. Washington, DC 20402. 1981. 17 pp. Free. A listing of many low-cost government publications which may be used in the classroom.

Your Fabulous Friend. Southern Forest Institute. 3395 N.E. Expy. Atlanta, GA 30341. 13 pp. Single copy free. Booklet about the forest industry and the uses of wood. Illustrated. el-ms.

NUTRITION

ADA Materials. American Dietetic Assoc. 430 N. Michigan Ave. Chicago, IL 60611. Sample titles are:

Food Facts Talk Back (#0803). Rev. 1974. 34 pp. $1.25. Explores major food myths; sections on additives, vegetarianism, weight reduction, pregnancy, and balanced diets. hs-ad.

Leaflets. Single copy free with self-addressed stamped envelope (#10). Titles are:

Meal Time—Happy Time (#0804). 1975. Pointers to parents on the nutritional needs of children between one and the teen years. ad.

Nutrition: What's It All About? (#0806). Rev. 1975. Discusses the four food groups and essential nutrients. el.

Be Informed on Nutrition. New Readers Press. Box 131. Syracuse, NY 13210. 1973. 40 pp. $1.20; prepay orders under $10.00. Topics include what food does, how to eat what you need, calories and activity, weight loss and gain, meal planning, and shopping. Includes teacher's guide with resource list. el-ms.

Booklets. General Mills, Inc. Nutrition Dept. 505. P.O. Box 1112. Minneapolis, MN 55440. Send for listing of pamphlets concerning nutrition. Titles include:

►**Carbohydrates: Good News for a Balanced Diet** (#39406). 1982. 8 pp. 30 cents. Explains the contribution of simple and complex carbohydrates to a healthful diet.

Choose to Lose—Eat Sensibly (#35767). 1980. 12 pp. 50 cents. Techniques and menus to encourage the individual to reach a desired weight. ms-hs.

Food for Fitness (#35711). Rev. 1980. 4 pp. 25 cents. Outlines facts and fallacies of nutrition for athletics. ms-hs.

►**Help Your Child Join the Cavity-Free Generation** (#35763). Rev. 1982. 10 pp. 50 cents. A parent's guide to good dental health. Explains factors that cause dental cavities and the relationship between diet and dental health. Sanctioned by the American Dental Association.

►**A New Perspective on Dental Caries and Diet** (#38661). 1982. 6 pp. 30 cents. Contains the American Dental Association's "Statement on Diet and Dental Health." Explains the relationship of carbohydrates to dental decay. el-ms-hs.

►**Salt/Sodium** (#38666). 1982. 5 pp. 25 cents. Explains the relationship between sodium intake and high blood pressure, differences between salt and sodium, and the role of sodium in the body. ms-hs.

Coloring Books.

►**Good Food to Eat Coloring Book** (#34581). 1979. 4 pp. 40 cents for a set of five in either English, Spanish or combination of both. Nutrition oriented. pr.

►**The Thing the Professor Forgot** (#38686). Rev. 1982. 18 pp. 45 cents. Teaches a simple but important nutrition message to children under 10 years. pr-el.

►**Tommy and Toni Teeth Coloring Book** (#34973). 1979. 4 pp. 40 cents for a set of five in either English, Spanish or combination of both. Nutrition and dental health oriented. pr.

Breakfast Your Way to a Better Day. Kellogg Co. Dept. T-2. 235 Porter St. Battle Creek, MI 49016. 1978. 2 posters, each 25″ x 20″. Free; limit of 1 poster per classroom; U.S. distribution only. 1 poster designed for grades K-6 and 1 for grades 7-12. Each four-color poster is accompanied by a 1-page teacher's guide for use in classroom activities. pr. to hs.

Brown Bagging It. C. J. Frompovich Publications. R.D. #1. Chestnut Road. Coopersburg, PA 18036. Undated. Pamphlet. 30 cents postpaid; quantity discounts. Contains interesting suggestions for nutritious lunches carried to school or work. ms-hs-ad.

Children's Materials. C. J. Frompovich Publications. R.D. #1. Chestnut Road. Coopersburg, PA 18036. School prices available. Sample titles are:

►**A Child's ABC's for Nutrition Coloring Book.** Rev. 1981. 30 pp. $1.85 postpaid. An alphabet coloring book which helps to teach good nutrition. ps-pr.

Kids Cooking Naturally. 1979. 11 pp. $2.25. Introduction to preparing foods without preservatives and the use of the kitchen and kitchen utensils. Contains recipes for natural foods. el.

Nutrition Workbook for Children. 1978. 28 pp. $2.35. Puzzles, riddles, coloring, and word games that teach good eating habits. el.

Consumer's Guide to Food Labels. Consumer Information Center. Pueblo, CO 81009. 1978. 4 pp. Free. Covers health, organic, and natural foods. hs-ad.

►**Energize at Sunrise™.** Kellogg Co. Dept. U-2. 235 Porter St. Battle Creek, MI 49016. 1977. $2.00 per unit; U.S. and Canada distribution only. A nutrition education unit designed for grades K-6. Each unit includes 13 spirit masters, 4-color overhead transparency, teacher's guide, and poster game.

Feeding Children. Tennessee Dept. of Public Health. Nutrition Services. State Office Bldg. Ben Allen Rd. Nashville,TN 37216. Single copy free; multiple copies available in Tennessee. Leaflets concerning foods for children. hs. Titles include:

Feeding Your Baby

Food for You and Your Baby Too

Foods to Help Children

The Natural Things to Do

►**PKU—What Is PKU?**

►**Weaning—Teaching Your Baby to Use a Cup**

►**When Your Baby Is on the Way**

►**Fitness Focus™.** Kellogg Co. Dept. V-2. 235 Porter St. Battle Creek, MI 49016. 1980. $2.50 per unit; U.S. and Canada distribution only. A nutrition education unit designed for grades 5-9. Each unit includes 6 duplicating masters, 2 overhead transparencies, a 4-color poster, and teacher's guide.

Food, Diet, and Nutrition (SB-078). U.S. Gov't. Printing Office. Washington, DC 20402. 1982. 19 pp. Free. A listing of many low-cost government materials.

Food for Thought. Chevron Chemical Co. Public Affairs. P.O. Box 3744. San Francisco, CA 94119. 1977. 8 pp. Single copy free. A booklet on the food value of carbohydrates, protein, minerals, and vitamins. el.

Food Value Materials. Stokely-Van Camp, Inc. Home Economics Dept. 941 N. Meridian St. Indianapolis, IN 46206. Payment must accompany order; no purchase orders accepted. A variety of materials on nutritional values, calorie content, cooking, and seasoning. Sample titles are:

Calorie Counting for a Better Looking You. 1977. Chart, 18″ x 24″. 5 cents. Calorie content of canned fruits and vegetables. ms-hs.

Enjoying Vegetables. 1977. Packet. $1.00. Contains a teacher's guide, six spirit masters, and a transparency for class activities. hs.

►**How to Be Your Body's Best Friend.** 1982. 29 pp. 50 cents. Booklet contains a nutritious weight control plan using basic 4 pattern and a diet exchange listing.

Fruit. Sunkist Growers. P.O. Box 7888. Van Nuys, CA 91409. Materials related to teaching about nutrition, especially Vitamin C. Titles include:

Nutrition Sports Mobile (#8810). Free; one per classroom. For elementary grade teachers, coaches, and school cafeterias.

►**Questions and Answers About Vitamin C in Fresh Citrus Fruit** (#8309). Rev. 1981. 4 pp. Free. ms-hs.

Vitamin C Makes a Difference (AV-78). 1977. $2.50. Filmstrip; 50 frames. Narrative and strip emphasize low-cost foods high in Vitamin C. el-ms.

Wall Posters. Free to teachers only. pr.-hs. Titles include:

Think Orange When You Choose a Snack (#8302).

What Vitamin C Does for the Body (#8301).

Good Diets. Tennessee Dept. of Public Health. Nutrition Services. State Office Bldg. Ben Allen Rd. Nashville, TN 37216. Single copy free; multiple copies available in Tennessee. Various pamphlets available. el-ms. Titles include:

The Good Foods Coloring Book. 16 pp. pr.

Happiness Is a Good Daily Diet

If You Want to Lose Weight, Choose Your Food Carefully!

►**Instant Nonfat Dry Milk**

Iron-Rich Foods Make a Difference

Nutrition and the Pill

►**Variety With Ground Beef**

Vitamin C—One of the Keys to Good Nutrition

►**What to Buy?**

►**Heinz Guide to Good Nutrition.** (M15923). Communications Dept. Heinz U.S.A. P.O. Box 57. Pittsburgh, PA 15230. 1981. 4 pp. Free. Emphasizes dietary needs from the basic food groups to obtain essential nutrients. Also in Spanish. ms-hs.

►**Nutrition: Food at Work for You.** Prudential Insurance Co. P.O. Box 36. Newark, NJ 07101. 1979. 16 pp. Free. A booklet of basic nutrition information and a "Daily Food Guide" that may be posted for easy reference. hs-ad.

Nutrition and Intellectual Growth in Children. Assoc. for Childhood Education International. 3615 Wisconsin Ave., N. W. Washington, DC 20016. 1969. 64 pp. $2.00 plus 10% for shipping; prepay in U.S. currency. Presents evidence of the grave effects of poor nutrition on intellectual growth. ad.

Nutrition Education Materials. Direct requests to the Dairy Council office of your area. If not served locally, send to: National Dairy Council. 6300 N. River Rd. Rosemont, IL 60018. 1980. 15 pp. Free. Illustrated and annotated catalog of a variety of booklets, posters, films and filmstrips for grades K-12, consumers, and health professionals. Teacher's guides, reference materials, and multi-media packages are also available. Sample title is:

►**Nutrition Source Book** (B074). Rev. 1980. 40 pp. $2.00. An educator's reference which emphasizes a nutrient approach to teaching and applies nutrient and food group information to plan daily meals. ad.

►**Nutrition Guide/Calculator.** California Apricot Advisor Board. 1295 Boulevard Way, Suite H. Walnut Creek, CA 94595. 1975. Free. A slide that tells what essential nutrients do for the body and what percentage of the U.S. RDA is in one cup of various canned fruits. el-ms-hs.

Nutrition Reports. Center for Science in the Public Interest. 1755 S St., N.W. Washington, DC 20009. Send for free list of publications. Titles include:

Midget Encyclopedia of Food and Nutrition. 1980. Set of 5 pamphlets. 8 pp. each. $1.25. Covers food issues such as chemical additives, manufactured and processed foods, fats, sugar, salt, and health problems. hs-ad.

Nutrition Posters. 18″ x 24″. $3.00 each; bulk prices available. Titles are:

►**Chemical Cuisine.** Rev. 1981. Lists and describes safe and unsafe food additives, from antioxidants to chelating agents. ms-hs.

New American Eating Guide. 1979. Guide to selection of foods for a balanced, nutritious diet and foods to avoid. ms-hs.

Nutrition Scoreboard. 1980. Indicates the relative nutritional values of many common foods. ms-hs.

►**Sodium Scoreboard.** 1982. Brand-name guide to sodium content of over 200 common foods.

►**Project Nutrition™.** Kellogg Co. Dept. W-2. 235 Porter St. Battle Creek, MI 49016. 1979. $4.00 per unit; U.S. and Canada distribution only. A nutrition education unit designed for grades 7-12. Each unit includes four 12-frame filmstrips with script, 25 spirit masters, 20-page teacher's guide, and 4-color poster, 17″ x 22″.

Raisins. California Raisin Advisory Board. P.O. Box 5172. Dept. S. Fresno, CA 93755. Titles include:

Questions You've Been Raisin' and Our Answers. Free. A pamphlet on uses and handling of raisins. hs-ad.

Raisin Nutrition. 1978. 4 pp. Free. A pamphlet on the nutritional substances and their value in raisins. hs-ad.

Selective Snackology. 1977. Kit. $1.00. A teaching kit to help children learn simple facts about good snacking. Includes teacher's guide, a 22″ x 34″ wall chart, 30 mini-posters, coloring sheets, class activities, and recipes. pr.

Ralston Materials. Ralston Purina. Corporate Consumer Services. Public Relations. Checkerboard Square. St. Louis, MO 63164. Titles are:

Cereals and Crackers. 1979. Free. A foldout of nutrition information about breakfast cereals and snacks. ms-hs.

►**Nutrient Analyses of Chicken of the Sea® Tuna Products.** Free. A foldout of nutrition information about tuna products. hs.

PERSONAL AND LEADERSHIP DEVELOPMENT

Hair Care. Johnson Wax. Consumer Services Center. Personal Care Division. P.O. Box 567. Dept. FI 83-HC. Racine, WI 53401. Undated. 16 pp. Free; request on postcard. A booklet covering such aspects of hair care as cutting and styling, products and treatments, appliances and problems. ms-hs.

Here's Looking At You! The Soap and Detergent Assoc. Consumer Affairs Dept. 475 Park Ave. S. New York, NY 10016. 1980. 31 pp. 25 cents. A grooming guide for teenage boys and girls. Includes tips on grooming, health, manners, and clothes care, and advice on getting a job and keeping it. ms-hs.

Interstate Booklets. The Interstate Printers & Publishers, Inc. 19-27 N. Jackson St. Danville, IL 61832. Quantity rates available. Titles are:

►**The "How" in Parliamentary Procedure** (LC 80-84460). 4th ed. 1981. 68 pp. $1.50. Stresses learning to hold efficient meetings through widely accepted procedures rather than expert parliamentarianship. ms-hs-ad.

►**Instant Meeting Planning** (#2223-X). 1982. 32 pp. $1.50. A "how-to" book to help you coordinate a successful meeting written by a person of long experience. hs-ad.

►**Instant Speaking Course** (#2176-4). 1981. 32 pp. $1.50. Provides pointers for speech-makers from gaining credibility with an audience to judging acoustics and handling interruptions. ms-hs.

Grooming and Beauty Tips. Johnson & Johnson Baby Products Co. Consumer and Professional Services. Skillman, NJ 08558. Titles include:

Grooming Hints for Girls and Guys. 1981. 13 pp. Free. Tips on skin and hair care for teenagers with an emphasis on the "natural look." ms-hs.

Ten Ways to Say Hello to Beautiful Skin. 1980. 6 pp. Free.

Sportshelf Booklets. Sportshelf. P.O. Box 634. New Rochelle, NY 10802. $1.00 each, postpaid. Titles include:

Agree to Disagree. 1970. 15 pp. How to make your opinions known on the job without being unpleasant. ms-hs.

Do It the Easy Way. 1971. 15 pp. Suggestions for increasing personal efficiency on the job and at home. ms-hs.

How to Make People Like You. 1971. 14 pp. Contains pointers for building successful relationships with others. ms-hs.

Making Your Point. 1971. 11 pp. Introductory logic used to guide personal interactions. ms-hs.

Time: Your Most Valuable Resource. 1971. 15 pp. How to develop the correct attitudes toward proper utilization of time. ms-hs.

Wake Up Your Memory! 1972. 11 pp. Facts and fallacies about memory; includes specific tips for remembering better. ms-hs.

Teen Times. Future Homemakers of America. National Headquarters. 1910 Association Dr. Reston, VA 22091. Four issues yearly. 22 pp. each. $4.00 subscription. A motivational magazine dealing with current teen concerns, giving suggestions for change. Back issues devoted to major topics are available for $1.00 each. Send for listing.

PHILOSOPHY AND RELIGION

Bible. Abingdon. Customer Service Dept. 201 8th Ave. S. Nashville, TN 37202. Payment should accompany all orders; schools and libraries entitled to 25% discount. Titles include:

Abingdon Glossary of Religious Terms. 1980. 94 pp. $1.50. A simplified reference for biblical and religious terms used in Judaism and Western Christianity. hs-ad.

The Autobiography of Jesus: What He Said About Himself. 1980. 155 pp. $1.95. Uses Biblical passages in which Jesus talked about himself to construct an "autobiography." hs-ad.

►**A Bible Who's Who** 1957. 64 pp. 95 cents. A selection of 620 short biographies of scriptural characters. hs-ad.

Strange Facts About the Bible. 1968. 350 pp. $2.25. A collection of unsolved riddles and unusual questions that have plagued scholars and laymen for centuries. hs-ad.

►**The Fourth "R": Religion in the Public Schools** (#11). American Jewish Committee. Institute on Human Relations. 165 E. 56th St. New York, NY 10022. 1982. 11 pp. Typewritten. $1.00. Focuses on the history and current emphasis of the national debate over religion in public schools. hs-ad.

Life After Life (#22735-1). Bantam Books. 666 5th Ave. New York, NY 10103. 1975. 184 pp. $3.50. Accounts of people declared clinically "dead" whose experiences raise new views about life, death, and spiritual survival. hs-ad.

Sun Songs: Creation Myths From Around the World (ME1810). New American Library. 1633 Broadway. New York, NY 10019. 1980. 402 pp. $2.95. Covers creation myths from ancient Egyptian beliefs to North American Indian fables to the recent legends of the Pacific islanders. hs-ad.

Teaching About Death (#342). Curriculum Bulletin. Oceanside, OR 97134. 1978. 16 pp. $2.50 postpaid; payment must accompany order. Contains lessons and activities directed toward increased awareness of death. hs-ad.

►**Understanding the Christian Faith** (42955-2). Abingdon. Customer Service Dept. 201 8th Ave. S. Nashville, TN 37202. 1974. 181 pp. $1.95. Payment should accompany all orders; schools and libraries entitled to 25% discount. A book written to set forth the basic convictions and beliefs of Christianity. ms-hs-ad.

PHYSICAL EDUCATION AND SPORTS

The ABC's of Archery—Fun for Everyone. Ben Pearson Archery, Inc. 2912 W. 2nd Ave. P.O. Box 7465. Pine Bluff, AR 71611. 1972. 15 pp. Free. Contains illustrated instructions for learning to use the bow and arrow. Includes the Archer's Code for safety. ms-hs-ad.

Basketball Was Born Here. Basketball Hall of Fame. Box 175V. Highland Station. Springfield, MA 01109. 1980. 23 pp. Free with self-addressed stamped envelope (#10). A history of basketball and the Basketball Hall of Fame. ms-hs.

►***College Sports.*** National Collegiate Athletic Assoc. P.O. Box 1906. Mission, KS 66201. Disseminates information about college athletics. Write for a free catalog that lists costs for *NCAA News,* books on college sports, rules of play, statistical-instructional guides, and research related to sports. hs-ad.

Cosom Publications. COSOM Div. Schaper Mfg. Co. P.O. Box 1426. Minneapolis, MN 55440. Send for free Safe-T-Play products catalog. Titles include:

> **Safe-T-Play Hockey Official Rule Book.** 26 pp. 75 cents. Includes chapters on organizing a hockey league and on wheelchair hockey for the handicapped. pr-el-ms-hs.

Safe-T-Play Scoop Games Official Rule Book. 22 pp. 75 cents. Diagrams, instructions, and pictures of 26 games. pr-el-ms-hs.

Don't Let Your Diet Let You Down (#1044). Cooperative Extension Service. University of Illinois at Urbana-Champaign. Urbana, IL 61801. 1980. 5 pp. 20 cents. Identifies foods and diets that athletes need. Contains a training table guide. ms-hs.

►**Ektelon's Total Racquetball.** Ektelon. Dept. FI. 8929 Aero Dr. San Diego, CA 92123. 1982. 29 pp. Free. Covers specifics of the court, equipment, strokes, serves, grips and fashions for wear on and off the court. Includes complete game rules. ms-hs.

Floor Tennis. Floor Tennis Co. 2030 W. Morse Ave. Chicago, IL 60645. 4 pp. Single copy free. Instructional pamphlet specifying equipment and regulations.

Handball Rules and Racquetball Rules. Champion Glove Manufacturing Co. 2200 E. Ovid. Des Moines, IA 50313. 20 pp. Free. Official rules for handball and racquetball. ms-hs-ad.

►**An Introduction to Physical Fitness.** The President's Council on Physical Fitness and Sports. Washington, DC 20001. 1982. 16 pp. Single copy free. A booklet discussing physical fitness and outlining an exercise program for adults. Contains illustrations and directions. ad.

►**The Olympic Games.** U.S. Olympic Committee. 1750 East Boulder St. Colorado Springs, CO 80909. Rev. 1982. 32 pp. Free in quantities up to 100. A brief description of the history, purposes, and operation of the Olympic Games. hs.

Olympic Games: What's to Become of Them? (Vol. 29, No. 7). Center for Information on America. Washington, CT 06793. 1980. 4 pp. 50 cents. Discusses the political nature of the Games and proposed changes to strengthen them as sporting events. hs.

Parents' Guide to Football Safety; or, How to Keep Your Son From Becoming a Statistic! Ginseng Press. Route 2, Box 1105. Franklin, NC 28734. 1978. 29 pp. $4.00. While aimed primarily at parents, this booklet offers much in an educational sense to teachers, coaches, students, and the public. ad.

P. E. Guides. American Alliance for Health, Physical Education, Recreation, and Dance. P.O. Box 704. Waldorf, MD 20601. Materials to assist the development and evaluation of physical education curriculum. ad. 10% discount on 10 or more copies. Titles include:

Assessment Guide for Secondary School Physical Education Programs (#020-9). 1977. 32 pp. $3.50.

Essentials of a Quality Elementary School Physical Education Program (#067-5). 1970. 16 pp. $1.95. A position statement.

Guidelines for Secondary School Physical Education: A Position Paper (#094-2). 1979. 16 pp. $1.50.

►**Recreational and Outdoor Activities** (SB-017). U.S. Gov't. Printing Office. Washington, DC 20402. 1982. 13 pp. Free. A listing of many low-cost government publications which may be used in the classroom.

Roller Skating. Chicago Roller Skate Co. 4458 W. Lake St. Chicago, IL 60624. Leaflets. Free; include 25 cents for handling and a self-addressed stamped envelope (#10). Titles include:

How to Roller Skate and Have Fun! 10 pp. Illustrated directions for learning, caring for skates, and games and tricks. el-ms-hs.

Roller Skating in Gyms or Recreation Areas. 7 pp. Discusses how roller skating can be introduced in school and recreation programs. ad.

Skating Skills. 8 pp. A comic book which gives directions for learning to skate and safety rules for indoor and outdoor skating. el-ms-hs.

The Rules of Golf (#001). U.S. Golf Association. Golf House. Far Hills, NJ 07931. 60 cents. United States Golf Association's official rules. hs-ad.

Skill Test Manuals. American Alliance for Health, Physical Education, Recreation, and Dance. P.O. Box 704. Waldorf, MD 20601. $3.95 each; 10% discount on 10 or more. Prescribes testing procedures and norms for sports skills most common to physical education programs in the elementary and middle school grades. Useful for standardized evaluation of performance and for motivating student improvement. Titles include:

Archery for Boys and Girls (#178-7). 1967. 35 pp.

Basketball for Girls (#179-5). 1966. 47 pp.

Football (#180-9). 1965. 47 pp.

Softball for Boys (#181-7). 44 pp.

Volleyball for Boys and Girls (#182-5). 1965. 36 pp.

Speed-A-Way: A Game for Boys and Girls. Marjorie Larsen. 1754 Middlefield. Stockton, CA 95204. 1970. 77 pp. $2.00. A complete guidebook to the "Speed-A-Way" game. Includes aids, rules, skill tests, and teaching hints. ms-hs.

Sports Safety Monographs. American Alliance for Health, Physical Education, Recreation, and Dance. P.O. Box 704. Waldorf, MD 20601. A series of guides for the prevention of injuries and control of hazards in sports and recreation. Titles include:

Safety in Aquatic Activities (#163-9). 1978. 72 pp. $3.95.

Safety in Individual and Dual Sports (#164-7). 1978. 72 pp. $3.95.

Safety in Outdoor Recreational Activities (#165-5). 1978. 72 pp. $3.95.

Safety in Team Sports (#162-0). 1977. 72 pp. $3.95.

Successful Jogging (#575J). Consumer Information Center. Pueblo, CO 81009. 1979. 4 pp. Free. Purpose of jogging, how to plan your program, and what equipment you will need. el. to ad.

Table Tennis. U.S. Table Tennis Assoc. Olympic House. 1750 E. Boulder St. Colorado Springs, CO 80909. Titles are:

The Official Rules of Table Tennis. 1979. 24 pp. $1.00. Easy-to-read illustrated rule book. hs-ad.

Table Tennis for Everyone. 1980. 24 pp. 25 cents. A brief history of table tennis, information about rules and equipment, tips for beginners, and terms and aspects of the sport. ms-hs-ad.

Tennis. U.S.T.A. Education and Research Center. Publications Dept. 729 Alexander Rd. Princeton, NJ 08540. Add $1.00 for postage to orders under $10.00; 20% for over $10.00. ms-hs-ad. Titles include:

►**The Code.** Rev. 1982. 45 pp. 75 cents.

►**Official Rules of Tennis and Cases and Decisions.** Annual. 16 pp. 50 cents.

►**Ten Tests for Better Tennis.** 1981. 24 pp. 25 cents.

►**Teaching Tennis to Groups.** 1974. 16 pp. $1.00.

►**The Tennis Teacher's Guide: Group Instruction and Team Coaching.** 1980. 96 pp. $4.50.

►**The Tennis Workbook** (Unit I). 1980. 64 pp. $2.95.

►**Your Body . . . Getting Ready for Sports.** Personal Products. Box FTBF. Milltown, NJ 08850. 1979. 16 pp. Classroom quantities free. Girls' and boys' versions. Discusses the importance of physical activity and sports for lifetime fitness. ms-hs.

POPULATION

Census Materials. College Curriculum Support Project. Data User Services Div. Bureau of the Census. U.S. Dept. of Commerce. Washington, DC 20233. Pamphlets, booklets, maps, and other materials based on U.S. census data are available. Titles include:

CCSP Update. Periodical. Free. Provides curriculum resources on selected themes of interest to instructors. hs-ad.

►**Census '80: Product Primers.** Series of classroom exercises. 4-8 pp. Single copy free. Each primer introduces one of the major 1980 census products. Includes lecture outlines, answer keys, and ready-to-use activities that develop statistical, analytical, and concept-related skills. hs-ad.

Factfinder for the Nation. Series of 22 brochures. Approx. 4 pp. each. Single copy free. Covers diverse aspects of the Bureau's statistical efforts, organization, programs, and products, and provides a bibliography of reference materials. A useful resource for a school library reference collection. hs-ad.

How America Studies Itself: The U.S. Census. 1980. 14 pp. Free. A teaching module on the 1980 census for high school students. A variety of activities for role playing and simulation are presented to demonstrate the purposes and procedures of the census and the importance of census information in daily life. hs-ad.

Population Analysis. Population Reference Bureau. Circulation Dept. 1337 Connecticut Ave., N.W. Washington, DC 20036. A variety of materials on population factors in the U.S. and the world is available. Request current listing.

Population Profiles. Center for Information on America. Box 276. Washington, CT 06793. A series of 17 units for the study of demography. Each unit contains charts, graphs, and text. Sample titles are:

►**The Middle East** (#5). 1980. $1.00. hs.

The Population of China (#2). 1980. 8 pp. $1.00. Discusses the history of Chinese population, distribution, growth rate, and other facts. hs.

Population of the Future (#13). 1975. 8 pp. 50 cents. A study of present population and growth trends for the future. hs.

►**The Population of India** (#3). 1980. 8 pp. $1.00. hs.

►**The Population of the Soviet Union** (#4). 1981. 8 pp. $1.00. hs.

Why Study World Population? (#1). 1980. 8 pp. $1.00. Gives essential population facts and shows the necessity for growth control if the human race is to survive. hs.

Population: The Human Dilemma (#471-14714). NSTA. 1742 Connecticut Ave., N.W. Washington, DC 20009. 1977. 104 pp. $5.00 prepaid; orders of $15.00 or less must include $2.00 for shipping. A bibliographic synopsis of authoritative literature for teachers and students. Also contains guides to curriculum materials, films, and resource organizations. ad.

Understanding Population. The Ford Foundation. 320 East 43rd St. New York, NY 10017. 1977. 39 pp. Free. Overview of the population growth and urbanization in developing countries. hs-ad.

►**U.S. Carrying Capacity: An Introduction.** Carrying Capacity. 1525 New Hampshire Ave., N.W. Washington, DC 20036. 1982. 77 pp. $3.00; additional copies $2.50 each. D.C. residents add 12 cents per copy sales tax. Urges the U.S. to reduce its population and consumption to avert economic and resource crises for future generations. hs-ad.

►**Vital and Health Statistics** (SB-121). U.S. Gov't. Printing Office. Washington, DC 20402. 1981. 6 pp. Free. A list of many low-cost government publications which may be used in the classroom.

World Bank Atlas: Gross National Product, Population, and Growth Rates. World Bank. 1818 H St., N.W. Washington, DC 20433. Rev. annually. 1981. 24 pp. $2.50. Presents estimates of population (1979); GNP at market prices and per capita (1979); and average annual growth rates (1970-79), and preliminary data for 1980, for 189 countries and territories by continent. hs-ad.

World Population. The Environmental Fund. 1302 18th St., N.W. Washington, DC 20036. Numerous materials describing present and probable future global conditions with respect to land and food supply and population growth. Sample titles are:

►**Immigration and the American Conscience.** 1981. 7 pp. $2.00. Rebuts the assumption that the U.S. is obliged to accept unlimited immigration. hs-ad.

The Other Side. Periodical. 4 pp. Free. Newsletter focused on population growth as a basic cause of most social problems. hs.

►**TEF Data: Immigration, the Labor Force, and Unemployment.** 1982. 5 pp. 25 cents. Counters the view that immigration is needed to offset a declining workforce in the U.S. hs-ad.

►**TEF Data #1: U.S. Immigration Facts.** 1981. 1 pp. 25 cents. Describes the cost of uncontrolled immigration, change in countries of origin, and population growth due to immigration. hs-ad.

RECREATION AND TRAVEL

About the Appalachian Trail. Appalachian Trail Conference. P.O. Box 236. Harpers Ferry, WV 25425. 1982. Pamphlet. Free. Contains illustrations and descriptions of the trail and how to plan a hiking trip on it. Request free brochure on available books, maps, newsletters, patches, and guides to the trail. el. to ad.

BB Rifles. Daisy Mfg. Co. Training Services Dept. Rogers, AR 72756. Single copy free to teachers. Titles include:

Daisy Rifle Book. 9 pp. How to set up a training program. hs-ad.

Suggested Course Outline for Gun Safety and Marksmanship Program. 28 pp. A 10-lesson curriculum on gun safety. hs-ad.

Bermuda. Bermuda Dept. of Tourism. Suite 2008. 235 Peachtree Street, N.E. Atlanta, GA 30303.

Bicycling—the Way to Go. Bicycle Manufacturers Association of America, Inc. 1101 15th St., N.W.—Suite 304. Washington, DC 20005. Pamphlet. 50 cents; quantity rates available. Gives advice on how to buy and inspect bicycles, rules of the road, and lists bicycling organizations and publications. el-ms-hs.

Books on the National Park System in the West. Southwest Parks and Monuments Assoc. Box 1562. Globe, AZ 85501. 1982. 10 pp. Free. An annotated listing of current offerings about western parks and related subjects. hs-ad.

Country Wisdom Bulletins. Garden Way Publishing Co. Ferry Road. Charlotte, VT 05445. 28-32 pp. each. $1.95 each; 5 or more copies $1.50 each. Add $1.00 postage and handling on orders under $5.00. A series of 80 illustrated guides to gardening, cooking, and preserving. Send for complete listing. el-ms-hs. Sample titles are:

Braiding Rugs (A-3)

Clay Flower Pots Handmade (A-29)

►**Grow Fifteen Herbs for the Kitchen** (A-61)

►**Making Cheese, Butter and Yogurt** (A-57)

►**Directory of Foreign Government Tourist Offices.** Travel Insider. P.O. Box 66323. O'Hare International Airport. Chicago, IL 60666. 1981. 24 pp. $2.00; in Canada $2.50. A comprehensive listing of official sources of information from foreign governments. Useful to teachers and students seeking literature and other materials. ad.

Duncan Yo-Yo Trick Book. Duncan Toys Co. P.O. Box 165. Baraboo, WI 53913. 1979. 45 pp. $1.00. Illustrations and instructions for performing yo-yo tricks. el-ms-hs.

Foreign Coins and Paper Money Packet. Jolie Coins. P.O. Box 68X. Roslyn Heights, NY 11577. $1.00 (U.S. currency only) for postage and handling. 18 pieces of money from such places as China, Indonesia, Hong Kong, Pakistan, India, Korea, Philippines, Finland, Israel, Formosa, El Salvador, Brazil, Belgium, and Honduras. el.

Gardening Books. Brooklyn Botanic Garden. 1000 Washington Ave. Brooklyn, NY 11225. Handbook series. $3.05 for one book; $2.05 for each additional. Well-illustrated handbooks providing authentic information and ideas to gardeners and amateur horticulturists. Send for free brochure of more than 60 titles. Titles include:

Gardening Under Lights (#93). 1960. 66 pp.

Gardening Without Pests (#89). 1979. 90 pp.

House Plants: Basic Care and Culture (#90). 1979. 66 pp.

►**Planting and Transplanting** (#97). 1982. 66 pp.

►**Pruning** (#95). 1981. 70 pp.

Rock Gardening (#91). 1980. 78 pp.

GPO Materials. U.S. Gov't. Printing Office. Washington, DC 20402. Lists of many low-cost government publications. Sample titles are:

►**Coins and Metals** (SB-198). 1981. 3 pp. Free.

►**Photography** (SB-072). 1981. 4 pp. Free.

A Guide for Disabled People. Smithsonian Institution. Visitor Information Center. Washington, DC 20560. 25 pp. Free. Brochure describing museum facilities for visiting handicapped persons. hs-ad.

Holiday Puzzlers. Hayes School Publishing Co. 321 Pennwood Ave. Wilkinsburg, PA 15221. 1976. 18 pp. $3.95. A book of duplication masters for 18 crossword puzzles related to annual holidays. el.

Introduction to Scale Model Railroading. Kalmbach Publishing Co. 1027 N. 7th St. Milwaukee, WI 53233. 1979. 31 pp. Free to libraries and schools in class quantities; 35 cents to others. A manual-type booklet which answers many questions for those interested in beginning a hobby of model railroads. Two free-loan films also available. ms-hs.

Let's Collect Rocks & Shells. Shell Oil Co. Public Affairs Dept. P.O. Box 2463. Houston, TX 77001. 21 pp. Free. A booklet on aspects of rocks and shells and on collecting them as a hobby. el-ms.

Olympic National Park. National Park Service. Olympic National Park. 600 East Park Ave. Port Angeles, WA 98362. Free guides to the park.

Philatelic Catalog. U.S. Postal Service. Philatelic Sales Div. Washington, DC 20265. 1980. Free. Listing of currently issued stamps including commemoratives. el-ms-hs.

Recreation for Disabled Persons (#571). Public Affairs Committee, Inc. 381 Park Ave. S. New York, NY 10016. 1979. 28 pp. 50 cents. Describes recreational programs desirable for handicapped persons and ways they can join in the normal activities of able-bodied persons. hs-ad.

Rocketry. Estes Industries, Inc. Robert L. Cannon, Manager of Educational Services. Dept. 165. Penrose, CO 81240. el-ms-hs. Titles include:

Camp Leader's Model Rocketry Manual (#2822). 18 pp. $1.20. A guide for introducing model rocketry into camp programs.

Guide for Aerospace Clubs (#2817). 30 pp. 95 cents. A source book for organizing and operating a successful model rocket club.

►**Model Rocket Contest Guide** (#2815). 1968. 18 pp. 95 cents. Gives rules for competitive events and suggestions for contest organization. ms-hs.

RECROC—Recreational Rocketry (#2826). 22 pp. $1.45. A guide for starting a community program in model rocketry.

Roses Are for You. All-America Rose Selections. P.O. Box 218. Shenandoah, IA 51601. 15 pp. Free. A handbook showing many uses for roses. hs-ad.

►**So You Want to Know About Orienteering** (#05010). Orienteering Services, USA. Box 1604. Binghamton, NY 13902. 1982. 11 pp. 50 cents. Tells how to begin orienteering—finding your way with map and compass over unknown ground for sport, fitness, or just fun. el-ms.

Stamp Packet. The Franklin D. Roosevelt Philatelic Society. 154 Laguna Court. St. Augustine Shores, FL 32084. Enclose 50 cents for handling and self-addressed envelope with 35 cents postage. Request Offer No. 1: A package of 10 foreign stamps and "Soliloquy of a Postage Stamp." el-ms-hs.

►***Yellowstone Park.*** National Park Service. P.O. Box 168. Yellowstone National Park, WY 82190. 1982-1983. Free; individual copies only. Brochures containing maps, points of interest, and other information about Yellowstone Park. el-ms.

SAFETY

Allstate Pamphlets. Allstate Insurance Co. Loss Prevention Director. Allstate Plaza, F-3. Northbrook, IL 60062. Free. Titles include:

Adventure by Bicycle. Tips for the young rider on bicycling fun, safety, and rules of the road. el-ms.

His Visit Just Cost You $1,553.34. Tips on how to burglarproof your home and valuables. ad.

The Joy of Bicycling (for adults only). Suggests ways to increase bicycling pleasure. ad.

A Matter of Minutes. Precautions to take against home fires. hs-ad.

Your Household Inventory Record. Charts for recording the value of articles in each room. hs-ad.

AMA Materials. American Medical Association. Order Department. P.O. Box 821. Monroe, WI 53566. Send for listing of current publications.

American Red Cross. Available from local Red Cross chapters. Materials include information on Red Cross services for safety.

Bicycle Safety. American Auto Assoc. 8111 Gatehouse Road. Falls Church, VA 22047. Materials available only from local AAA Club offices; request prices.

Can You Give First Aid? New Readers Press. Box 131. Syracuse, NY 13210. 1979. 32 pp. 95 cents. Payment must accompany order under $10.00. Simple and basic steps to follow in emergencies at home and on the highway. ms-hs-ad.

Eye Safety. National Society to Prevent Blindness. 79 Madison Ave. New York, NY 10016. Catalog of publications sent on request. Materials include:

The Eyes Have It (P620). 1975. Teaching packet. $2.00 each. Guide to teaching eye safety with seven spirit masters for classroom activities. Can be used with or without companion film (16 mm, sound-color, 8 min.) which may be borrowed for a $5.00 handling charge. ps-pr.

An Option to See (P621). 1977. Teaching packet. $3.95 per packet. Designed to encourage use of eye protection in lab and shop classes. Includes teacher's guide, a poster, overhead transparencies, 10 spirit masters, and a first aid sticker. Can be used with or without companion film (16 mm, sound-color, 17 min.) which may be borrowed for $5.00 handling. ms-hs.

See Your Future. Poster. 24″ x 31″. $1.00. Three-color wall poster encouraging use of safety eyewear in lab and shop classes. hs.

Fire Safety. Burger King Corporation. 7360 N. Kendall Dr. Miami, FL 33156. Titles include:

Snuffy's Fire Safety Brigade. 16 mm film. Color. Sound. 14 min. Free-loan; user pays return postage. Available from participating Burger King restaurants and from Modern Talking Picture Service. 5000 Park St. N. Petersburg, FL 33709. el.

►**Make Time for Fire Safety.** 2nd ed. 1981. $5.00. A classroom unit for grades K-6 containing 16 oversized flash cards, 12 duplicating worksheets, two poster-sized game boards, and an educator's resource guide. Send check or money order payable to Burger King Fire Safety Program to: Robert Landau Distribution and Fulfillment Center. 179 Saw Mill River Rd. Yonkers, NY 10701. Attn: Fire Safety Order Dept.

For Safety's Sake (N81100). American Gas Assoc. 1515 Wilson Blvd. Arlington, VA 22209. Also available from local gas companies. 35 frames with cassette. 35 mm. Color. Free. Cartoon characters present information of gas appliance safety as well as what to do if one smells gas. Includes teacher's guide. K-G4.

Games That Teach (MP-59). Federal Emergency Management Agency. Defense Civil Preparedness Agency. Washington, DC 20472. Rev. 1975. 96 pp. Free. Describes classroom games designed to teach concepts of civil preparedness for natural disaster and nuclear attack. el-ms-hs.

GPO Materials. U.S. Gov't. Printing Office. Washington, DC 20402. Lists of many low-cost government publications. Sample titles are:

►**Accidents and Accident Prevention** (SB-229). 1982. 6 pp. Free.

►**Fire Fighting, Prevention, and Forest Fires** (SB-076). 1981. 10 pp. Free.

Health and Safety Educational Materials Catalog. Metropolitan Life Insurance Co. Health and Safety Education Div. 1 Madison Ave. New York, NY 10010. 11 pp. Free in reasonable quantities for educational programs. Catalog describes inexpensive leaflets, posters, films, and other teaching aids for health and safety subjects. Many are free in single copies. ad.

Home Is Where the Hurt Is. The Travelers Film Library. 1 Tower Square. Hartford, CT 06115. 35 mm color slides with audio cassette. 10 min. Free loan; borrower must pay return postage. Shows how to eliminate unsafe work and play conditions that cause over four million home accidents yearly. ms-hs.

►**It's Your Move.** The Travelers Film Library. 1 Tower Square. Hartford, CT 06115. 16 mm. 10 min. Color. Free-loan; borrower must pay return postage. Presents ten common auto-bicycle accident situations and lets the viewer decide on evasive action. Includes teacher's discussion guide, wall poster, and bicycle safety club materials. Spanish version available. G4-6.

Let's Learn About Safety. Eli Lilly and Co. Public Relations Services. 307 E. McCarty St. Indianapolis, IN 46285. 8 pp. Free in classroom quantities to teachers of grades K-5. Request on school letterhead. Designed to teach children the concepts of safety. Illustrated. pr-el.

Life Saving Kit. Institute of Makers of Explosives. Suite 550. Attn: Dept. A. 1575 Eye St., N.W. Washington, DC 20005. Free; limit 5 per order. Contains posters and bookmarks. Explains the potential danger of blasting caps which might be found near sites of blasting operations. el.

McDonald's Films. McDonald's Corporation. 16 mm films. Color. Sound. Available through the Community Relations Representative at local McDonald's restaurants. Also available for purchase from: Dennis Films, Inc. 161 Erie St. Chicago, IL 60611. Titles are:

> **Bicycles Are Beautiful.** 26 min. A film narrated by Bill Cosby which presents an amusing history of bicycles and features a bicycle safety quiz. Teacher's guide with spirit masters and reproducible test blanks accompany film. el.
>
> **Home Safe Home.** 21 min. A film starring Barbara Eden which teaches elementary students valuable lessons about safety in the home. Includes teacher's materials and a poster.

Motorcycle Safety. U.S. Dept. of Transportation. National Highway Traffic Safety. Washington, DC 20590. 1976. 20 pp. Free. Points out risks involved and measures necessary to insure safety in motorcycle operation. hs.

Product Safety Materials. U.S. Consumer Product Safety Commission. Washington, DC 20207. Many pamphlets, leaflets, and other materials are available; request catalog.

Safeco Booklets. Safeco Insurance Co. Attn: Marketing, T-21. Safeco Plaza. Seattle, WA 98185. Available free to nonprofit organizations in moderate quantities. Titles are:

►**Auto Insurance Handbook.** 1982. 16 pp. Explains basic auto insurance coverages. hs-ad.

►**Safe Boating Guide.** 1981. 52 pp. Covers boating do's and don'ts, Coast Guard rules, equipment, requirements, emergency procedures, glossary, and more. el. to ad.

►**Safe Driving Guide.** 1979. 48 pp. Covers defensive driving techniques, recreational vehicle safety, what to do if an accident occurs, and ways to get better gas mileage. hs-ad.

►**Stop Thief.** 1981. 28 pp. Tips on protecting oneself from crime losses, including burglary, street crime, auto theft, sexual assault, and confidence rackets. hs-ad.

Safety Pamphlets. American Mutual Insurance Cos. Institute for Safer Living. Wakefield, MA 01880. Up to 200 copies free when requested on official stationery. Titles are:

Babysitter's Pledge. Outlines the major responsibilities of a babysitter including those for emergencies. ms-hs.

How Not to Get the Break of Your Life. How to build safe stairways, keep them safe, and use them safely. hs-ad.

►**Night Fires.** What to do and how to plan an escape. hs-ad.

So You Think You Know All About Ladders. Rules for using a ladder. hs-ad.

Questions to Help You Be a Safe Driver. A test that determines ability to handle a car accident-free under varying conditions. hs-ad.

Your Home Can Be as Safe as You Make It. Safety checklist for all areas of the home. el-ms-hs-ad.

Safe Water Skiing. American Water Ski Assoc. P.O. Box 191. Winter Haven, FL 33880. Free. Titles include:

Safe Boat Driving for Water Skiing. 4 pp.

Safety in Water Skiing. 8 pp.

Water Skiing Fundamentals. 8 pp.

►**Sparky's Fire Department.** National Fire Protection Assoc. Batterymarch Park. Quincy, MA 02269. 1982. 50 cents. A fire prevention kit that includes a badge, membership card, and inspection handbook for checking your home for fire hazards. ps-el.

State Farm Leaflets. State Farm Insurance Cos. Public Relations Dept. 1 State Farm Plaza. Bloomington, IL 61701. Free in classroom quantities. A variety of pamphlets on safety and accident prevention. el-ms. Titles include:

►**The Car, the Road and You**

Don't Make Waves (Boating)

Enjoy Your Wood Burning Stove . . . the Safe Way

Legend of Fire

Safe Bicycling Quiz

State Farm Safe Home Guide

Surelocked Homes: Making Entry Less Elementary

►**WATCH: A Safe Neighborhood Is Everyone's Concern**

►**Your Dollars Are Burning**

Teaching Safety in the Elementary School (#188-4). American Alliance for Health, Physical Education, Recreation, and Dance. P.O. Box 704. Waldorf, MD 20601. Rev. 1972. 32 pp. $1.95. General safety information for teachers, methods for teaching, and utilization of learning experiences. ad.

We Ride the School Bus. Dept. of Public Instruction. Attn: Connie Storley. GEF III Bldg. 125 S. Webster St. Madison, WI 53707. Undated. Pamphlet. Sample copy free when requester sends stamped, self-addressed, long envelope; 50 copies for $1.50. Rules for riding a bus presented to encourage safe habits and good bus riding attitudes. el.

SCIENCE

►**AAAS Products.** AAAS. Product Marketing Dept. 10th Flr. 1101 Vermont Ave. N.W. Washington, DC 20035. Free upon request. Brochures describing books, tapes, reprints, and items available from the American Association for the Advancement of Science.

Air Pollution Experiments. High School Edition. Prof. Joseph J. Soporowski, Jr. Dept. of Environmental Science. Rutgers University. P.O. Box 231. New Brunswick, NJ 08903. Rev. 1970. 20 pp. Single copy free. Presents five experiments which tell the story of contaminated air. hs.

Ancient Astronauts: (#53). Pro and Con P.P.I. Publishing. P.O. Box 335. Dayton, OH 45459. 1979. 41 pp. $2.75. Examines the arguments for and against the earth having been visited by astronauts in ancient times. ms-hs.

A Century of Light. Thomas Alva Edison Foundation. Cambridge Office Plaza. Suite 143. 18280 W. Ten Mile Rd. Southfield, MI 48075. Undated. Three graded activity kits; K-3, 4-6, or upper level. Each kit contains a 17″ x 22″ chart, six spirit-duplicating activity masters, and teacher's guide printed on a file folder. $2.50 postpaid; 10 or more kits, $2.00 each plus shipping. Interdisciplinary materials that lead students into an exploration of some aspect of social studies, science, or the language arts. pr-el-ms.

►**A Chemistry Project From Start to Finish.** American Chemical Society. Education Div. Career Services. 1155 16th St., N.W. Washington, DC 20036. 1982. 13 pp. 50 cents; quantity rates available. Tells how to approach a project in an organized manner from selecting an idea to preparing an exhibit. hs.

The Child and Science: Wondering, Exploring, Growing. Assoc. for Childhood Education International. 3615 Wisconsin Ave., N.W. Washingon, DC 20016. 1977. 48 pp. $2.75 plus 10% for postage; prepay in U.S. currency. Thirty suggestions for innovative and practical science activities for 2 to 12 year olds.

►**The Earth: Our Restless Blue Planet** (SC-4304). World Book, Inc. Merchandise Mart Plaza. Chicago, IL 60654. 1983. 8-page foldout. 20 cents. A guide for the student's independent study of our planet on its journey through space; its atmosphere, the land and the oceans on its surface, and the forces at work on it and inside it. hs.

►**Exceptional Black Scientists.** CIBA—GEIGY Corp. Ardsley, NY 10502. 1980. Posters. 16″ x 20″. First set free; additional sets $1.00 each. Series of nine color posters that depict black scientists and give synopses of their contributions. ms-hs.

Experiments. Fisher Scientific Co. Educational Materials Div. 4901 West LeMoyne St. Chicago, IL 60651. Titles are:

- ►**How Book of Science** (AS51324). 1982. 144 pp. $4.00. Contains 149 unusual experiences to illustrate basic principles of life science, air, heat, sound, chemistry, mechanics, light, electricity, astronomy, and health. Also an activity supplement for advanced students. el-ms-hs.

- ►**pH Educational Lab Experiment Manual** (AS60005). 1980. 48 pp. $4.95. Introduces acids and bases, concept of pH, and electrodes and their reactions. Includes formulas, equations, and diagrams. Outlines twelve lab experiments with theory, step-by-step procedures, and study questions. hs-ad.

Experiment Booklets. Thomas Alva Edison Foundation. Cambridge Office Plaza. Suite 143. 18280 W. Ten Mile Rd. Southfield, MI 48075. A series of nine 32-page booklets containing simple experiments in such areas as energy sources, energy conservation, electricity, magnetism, and the environment. 50 cents each; 3 for $1.00. el-ms-hs. Send for complete listing. Titles are:

Alternative Energy Sources

Electrical and Chemical Experiments

Energy Conservation

Environmental Experiments

Lewis Latimer . . . A Black Inventor

Nuclear Experiments

Selected Experiments

Simple Experiments on Magnetism and Electricity

Useful Science Projects

►**General Science Laboratory Experiences Using Dixie Cups.** James River-Dixie/Northern, Inc. Consumer Affairs Dept. P.O. Box 2260. Greenwich, CT 06830. 1956. 41 pp. Free. Step-by-step procedures that demonstrate principles in areas of matter, air, heat, light, sound, and plants. Illustrated. el.

Glossary of Electronic Terms. Henry Lavin Associates, Inc. 12 Promontory Dr. Cheshire, CT 06410. 1972. 38 pp. $1.50. Provides the user with definitions and helpful descriptions of electronic expressions. hs-ad.

Golden Guides. Western Publishing Company, Inc. Education Div. 150 Parish Dr. Wayne, NJ 07470. $2.95 each. Easy-to-use science guides which contain a remarkable amount of information. Request current listing.

GPO Materials. U.S. Gov't. Printing Office. Washington, DC 20402. Lists of many low-cost government publica ions. Sample titles are:

►**Anthropology and Archeology** (SB-205). 1981. 5 pp. Free.

►**Earth Sciences** (SB-160). 1981. 29 pp. Free.

►**Oceanography** (SB-032). 1981. 12 pp. Free.

►**Science Experiments and Projects** (SB-243). 1981. 14 pp. Free.

"How-To" Materials. National Science Teachers Assoc. 1742 Connecticut Ave., N.W. Washington, DC 20009. Titles include:

How to . . . Activities in Meteorology. 1978. 121 pp. $1.50. An activity guide. ms-hs.

How to . . . Activities in Physical Oceanography. 1978. 8 pp. $1.50. An activity guide. ms-hs.

How to Ask the Right Questions. 1975. 8 pp. $1.50. A guide to using a classroom questioning strategy. ad.

How to Teach Measurements in Elementary School Science. 1969. 12 pp. $1.50. How to help youngsters develop concepts about measurement in science activities. Illustrated. pr-el.

International Atomic Weights and Periodic Chart of the Elements. Allied Chemical Advertising Dept. P.O. Box 2064R. Morristown, NJ 07960. Classroom quantities free to teachers when requested on school stationery. A table of international atomic weights and periodic chart. hs-ad.

Light. GTE Lighting Products. Public Affairs Dept. Sylvania Lighting Center. Danvers, MA 01923. Leaflets. Films also available on cost-free basis; write for information. Titles are:

> **Light and Man: A History of Human Achievement.** 1973. 6 pp. Free. Recounts the development of the light bulb. el-ms.
>
> ►**Light and Man: Saving Lighting Energy.** 1981. 6 pp. Free. Discusses ways to save lighting energy. el-ms.
>
> **Light and Man: Radiant Energy.** 1977. 5 pp. Free. Discusses applications of radiant energy. el-ms.
>
> **Light and Man: The Evolution of Lighting.** Wall poster. Free. el-ms.

The Microscope. Bausch & Lomb, Inc. Dept. 6606. Optics Center. Rochester, NY 14602. Request current listing of publications. Also request information about free-loan science and vision films.

Mini-Experiments. Edmund Scientific Co. 7082 Edscorb Bldg. Barrington, NJ 08007. Send for listing of current materials.

Motion Picture Film Services of the U.S. Geological Survey. U.S. Dept. of the Interior. Geological Survey. Visual Services. 303 National Center. Reston, VA 22092. 1980. 19 pp. Free. A catalog of free loan films. Subjects include topographic mapping, geology, water resources, astrogeology, and aerial photo interpretation. hs-ad.

Natural Gas. American Gas Assoc. 1515 Wilson Blvd. Arlington, VA 22209. Materials also available free from local gas companies. Request catalog, *Natural Gas Teaching Aids,* for listing. Sample titles are:

> **Experiments: Properties of Gas and Heat Energy** (N00085). 1971. 48 pp. 17 experiments on properties of gas and 14 experiments on heat energy. Prepared on spirit masters for reproduction by the teacher. ms-hs.
>
> **Science Behind Your Burner** (N00010). 35 mm. Color. A film strip kit with charts, pupil materials, a gas pipeline map of the U.S., and teacher's guide. ms.
>
> **Science Principles and Gas Appliances With Experiments** (N00500). 1970. 32 pp. Booklet on science principles used in six gas home appliances and twelve classroom experiments. Includes materials for overhead projection and a spirit master for student report sheets. el-ms-hs.

What Is a Gas? (N00550). 1972. 44 pp. A book of 12 classroom demonstrations and experiments for learning about matter that exists in a gaseous state—colorless, odorless, tasteless, and silent. el-ms.

Oceanography Publications. National Ocean Survey, NOAA. Physical Science Services Branch. Rockville, MD 20852. Titles include:

List of Free and Inexpensive Educational Materials. 2 pp. Free. List of maps, pamphlets, photos, films, and charts available in limited quantities. An Oceanography Packet and a Science Packet are offered to instructors.

Our Restless Tides. 1978. 21 pp. Free. Describes sea motions and tidal waves, and the types, ranges, and prediction of tides. ms-hs.

Summary of National Ocean Survey Technical Publications and Charts. 1978. Free. Lists hundreds of technical and over 50 non-technical materials obtainable from the NOS.

Periodic Chart of the Elements. Merck and Co., Inc. P.O. Box 2000. Rahway, NJ 07065. 1976. 4 pp. Free. Chart of 103 natural elements in order of their nuclear charge; gives atomic number, atomic symbol, atomic weight, electronic configuration, and other data for each. hs-ad.

►**Popular Publications of the U.S. Geological Survey.** U.S. Geology Survey. Eastern Distribution Branch. Text Products Section. 604 S. Pickett St. Alexandria, VA 22304. 1980. 26 pp. Free. A catalog describing popular titles presently available from the Geological Survey.

►**Science Challenge.** Curriculum Innovations, Inc. 3500 Western Ave. Highland Park, IL 60035. Magazine. 9 issues yearly. Sample issue free to teachers. Each issue contains a variety of articles on science and its impact on society. ms-hs.

Science Education. National Science Teachers Assoc. 1742 Connecticut Ave., N.W. Washington, DC 20009. Sample titles are:

American Black Scientists and Inventors. 1975. 79 pp. $5.00. Motivation stories of 12 black Americans who made great contributions to science and technology.

Science Education for You? 1975. 20 pp. $2.00. Describes the many kinds of positions in science education, helps students evaluate their abilities and interests, and suggests ways to prepare for a career in science education. hs.

Science Experiments. Chevron Chemical Co. Growing Ideas. P.O. Box 3744. San Francisco, CA 94119. Single copy free to teachers; 1-49 copies, 50 cents each. Kit includes:

Growing Ideas Kit. 1977. Eleven cards with numerous classroom experiences about weather, seasonal changes, how plants grow, and so on. pr-el.

Learning on the Light Side. 1977. 8 pp. A science unit on how light and gravity affects plants. pr-el.

Science Experiments for Children. Dover Publications, Inc. 180 Varick St. New York, NY 10014. Each book contains basic information and a number of experiments ranging from simple to complex. Titles include:

Chemistry Experiments for Children. 1968. 95 pp. $2.50. el.

Electricity Experiments for Children. 1968. 95 pp. $2.50. el.

Physics Experiments for Children. 1968. 95 pp. $2.50. el.

Science Experiments for Children. 1968. 95 pp. $2.25. el.

The Search for Solutions. The Search for Solutions Booking Center. 708 3rd Ave. New York, NY 10017. A free-loan film series of nine 18-minute, 16 mm, color-sound films. Teaching guide and materials available. Concepts are taught through the study of the scientific process. Looks at all phases of science and relates them to everyday environment. ms-hs.

►**Thousands of Science Projects.** Science Service. 1719 N St., N.W. Washington, DC 20036. $1.00 prepaid. A listing of several thousands of projects performed and shown at science fairs. Arranged in Library of Congress subject classification. hs.

The Woods Hole Oceanographic Institution. The Woods Hole Oceanographic Institution. Woods Hole, MA 02543. 1980. 4 pp. Free. Describes the institution's history and current day function. hs-ad.

Words of Science and the History Behind Them. New American Library. 1633 Broadway, New York, NY 10019. 1959. 319 pp. $1.95. Explores, explains, and illuminates the scientific vocabulary by tracing 1,500 terms from their simple roots. hs-ad.

SEX EDUCATION

AMA Materials. American Medical Assoc. Order Dept. P.O. Box 821. Monroe, WI 53566. Send for listing of current materials.

Female Development and Hygiene. Personal Products. Consumer Information Center. Box FIL. Milltown, NJ 08850. A variety of aids for instruction on menstruation and female development are available, including booklets, transparencies, spirit masters, a teacher's guide, and free-loan film (English, Spanish, or captioned). Request catalogue. Single copies of booklets are free (including Braille editions). Sample titles are:

►**For Boys—A Book About Girls.** 1981. 10 pp. Set of 25 copies, $2.00; Braille edition $1.50 each. For boys 9 to 13 years old.

►**Growing Up and Liking It.** 1982. 25 pp. Set of 25 copies, $2.50; Braille edition $1.50 each. For girls 9 to 13 years old. Also available in Spanish.

►**How Shall I Tell My Daughter?** 1981. 13 pp. Set of 25 copies, $2.00. For parents. ad.

►**The Menstrual Cycle . . . More Than Your Period.** 1980. Limited quantities free. For women 18 to 35 years old. Also available in Spanish.

►**Your Body After Childbirth.** 1982. 4 pp. Limited quantities free. For new mothers.

►**Your Teenage Menstrual Cycle.** 1980. 4 pp. Limited quantities free. For girls 13 to 18 years old. Also available in Spanish.

►**Finding Yourself** (#070-5). American Alliance for Health, Physical Education, Recreation, and Dance, P.O. Box 704, Waldorf, MD 20601. Rev. 1981. 32 pp. $2.95. For use by boys and girls of junior high school age and their teachers. ms.

Guides. Planned Parenthood Assoc. of Southeastern Pennsylvania. 1220 Sansom St. Philadelphia, PA 19107. Titles include:

Love, Sex, and Birth Control for the Mentally Retarded: A Guide for Parents. 1971. 40 pp. $2.25; prepaid orders only. Offers advice for providing sex education to retarded children.

Sexuality . . . Decisions, Attitudes, Relationships. 1979. 35 pp. $2.30; prepaid orders only. Presents ways to clarify your own feelings about your relationships and your sexuality. ms-hs.

Having a Baby Series. New Readers Press. Box 131. Syracuse, NY 13210. Payment must accompany order under $10.00. ms-hs. Titles include:

Having a Baby. 1975. 168 pp. $3.50. Presents every aspect of pregnancy with related medical information. Reading level 5.1. ms-hs.

Pamphlets. Information from the book presented in pamphlet form. Titles are:

The Baby and the Family. 1973. 24 pp. 60 cents.

Conception and Pregnancy. 1973. 20 pp. 60 cents.

The First Six Weeks. 1974. 40 pp. 75 cents.

Giving Birth. 1973. 24 pp. 60 cents.

Prenatal Care. 1973. 28 pp. 60 cents.

Unwed Mother. 1975. 24 pp. 60 cents.

Life Cycle Instructional Aid. Kimberly-Clark Corp. P.O. Box 9474. St. Paul, MN 55194. Four booklets and related instructional aids such as filmstrip, film, and chart. Booklets are 10 cents each; send payment with orders of $5.00 or less. Titles are:

►**The Miracle of You.** Rev. 1981. 23 pp. Discusses the female reproductive system and its development. ms-hs.

►**Tell It Like It Is.** Rev. 1981. 10 pp. Explains the use of tampons. Illustrated instructions. ms-hs.

►**Very Personally Yours.** Rev. 1981. 22 pp. Covers menstruation, exercise, and nutrition. ms-hs.

►**Your New Self-Discovery.** Rev. 1981. 39 pp. Focuses on emotional and sexual maturity, and health and medical care. ms-hs.

Life Cycle Materials. Kimberly-Clark Corp. The Life Cycle Center.® P.O. Box 2001. Neenah, WI 54956. Write for details and sample copies of family life student booklets and catalog of related aids.

Materials in Spanish. U.S. Gov't. Printing Office. Washington, DC 20402. Also send for *Publicaciones en Espanol* (SB-130) for a free listing of other low-cost government publications which may be used in the classroom. Sample title is:

Methodos Anticonceptivos en la Planification Familiar (Contraceptive Methods in Family Planning). (SN 017-031-00018-0). 1977. 1 p. 50 cents.

Menstruation. Tampax Inc. Dept. GP. P.O. Box 7001. Lake Success, NY 11042. Available without charge to teachers, students, advisers, librarians, and parents. Also ask about the free-loan film *Accent on You.* ms. Titles include:

Accent on You. Classroom quantities. A booklet for girls ages 9 to 14.

Dispelling the Menstrual Myth. One to a teacher. Outlines topics to include in a menstrual health teaching unit.

Female Anatomical Charts. 8½" x 11"; classroom size 17" x 22". Limited classroom quantity available to teachers and school nurses.

From Fiction to Fact. One to a teacher. A teaching guide to the correct understanding of menstrual health.

Oral (and other) Contraceptives (#219). Do It Now Foundation. P.O. Box 5115. Phoenix, AZ 85010. 1979. 12 pp. 50 cents. Discusses ways to control family size and the effects on the body of birth control pills. hs-ad.

Pamphlets. U.S. Public Health Service. Health Resources Services Administration. Room 7-15. Rockville, MD 20857. Titles are:

Changes (HSA 80-5648). 16 pp. Free. An explanation of puberty written for adolescents. el-ms.

Changes and Choices (HSA 80-5647). 16 pp. Free. Suggestions for parents on how to discuss sex with children and teenagers. ad.

Choices (HSA 80-5699). 16 pp. Free. Suggestions for teenagers on how to think through decisions regarding behavior. ms-hs.

Planning Your Family. New Readers Press. Box 131. Syracuse, NY 13210. Rev. 1975. 24 pp. 50 cents prepaid. Explains birth control and various contraceptives available. el-ms.

Public Affairs Pamphlets. Public Affairs Committee, Inc. 381 Park Ave. S. New York, NY 10016. 50 cents each; quantity rates available. Sample titles are:

> **Changing Views of Homosexuality** (#563). 1978. 28 pp. Explains what homosexuality is, presents different views of its origins, traces past and present attitudes and laws, and offers guidance to parents. hs-ad.
>
> **Family Planning—Today's Choices** (#513A). 1980. 28 pp. Summarizes findings on methods of contraception and considers special problems of unwanted pregnancies among teenagers. ad.
>
> **Schools and Parents—Partners in Sex Education** (#581). 1980. 28 pp. Proposes a curriculum for family life education programs; includes resource list. hs.
>
> **Sex Education: The Parents' Role** (#549). 1977. 28 pp. Contains information for parents to use in answering children's questions about sex. ad.
>
> **Talking to Preteenagers About Sex** (#476). 1972. 25 pp. A consultant on child development and parent education stresses the significance of the attitudes transmitted from parent to child. ad.
>
> ►**Teenage Pregnancy—What Can Be Done?** (#594). 1981. 28 pp. Presents the problem of teenage pregnancy, the options for dealing with it, and the controversy over those options. hs-ad.

Sex Education for Adolescents: A Bibliography of Low-Cost Materials. American Library Assoc. Order Dept. 50 E. Huron St. Chicago, IL 60611. 1980. 32 pp. $2.00. Offers commentary on the content and style of 83 publications on sexuality. Entries are classified and cross-referenced. ad.

Sex Education for the Visually Handicapped in Schools and Agencies: Selected Papers. American Foundation for the Blind, Inc. 15 W. 16th St. New York, NY 10011. 1975. 76 pp. $4.50. An informative analysis and instructional approach to be used in teaching blind-born children about sexuality. ad.

SIECUS Publications. Sex Information and Education Council of the U.S. 80 5th Ave., Suite 801. New York, NY 10011. Several resource publications for sex educational programs; request free catalog. Order must include self-addressed stamped envelope (#10). Titles include:

> **Bibliography of Religious Publications on Sexuality and Sex Education.** 1980. 2 pp. 25 cents.
>
> **Bibliographies of Holdings of the SIECUS Resource Center and Library at New York University.** 2 pp. Free.

Human Sexuality: A Selected Bibliography for Professionals. $1.00.

Human Sexuality: Books for Everyone. $1.00.

►**Sexuality and Disability: A Selected Annotated Bibliography.** $1.00.

VD Education. American Social Health Assoc. 260 Sheridan Ave., Suite 307. Palo Alto, CA 94306. A variety of materials on venereal diseases are available. Send for current listing.

SOCIAL PROBLEMS

Developing Insights Into Aging. Minnesota Home Economics Assoc. c/o Karen S. Foot. 5702 Holiday Rd. Minnetonka, MN 55343. 1978. 73 pp. $4.75; 10% discount on ten copies or more. An annotated bibliography of over 500 resources on aging. ad.

Hunger on Spaceship Earth Simulation Game. American Friends Service Committee. 15 Rutherford Pl. New York, NY 10003. 1976. $2.00 postpaid. Creates understandings of some inequities present in the world social and economic situation and of some feelings of helplessness they cause. ms-hs.

Public Affairs Pamphlets. Public Affairs Committee, Inc. 381 Park Ave. S. New York, NY 10016. 50 cents each; quantity rates available. Titles include:

Ageism—Discrimination Against Older People (#575). 1979. 28 pp. Discusses the forms of ageism and what can be done about them. Includes resource list. hs-ad.

►**Compulsive Gambling** (#598). 1981. 28 pp. Describes the illness of compulsive gambling, its causes and signs, and some techniques of treatment. Also outlines gambling's popularity and the issue of legalized gambling. hs-ad.

Compulsory Retirement: Pros and Cons (#555). 1978. 28 pp. Presents the arguments of proponents and opponents to this complex issue, the problems of retirement in general, and some alternatives. hs-ad.

►**Family Neglect and Abuse of the Aged: A Growing Concern** (#603). 1982. 28 pp. Discusses reasons that elderly persons are neglected and abused, that their plight is often unknown, and that protective services are lacking. hs-ad.

Jobs for Handicapped Persons: A New Era in Civil Rights (#557). 1978. 28 pp. Covers removal of architectural barriers, reasonable accommodation, job discrimination, and programs to increase opportunities. hs-ad.

Nursing Homes: Strategy for Reform (#561). 1979. 28 pp. Analyzes the problems of nursing home care and suggests actions to make certain that nursing homes provide a high quality care. hs-ad.

Public Welfare: Facts, Myths, and Prospects (#554A). 1980. 28 pp. Identifies various programs of social welfare, explains how and for whom they work, cites persistent problems, and analyzes recent reform proposals. hs-ad.

Runaway Teenagers (#552). 1977. 28 pp. Discusses the reasons young people leave home, some programs to help runaways and their parents, and some advice on family relations. hs-ad.

►**To Combat and Prevent Child Abuse and Neglect** (#588). 1981. 28 pp. Discusses causes of child maltreatment, ways of helping abused children and their parents, and steps that can be taken to prevent abuse and neglect. hs-ad.

►**The Unseen Alcoholics—the Elderly** (#602). 1982. 24 pp. Explains why older people can be especially vulnerable to becoming problem drinkers, but often they are neither noticed nor helped. hs-ad.

Where Older People Live: Living Arrangements for the Elderly (#556). 1978. 28 pp. Examines different types of housing and services for the elderly and why more public action is needed for affordable housing which also meets other needs of the elderly. hs-ad.

Racial and Economic Problems. Southern Regional Council, Inc. 52 Fairlie St., N.W. Atlanta, GA 30303. Request an annotated listing of publications focusing on the problems of discrimination and poverty in the southern region.

Silicon Valley: Paradise or Paradox? The Impact of High Technology Industry on Santa Clara County. Pacific Studies Center. 222B View St. Mountain View, CA 94041. 1977. 62 pp. $2.50. An analysis of various social costs of high technology industry in one U.S. region. ad.

Some Options for the Aging. Hogg Foundation for Mental Health. University of Texas, Austin, TX 78712. 1978. 23 pp. 90 cents. A reprint from the *Pursuit of Dignity* in which some alternative living patterns for the elderly that may lessen the need for institutional care are examined. hs.

Vital Issues. Center for Information on America. Washington, CT 06793. A continuous series of discussion guides on current public and social issues designed for high school classes. Teacher's guide available for each edition. Sample titles are:

The American Eater: Some Nutritional Problems and Some Solutions (Vol. 29, No. 2). 4 pp. 50 cents. Points out the danger of Americans becoming undernourished due to their lifestyle and ways to remedy these deficiencies. hs.

Attitudes Toward the Elderly: Do We Honor and Respect Our Senior Citizens? (Vol. 20, No. 6). 1980. 4 pp. 50 cents. Examines ill effects of ageism and how this problem is gradually being changed through education and training. hs.

Blacks in the Suburbs: Their Number Is Rising, but Patterns of Segregation Persist. What Are the Causes? (Vol. 27, No. 4). 1977. 4 pp. 45 cents. Explains how suburbs are becoming as segregated as inner cities. hs.

Child Abuse: What Resources for Meeting the Problem? (Vol. 28, No. 2). 1978. 4 pp. 45 cents. Covers the serious problem of child abuse, several sample cases, and methods of prevention and treatment. hs.

The Impact of Social Change on Children and Young People (Vol. 27, No. 5). 1978. 4 pp. 45 cents. Teaching young people to live responsibly as adults entails meeting the effects of social change. hs.

Latchkey Children (Vol. 30, No. 3). 1980. 4 pp. 60 cents. Focuses on the risks associated with children whose parents work. hs.

Our Dietary Habits (Vol. 24, No. 2). 4 pp. 45 cents. Presents livestock consumption trends in developed nations and the economic, ecological, health, and moral reasons to modify diets. hs.

The Public Library: What Is Its Place and Function in the United States? (Vol. 29, No. 3). 1979. 4 pp. 50 cents. Discusses the precarious financial situation which threatens the well-being of public libraries in the U.S. hs.

The Suburbanization of Corporate Headquarters: What Are the Trends and Consequences? (Vol. 27, No. 8). 1978. 4 pp. 45 cents. Discusses the effects of the trend for corporations to relocate to the suburbs. hs.

Youth Unemployment: A Critical Problem. How to Respond to It. (Vol. 26, No. 9). 1977. 4 pp. 45 cents. Presents the problems of youth unemployment and possible solutions through public and private action. hs.

SOCIAL STUDIES

America, My Country. Hayes School Publishing Co., Inc. 321 Pennwood Ave. Wilkinsburg, PA 15221. 1976. 48 pp. $1.95; quantity prices available. A social studies book for primary grades. pr.

Circus! (#332). Curriculum Bulletin. Oceanside, OR 97134. 1976. 24 pp. $1.50 postpaid; payment must accompany order. A teaching unit; includes history, terminology, activities for teaching, and bibliography. pr-el.

Clarifying Values Through Subject Matter. Winston Press. 430 Oak Grove. Suite 203. Minneapolis, MN 55403. 1973. 146 pp. $4.95. Contains sample lessons for 20 different subjects using the three-level approach of facts, concepts, and value teaching. el-ms.

Days to Celebrate. Women's International League for Peace and Freedom. United States Section. 1213 Race St. Philadelphia, PA 19107. 1978. 47 pp. $3.75 postpaid. Traditional and untraditional holidays and celebrations are described, particularly special days that stress independent thought and individual initiative. el-ms.

Earthbeats (#2). Communications Office. University of Wisconsin. Sea Grant Institute. 1800 University Ave. Madison, WI 53706. 1978. 10 pp. 60 cents. A newspaper edition about how the Great Lakes came into being, the problems they are facing, and what life is like in and around these inland seas. ms-hs.

Earth's People: The Four Billion (SC-4305). World Book, Inc. Merchandise Mart Plaza. Chicago, IL 60654. 1977. 8-page foldout. 20 cents. A guide for the student's independent study. Explores the interesting people who share our planet through *World Book* articles about the nations of the world and their peoples' lives. ms-hs.

►**A Fact Sheet for Americans.** International Labor Organization. Washington Branch. 1750 New York Ave., N.W. Washington, DC 20006. Free. A leaflet describing the purposes and work of the ILO, created in 1919 and now having 132 member nations. hs.

Family Life. National Council on Family Relations. 1219 University Ave., S.E. Minneapolis, MN 55414. Reports, reprints, books, and pamphlets on various aspects of family life and family relations. Send for publications lists.

Fawcett Books. Fawcett Books. Educational Marketing Dept. 1515 Broadway. New York, NY 10036. Write for list of books in the category of social studies.

Future Planning Games Series. Greenhaven Press. 577 Shoreview Park Rd. St. Paul, MN 55112. 1973 to 1980. $1.95 each; add 7% for shipping ($2.00 min.). A series of 13 simulation games that provide one or two weeks of classroom activities. hs. Titles include:

Constructing a Life Philosophy

►**Constructing a Political Philosophy**

Determining America's Role in the World

Determining Economic Values

Determining Family and Sexual Roles

Protecting Minority Rights

Geography. National Ocean Survey, NOAA. Physical Science Services Branch. 6001 Executive Blvd. Rockville, MD 20852. Several non-technical pamphlets are available. Request listing. Sample titles are:

Geographic Center of the United States. 1 p. Free. Shows the changing geographic center from 1918 to present. ms-hs.

The Gulf Stream. 1968. 5 pp. Free. Describes the Gulf Stream current and includes three maps. ms-hs.

►**Principal Rivers and Lakes of the World.** 1982. 54 pp. Free. Information on rivers and lakes including location, size, and length. el. to ad.

►**Global Education Resource Guide.** Global Education Associates. 552 Park Ave. East Orange, NJ 07017. 1981. 72 pp. $4.00 plus 50 cents for shipping. An annotated listing of books, audio-visual materials, teaching aids, and other resources arranged by topics. Also lists addresses of organizations and publishers. el. to ad.

The House of the Americas Through Eyes of Children. Organization of American States. Sales and Promotion. 17th St. & Constitution Ave., N.W. Washington, DC 20006. 1979. 24 pp. $1.00. Letters and drawings by children describing the OAS headquarters and replies which provide information about the OAS and member countries. Color illustrations. el.

►**Human Rights.** Detroit Public Library. Public Relations. 5201 Woodward Ave. Detroit, MI 48202. Rev. 1980. 14 pp. $2.00. Graded, annotated bibliography of books relating to the Universal Declaration of Human Rights. el-ms-hs.

Jews in the Soviet Union. The American Jewish Committee. Institute of Human Relations. 165 E. 56th St. New York, NY 10022. 1975. 44 pp. $1.50. A bibliography of articles and other writings, covering the years 1967-74, on the condition of the Russian Jewish people. hs-ad.

OVP Pamphlet Series. Greenhaven Press, Inc. 577 Shoreview Park Rd. St. Paul, MN 55112. Reprints of chapters from books in the *Opposing Viewpoints* series. 105 titles are available at $1.65 each. Send for listing. Sample titles are:

►**Are Science and Religion Compatible?**

►**Communism, Socialism, or Capitalism?**

►**Is Our Legal System Fair?**

►**Should Abortions Be Permitted?**

►**What Is Patriotism?**

P.P.I. Booklets. P.P.I.—Publishing. P.O. Box 335. Dayton, OH 45459. Request free catalog for discriptions of booklets on a variety of contemporary topics and controversial issues. Prices mostly at $2.75 each plus $1.00 postage for 1-6 copies. Sample titles are:

►**Acid Rain: The Controversy.** 1982. 36 pp. Discusses the origin, content, and damage of acid rain and possible solutions to the danger. Includes charts, diagrams, and pictures. ms-hs.

►**Capital Punishment: An Issue Once Again.** 1981. 60 pp. Provides historical background and numerous cases in point on both sides of the debate. ms-hs.

►**Legalize Marijuana: Pro and Con—an Update.** 1981. 56 pp. Presents changing views of decriminalization, research on the effects of marijuana, possible medicinal uses, and harmful/useful effects on the body and mind. ms-hs.

Social Studies Materials. Center for Information on America. Washington, CT 06793. Materials include:

Grass Roots Guides. Series of booklets relating to citizen, political, and community affairs. Single copies either 50 cents or $1.00 each; quantity rates available. Send for listing.

Vital Issues Discussion Guides. 10 issues yearly. Subscription $6.00; single copies 35 to 75 cents each; quantity rates available. Four large pages on current topics. Send for listing.

Teaching for Social Values in Social Studies. Association for Childhood Education International. 3615 Washington Ave., N.W. Washington, DC 20016. 1974. 72 pp. $2.75 plus 10% for postage and handling; prepay in U.S. currency. Emphasizes the need for value clarification as part of the social studies curriculum. Includes classroom exercises for teachers and students. ms-hs.

►**Through the Legal Looking Glass: Reflections of Peoples and Cultures** (Intercom #100). Global Perspectives in Education, Inc. 218 East 18th St. New York, NY 10003. 1981. 40 pp. 8½" x 11". $4.50 postpaid. Explores methods of resolving conflict as an avenue to learning about other societies and their values. Prepared cooperatively with the American Bar Association. hs.

►***Unions.*** American Federation of Labor and Congress of Industrial Organizations. 815 16th St., N.W. Washington, DC 20006. Free. A packet of materials giving information on union structure, solidarity, collective bargaining, and the AFL-CIO. hs-ad.

Using Questions in Social Studies (Series 2, No. 4). NCSS. 3615 Wisconsin Ave., N.W. Washington, DC 20016. 1977. 8 pp. $1.75. A *How-To-Do-It* guide to using questions as tools to develop skills and knowledge. ad.

Visual Geography Series. Sterling Publishing Co. 2 Park Ave. New York, NY 10016. 64 pp. each. $2.95 each. Pictorial booklets on the history, government, people, and geography of approximately 64 countries and regions. Send for list. ms.

►**World Newsmap of the Week.** Curriculum Innovations, Inc. 3500 Western Ave. Highland Park, IL 60035. Newsweekly. 30 issues yearly. Sample issue free to teachers. Each issue contains the latest world news, maps, and activities. G5-12.

SPECIAL EDUCATION

►*AAHPERD Materials.* American Association for Health, Physical Education, Recreation and Dance. P.O. Box 704. Waldorf, MD 20601. 1982. 5 pp. Free. Send for catalog of 92 publications and audio-visuals for people who work with the handicapped. ad.

Booklets. National Easter Seal Society for Crippled Children and Adults. 2023 W. Ogden Ave. Chicago, IL 60012. Quantity rates available. Sample titles are:

►**Children on Medication . . . a Guide for Teachers** (A-288). 3 pp. 40 cents. An aid to understanding the most commonly utilized medications for school children. ad.

►**Dos and Don'ts for Parents of Children With Hearing Problems** (A-217). Rev. 1979. 3-fold leaflet. 40 cents. ad. (Also available in Spanish.)

Let's Play Games! (E-60). 1978. 62 pp. $2.25. A compilation of more than 50 group games for children and young adults with physical handicaps.

Yes You Can! (E-61). 1978. 26 pp. $1.00. A booklet to help young people with learning disabilities understand and help themselves.

Your Child Has a Future (E-62). 1978. 49 pp. $2.00. A primer giving guidance to parents of young children diagnosed as having a disability. ad.

Braille and Hand Signs. American Foundation for the Blind. 15 W. 16th St. New York, NY 10011. Single copy free. pr. to ad. Sample titles are:

Braille Alphabet and Numerals. A 6½″ x 3¼″ card showing the Braille and Roman alphabet and numerals.

The One-Hand Manual Alphabet. 4 pp. Photographs showing the positions of the hands in making each of the 26 letters.

Understanding Braille. 12 pp. A brief description of how Braille works.

►**Captioned, Subtitled, Non-narrated, Silent, and Signed Language Films.** Enoch Pratt Free Library. Publications Dept. 400 Cathedral St. Baltimore, MD 21201. 1980. Mimeographed. 48 pp. $2.00. An annotated list of 16 mm films suitable for use with the deaf and hearing-impaired.

CEC Booklets. Council for Exceptional Children. 1920 Association Dr. Reston, VA 22091. Resources for special education teachers. Orders under $25 must be prepaid. Sample titles are:

Cliffs Speech and Hearing Series. Cliffs Notes, Inc. Attn: Faculty Coordinator. Box 80728. Lincoln, NE 68501. A new series of 13 titles ranging in price from $2.75 to $4.95 that covers specific conditions and general problems. Request free brochure. ad.

Dyslexia: Fact or Fiction? The Woods Schools. Langhorne, PA 19047. 1977. 16 pp. 50 cents. A monograph which considers research on dyslexia, a specific learning disability. Includes references. ad.

Guidelines. Guidance Awareness Publications. Box 106. Rancocas, NJ 08073. Titles include:

Career Assessment Guidelines for Middle and High School Students With Special Needs. 1978. 44 pp. $2.00. Gives guidelines on evaluation of special education students in regard to career goals. ad.

Mainstreaming: Who? Why? When? How? 1978. 20 pp. $2.00. Discusses mainstreaming philosophy as developed by teachers and gives illustrations of the mainstreaming process in the public schools. ad.

Hard-of-Hearing Aids. A. G. Bell Assoc. for the Deaf. 3417 Volta Place, N.W. Washington, DC 20007. Many materials are available. Sample titles are:

I Heard That! (D-2552). 36 pp. $3.75. A developmental sequence of listening activities for the young child. References. ad.

My Child Comes With Directions (I-5567). 1978. 28 pp. $1.50. A workbook for recording medical and educational history, developmental skills, needs, and other information about a hearing impaired child. A guide to the user is included. ad.

Hearing Impaired Children. A. G. Bell Assoc. for the Deaf. Publications Sales. 3417 Volta Place, N.W. Washington, DC 20007. Reprints from *The Volta Review*. Titles include:

The Hard-of-Hearing Child in the Classroom: A Guide for the Classroom Teacher (N-7105). 1962. 7 pp. 75 cents. Lists general do's and don'ts for handling a hard-of-hearing child in school. ad.

Reading and Writing Skills and the Deaf Adolescent (Q-3928). 1978. 13 pp. $1.50. Deals with assessment, planning, and evaluation of a reading and writing skills program for deaf adolescents. ad.

Interstate Printers and Publishers Materials. Interstate Printers and Publishers, Inc. 19-27 N. Jackson St. Danville, IL 61832. Sample titles are:

Alike—but Unalike. 1974. 32 pp. 50 cents. Presents important facts about abilities of exceptional children and how to understand them. el-ms.

Deaf Child in the Public School. 2nd ed. 1978. 149 pp. $4.75. A handbook for parents of deaf children who are or will be in a public school to help them make decisions about educational experiences for their children. ad.

Early Recognition of Speech, Hearing, and Language Disorders in Children Under Six Years Old (#1961). 1977. 16 pp. $1.00. A quick reference of typical speech, hearing, and language "norms" to aid in the detection of children in need of specialized services. ad.

For Parents of a Child Whose Speech Is Delayed. 2nd ed. 1980. 32 pp. 50 cents. Discusses how children learn speech and the causes of delayed speaking ability. Gives twenty suggestions which parents can use in helping good oral communication. ad.

►**Helping the Child With a Learning Disability: Suggestions for Parents.** 2nd ed. 1982. 12 pp. 30 cents; quantity rates available. A pamphlet to help parents know what they can contribute toward teaching a child with a learning disability. ad.

The Three Bears and Other Plays. 1977. 54 pp. $2.95. For children educationally handicapped. Six easy plays chosen for their simplicity and common usage with opportunities for students to play-act, sing, and dance. pr-el-ms.

Learning Can Be Child's Play. Abingdon. Customer Services Dept. 201 8th Ave. S. Nashville, TN 37202. 1976. 64 pp. $3.95. Payment should accompany all orders; schools and libraries entitled to 25% discount. Presents teaching techniques through play for slower-than-average preschoolers. ad.

Learning Disabilities. Academic Therapy Publications. 20 Commercial Blvd. Novato, CA 94947. Prepay orders and include 10% handling charge (minimum $1.50). Official purchase orders over $15 may be billed. U.S. currency only; California residents must include sales tax. Titles include:

Fun and Fundamentals: Activities for the Classroom (#179-5). 1977. 80 pp. $3.00. Suggests activities in all curriculum areas for motivating and stimulating individuals and groups in special and resource classes. pr-el.

Oh Dear, Somebody Said "Learning Disabilities"! (#127-2). 1975. 96 pp. $3.00. Explains, in practical terms, learning problems, how to recognize them, and ways of coping with them. ad.

Living Skills. Pitman Learning, Inc. 19 Davis Dr. Belmont, CA 94002. Prepay orders and add 8% to total (min. $1.50) for shipping. Teacher's manuals included. ms-hs. Titles are:

►**Checking Account** (#1363-Z090). 1982. 80 pp. $4.40; school $3.30. Text-workbook that explains how to open and maintain a checking account. 4.0 reading level.

Eddie in School (#2590-Z090). 1967. 60 pp. $3.20; school $2.40. A text-workbook to help students adjust to school and community life. 2.2 reading level.

Going Places With Your Personality (#3495-Z090). 1971. 52 pp. $3.20; school $2.40. Workbook which focuses on personal attitudes and habits important for successful living. 2.7 reading level.

Jerry Works in a Service Station (#4025-Z090). 1967. 60 pp. $3.20; school $2.40. Supplementary reading material and guide for training pre-vocational skills and attitudes. 2.2 reading level.

►**Planning Meals and Shopping** (#5450-Z090). 1970. 58 pp. $3.52; school $2.64. A text-workbook designed to teach planning of meals, shopping, and proper food storage. 2.5 reading level.

►**Plans for Living** (#5465-Z090). 1973. 58 pp. $3.52; school $2.64. A text-workbook which establishes basic goals for good health and safety. Stresses independence and self-reliance. 2.6 reading level.

►**What It Takes** (#7400-Z090). 1972. 140 pp. $4.64; school $3.48. A textbook for special education students on important aspects of contemporary living. Emphasizes discussion. 2.4 reading level.

Mime: Techniques and Class Formats. American Foundation for the Blind. 15 W. 16th St. New York, NY 10011. 1980. 75 pp. $3.50. Gives directions for ten one-hour sessions for a movement program for the visually handicapped. ad.

The Open Door. The Hogg Foundation for Mental Health. The University of Texas. Austin, TX 78712. 1979. 48 pp. 1.00. Describes a program for preschoolers—normal and handicapped—based on mainstreaming concepts. ad.

►**Outline for Remediation of Problem Areas for Children With Learning Disabilities** (B-41). National Easter Seal Society. 2023 W. Ogden Ave. Chicago, IL 60612. Rev. 1980. 36 pp. $3.25. An outline of some common problems, the identifiable behaviors, and suggestions for remediations. Available in Spanish. ad.

Personal Competency. Globe Book Company. 50 W. 23rd St. New York, NY 10010. Two text-workbooks designed to develop practical living skills. Accompanying teacher's guide free upon request. G5 reading level. Titles are:

Going Out/Getting Around. 1979. 112 pp. $3.56; 10 or more copies, $2.97 each. A series of exercises through which students learn to handle everyday situations. ms-hs.

You, the Buyer. 1980. 128 pp. $3.56; 10 or more copies, $2.97 each. Uses facsimiles and exercises to develop the basic skills to be a critical buyer. ms-hs.

Professional Resources. National Center for Research in Vocational Education. The Ohio State University. 1960 Kenny Road. Columbus, OH 43210. Offers many publications and services of interest to professionals in special education. Write or call for brochures and listings. Toll free outside Ohio: 800-848-4815.

Public Affairs Pamphlets. Public Affairs Committee, Inc. 381 Park Ave. S. New York, NY 10016. 50 cents each; quantity rates available. Titles include:

Helping the Child Who Cannot Hear (#479). 1972. 28 pp. Discusses causes of hearing loss and types of educational methods available for use with those who do not hear. ad.

Helping the Handicapped Teenager Mature (#504). 1974. 28 pp. A psychologist who has worked with handicapped children discusses the difficulties in their social development and how psychologists may help. ad.

Learning Disabilities: Problems and Progress (#578). 1979. 28 pp. A guide for parents and teachers to help children with learning disabilities. Explains disabilities and their causes, prevention, and treatment; lists resources. ad.

Reading. Human Policy Press. Box 127. University Station. Syracuse, NY 13210. Titles are:

Amy Maura (C-2). 1975. 32 pp. $1.75 plus $1.50 for shipping. The story of a young girl's self-concept and the real life drama she participates in when her family's home catches fire. el.

The Sneely-Mouthed Snerds and the Wonderoctopus (C-1). 1975. 32 pp. $1.75 plus $1.50 for shipping. Snerds pick on each other and Wonderoctopus grows more frightening. Willie Two Poles (disabled) makes all the difference. A book that may change your thinking. el.

Sharing the Street: Activities for All Children. Community Education Services. Children's Television Workshop. 1 Lincoln Plaza. New York, NY 10023. 1978. 96 pp. $2.00; 25 copies or more $1.60. An activity book for individuals working with children who have impairments and disabilities; based on the entertainment approach used on TV's "Sesame Street." Spanish version available.

Speech Therapy. The Interstate Printers & Publishers, Inc. 19-27 N. Jackson St. Danville, IL 61832. Educational discounts available. Titles are:

►**Conversation Starters for Speech-Language Pathology** (#2186-1). 1981. 17 pp. $2.75. Designed for helping people with oral communications problems. Can be used for articulation remediation, voice improvement, fluency training, and other purposes. el. to ad.

►**Speech Chief—a Speech Therapy Workbook for Any Sound** (#2108-X). 1980. 61 pp. $1.00. Uses words from the child's textbook to progress from word discrimination to target sound in isolation, syllables, words, sentences, and conversation. pr-el.

Stuttering. Speech Foundation of America. P.O. Box 11749. Memphis, TN 38111. Several publications on the prevention and treatment of stuttering for speech pathologists are available. ad.

Visual Impairment. National Association for Visually Handicapped. 305 E. 24th St., 17-C. New York, NY 10010. Single copy free. Sample titles are:

►**About Children's Eyes.** 2 pp. Identifies common indications of a visual problem and steps to take. Also in Spanish. ad.

►**Catalog of Large Type Materials.** 1982. 32 pp. Lists books available for literature, science, social studies, and other subjects. ad.

Problems of the Partially Seeing. 1980. 12 pp. Discusses some aids, activities, and services which can help partially seeing people. hs-ad.

►**Professional Guide.** 1975. 22 pp. Discusses the growth and development of the partially seeing child. ad.

Large Type Storybooks. Series of four children's books about partially seeing children. 29-37 pp. each. $1.00 each. K-G4. Titles are:

Cathy

Larry

Monocular Mac

Susan

When You Have a Visually Handicapped Child in Your Classroom: Suggestions for Teachers. American Foundation for the Blind. 15 W. 16th St. New York, NY 10011. 1977. 28 pp. Single copy free. Helpful pointers for the regular classroom teacher in offering instruction to children who have visual handicaps. ad.

►**The Woods Review and Digest.** The Woods Schools. Lanhorne, PA 19047. Published quarterly. 26 pp. 75 cents. Each issue reviews articles from professional journals for those in educational, community, and institutional services for the developmentally disabled. ad.

TRANSPORTATION

Airports and Jets. Dept. of Airports. Public relations. Los Angeles International Airport. 1 World Way. Los Angeles, CA 90009. Free. A packet of mimeographed materials on how an airport operates, air traffic control vocabulary; Boeing, Douglas, and other types of aircraft; and captioned photographs of the Los Angeles airport.

America on the Move! U.S. Dept. of Transportation. Federal Highway Administration. Washington, DC 20590. 1980. 40 pp. Single copy free. The story of the federal-aid highway program. ms.

Aviation. Dept. of Transportation. Federal Aviation Admin. Washington, DC 20591. Send for *List of FAA Aviation Education Materials.* Educational aids for elementary and secondary students.

Cars and Trucks. Motor Vehicle Manufacturers Assoc. of the U.S., Inc. 300 New Center Bldg. Detroit, MI 48202. Free; shipping charges on bulk orders. Sample titles are:

America Runs on Wheels. 1980. 32 pp. Portrays the national economic impact of the motor vehicle industry. el-ms.

Saving Energy. 1980. 13 pp. Discusses energy-saving programs in the motor vehicle industry. ms-hs.

Trucks. 1976. An educational game designed to combine skill and concept development with learning about the role of trucks. el.

Trucks and Buses Serve America. Wall chart, 22″ x 35″. A poster depicting the different types and uses of trucks and buses and some general aspects of the trucking industry. Includes suggestions for related learning activities in language arts, social studies, and art. el.

Your Way to Better Fuel Economy. 1979. 21 pp. Offers consumers advice on how to improve the fuel efficiency of their vehicles. ms-hs.

Flight History. National Air and Space Museum. Smithsonian Institution. Washington, DC 20560. Free. Pamphlets on the history of aviation and on some pioneers of flight. ms-hs-ad. Sample titles are:

Amelia Earhart

Charles A. Lindbergh and the Spirit of St. Louis

Langley's Aerodrome

Otto Lilanthal and Octave Chanute: Pioneers of Gliding

►**The Pan-American Goodwill Flight of 1926-1927**

►**The T-2 Airplane and the First Nonstop Coast-to-Coast Flight**

►**Wiley Post's "Winnie Mae"**

The Wright Brothers

Maritime Administration Materials. U.S. Dept. of Transportation. Maritime Administration. 400 7th St., N.W. Washington, DC 20590. Free. Pamphlets and photographs on the work and purposes of the federal maritime agency. ms-hs. Titles are:

►**Introducing the Maritime Administration.** 20 pp.

►**U.S. Essential Foreign Trade Routes.** Map, 20″×10″.

►**U.S. Merchant Marine: A Brief History.** 7 pp.

►**U.S. Merchant Marine Fleet Pictures.** 1976. A set of 15 captioned photographs.

Shipping and Transportation (SB-040). U.S. Gov't. Printing Office. Washington, DC 20402. 1981. 10 pp. Free. A listing of many low-cost government publications which may be used in the classroom.

Trucking Materials. American Trucking Associations, Inc. Educational Services Dept. 1616 P St., N. W. Washington, DC 20036. A variety of pamphlets and leaflets concerning trucking in our transport system. Titles include:

How Trucks Serve You. 6 pp. Free. Describes the retail market's dependence upon truck transport. ms.

Milk. 6 pp. Free. Describes how milk is transported from farm to store. el.

Travel Fun With Trucks. 10 pp. Free. Puzzles, games, and riddles featuring trucks. pr.

The Truck Driver. 1965. Poster, 12″x15″. Free. Highlights the work of truck drivers. pr.

Trucks and Things You'll Want to Know About Them. 14 pp. Free. Tells how trucks serve the community, the farm, business, and industry. el.

UNITED NATIONS

FAO Fact Sheets. Food and Agriculture Organization of the U.N. Information Office. 1776 F St., N.W. Washington, DC 20437. Free. Summaries of work carried out by FAO. Leaflets. ms-hs-ad. Titles are:

The Farming World

The Field Programs of FAO

Information From FAO

World Food Day

World's Forests

Human Rights. UNESCO. Room 2401. U.N. Building. New York, NY 10017. Offers several free items related to human rights. el. to ad. Sample titles are:

►**Declaration of the Rights of the Child.** Reprint of the ten articles as adopted in 1959 by the United Nations.

►**UNESCO and Human Rights.** Foldout, 17″×26″. Several black and white photos illustrating significant portions of the Universal Declaration of Human Rights.

►**The Universal Declaration of Human Rights.** 2 pp. The thirty-article declaration as proclaimed by the United Nations in 1948.

►**Human Rights Are for Everyone.** U.S. National Commission for UNESCO. Dept. of State. Washington, DC 20520. Large wall posters. Free. Compares selections from American documents with the Universal Declaration of Human Rights adopted by the United Nations. ms-hs.

►**Publications and Educational Materials.** U.S. Committee for UNICEF. 331 East 38th St. New York, NY 10016. 1982. 6 pp. Free. Current catalog of UNICEF materials. Includes teachers' kits, displays, music, craft books, puzzles, etc., related to children around the world. Also available are free information packets on UNICEF programs in general and in specific countries. pr. to ad.

UNA Materials. United Nations Assoc. of the United States of America. Publications Service. 300 E. 42nd St. New York, NY 10017. Materials on the United Nations for schools are available. Free publications are available. Titles include:

Helping Boys and Girls Discover the World. 1978. $2.50. Designed for teaching about global concerns and the UN in elementary and middle schools.

A List of Recommended Films. 1980. 9 pp. 75 cents handling charge. Lists films for student and adult UN programs and hints for a successful film show. Gives procurement information.

►**Partnerships in Meeting Basic Needs.** 1981. 45 pp. $3.50. An examination of UN efforts in Asia, Africa, and Latin America. Includes background information on each country as well as UNICEF, WHO, and the United Nations Development Program. Provides discussion questions and classroom activities. el-ms.

UNESCO. U.S. National Commission for Unesco. 1015 20th St., N.W. Washington, DC 20520. Write for information on free materials available.

►**UNESCO: What It Is, What It Does, How It Works.** UNESCO. Room 2401. U.N. Building. New York, NY 10017. 1981. 24 pp. Free. A pamphlet on the purposes and work of the United Nations Educational, Scientific, and Cultural Organization. ms-hs.

►**The United Nations, the Human Rights Covenants, and the United States** (#595). Public Affairs Committee. 381 Park Ave. S. New York, NY 10016. 1981. 28 pp. 50 cents. Discusses the UN's program in human rights since 1966 and the issues stemming from America's failure to ratify the Universal Declaration of Human Rights. hs-ad.

United Nations Information Kit. United Nations. Public Inquiries Unit. GA-57. New York, NY 10017. Free; limit one kit per person or school. Contains materials on the structure and work of the U.N. Includes maps, charts, pamphlets, bibliographies, and information sheets. el-ms-hs.

U.S. and the UN. League of Women Voters Education Fund. 1730 M St., N.W. Washington, DC 20036. Titles include:

North and South at the UN: The Economic Challenge (#642). 1976. 6 pp. 40 cents. Examines tensions between developed and developing nations at the UN, especially over a "New International Economic Order." hs-ad.

Sharing UN Successes (#129). 1977. 4 pp. 30 cents. Offers tips on reaching the public with the "good news" about the UN's many success stories. ad.

World Hunger. Food and Agriculture Organization of the U.N. Liaison Office for North America. 1776 F St., N.W. Washington, DC 20437. Two pamphlets on the work of the FAO to relieve hunger worldwide. el-ms. Free. Titles are:

►**FAO: What Is it, What It Does, How It Works.** 1980.

►**World Food Program: What Is It, What It Does, How It Works.** 1981.

UNITED STATES AND TERRITORIES

Sources of Materials About Each State. A variety of booklets, maps, posters, and other materials may be obtained free or for a small charge from sources within many of the 50 states. Since supplies of all materials become depleted and new publications appear at frequent intervals, only general listings are given below. Teachers should direct inquiries to these sources asking either for a list of available items or stating clearly the grade level taught, the subject area, and other details to guide the agency in filling the request. Requests for large quantities of "everything you have" are unreasonable and should not be made.

Alabama. Alabama Bureau of Publicity and Information. 532 S. Perry St. Montgomery, AL 36130; or call toll free 1-800-633-5761 (in Alabama 1-800-392-8096).

Alaska. Dept. of Commerce and Economic Development. Div. of Economic Enterprise. Pouch EE. Juneau, AK 99811.
Alaska State Div. of Tourism. Pouch E. Juneau, AK 99811.

Arizona. Arizona Dept. of Transportation. 206 S. 17th Ave.—Rm. 159A. Phoenix, AZ 85012.
Arizona Office of Tourism. 3507 N. Central Ave.—Suite 506. Phoenix, AZ 85004.

Arkansas. Arkansas Dept. of Parks & Tourism. One Capitol Mall. Little Rock, AR 72201.
Secretary of State. State Capitol. Little Rock, AR 72201.

Colorado. The State Historical Society of Colorado. Heritage Center. 1300 Broadway. Denver, CO 80203.

Connecticut. Connecticut Department of Economic Development. 210 Washington St. Hartford, CT 06106.
State Department of Environmental Protection. Parks and Recreation Div. State Office Bldg. Hartford, CT 06115.

Delaware. Delaware State Travel Service. 99 Kings Highway. P.O. Box 1401. Dover, DE 19901.

Florida. Dept. of Commerce. Direct Mail. 126 Van Buren St. Tallahassee, FL 32301.

Georgia. Georgia Dept. of Natural Resources. Parks, Recreation and Historic Sites Div. 270 Washington St., S. W. Atlanta, GA 30334.

Hawaii. Hawaii Visitors Bureau. P.O. Box 8527. Honolulu, HI 96815.

Idaho. State of Idaho. Transportation Dept. P.O. Box 7129. Boise, ID 83707.

Illinois. Illinois Information Service. 201 W. Monroe. Springfield, IL 62706. Illinois State Museum. Spring and Edwards Sts. Springfield, IL 62706.

Kansas. Kansas Dept. of Economic Development. Travel Div. 503 Kansas Ave. —6th Flr. Topeka, KS 66603.

Louisiana. Louisiana Office of Tourism. P.O. Box 44291. Capitol Station. Baton Rouge, LA 70804.

Maine. Maine Publicity Bureau. 97 Winthrop St. Hallowell, ME 04347. Order in limited quantities.

Maryland. Maryland Tourism. 1748 Forest Dr. Annapolis, MD 21401. Offers a Teacher's Kit and a Student's Kit. Students must write individually for kits.

Michigan. Michigan History Div. Dept. of State. Lansing, MI 48918.

Minnesota. Minnesota Tourist Information Center. 240 Bremer Bldg. 419 N. Robert St. St. Paul, MN 55101.

Missouri. Missouri Div. of Tourism. 308 E. High St. P.O. Box 1055. Jefferson City, MO 65102.

Montana. Montana Travel Promotion Bureau. Dept. of Commerce. Helena, MT 59620.

Nebraska. Nebraska Secretary of State. State Capitol. Lincoln, NE 68509. Nebraska Game and Parks Commission. 2200 N. 33rd St. P.O. Box 30370. Lincoln, NE 68503.
Nebraska Dept. of Economic Development. 301 Centennial Mall S.—4th Flr. P.O. Box 94666. Lincoln, NE 68509.

Nevada. Nevada Dept. of Economic Development. Carson City, NV 89710.

New Jersey. State Div. of Travel and Tourism. Dept. of Commerce. Box CN384. Trenton, NJ 08625.

New Mexico. New Mexico Tourism and Travel Div. C-10 Bataan Memorial Bldg. Santa Fe, NM 87503.

North Dakota. North Dakota Tourism Promotion. Capitol Grounds. Bismarck, ND 58505.

Ohio. The Ohio Historical Society. Ohio Historical Center. I-71 at 17th Ave. Columbus, OH 43211.
Ohio Secretary of State. 14th Flr. 30 E. Broad St. Columbus, OH 43215.

Oklahoma. Oklahoma Historical Society. 2100 N. Lincoln. Historical Bldg. Oklahoma City, OK 73105.
Oklahoma Tourism and Recreation Dept. Literature Distribution Center. 215 N.E. 28th. Oklahoma City, OK 73105.

Pennsylvania. Commonwealth of Pennsylvania. Historical and Museum Commission. Box 1026. Harrisburg, PA 17120.
Pennsylvania Dept. of Commerce. South Office Bldg. Harrisburg, PA 17120.

Rhode Island. Rhode Island Dept. of Economic Development. Tourist Promotion Div. 7 Jackson Walkway. Providence, RI 02903.

South Dakota. South Dakota Industrial Development Expansion Agency. 221 S. Central. Pierre, SD 57501.
South Dakota Dept. of Transportation. Pierre, SD 57501.
Office of Indian Affairs. Capitol Bldg. Pierre, SD 57501.

Tennessee. Tennessee Dept. of Tourist Development. P.O. Box 23170. Nashville, TN 37202.
Tennessee Wildlife Resources Agency. P.O. Box 40747. Nashville, TN 37204.

Vermont. Vermont State Chamber of Commerce. Box 37. Montpelier, VT 05602.
State of Vermont. Travel Div. 61 Elm St. Montpelier, VT 05602.

Virginia. Virginia Dept. of Conservation and Economic Development. 1100 Washington Bldg. Capitol Square. Richmond, VA 23219.
Williamsburg Area Chamber of Commerce. Drawer HQ. Williamsburg, VA 23185.

West Virginia. West Virginia Travel Development. Bldg. 6—Room B-553. State Capitol. Charleston, WV 25305.

Wisconsin. Wisconsin Dept. of Transportation. Office of Information/Safety. P.O. Box 7910. Madison, WI 53707.

Wyoming. Wyoming Archives, Museums, and Historical Dept. Barrett Bldg. Cheyenne, WY 82002. Single copy of historical booklet available to teachers, students, and travelers.

►**Public Buildings, Landmarks, and Historic Sites of the United States** (SB-140). U.S. Gov't. Printing Office. Washington, DC 20402. 1981. 15 pp. Free. A listing of many low-cost government publications which may be used in the classroom.

Puerto Rico. Puerto Rico Federal Affairs Administration. Puerto Rico News Service. 734 15th St., N.W. Washington, DC 20005. Classroom series kit. Free to teachers. Kit includes: booklets on Puerto Rico's culture, science and industry, politics and government; a full-color historical map; a pamphlet of contemporary facts; a current issue of the quarterly magazine "Dateline . . . Puerto Rico, U.S.A." G7-12.

►**Rhode Island, the Biggest Little State in the Union.** R.I. Dept. of Economic Development. 7 Jackson Walkway. Providence, RI 02903. 1981. 28 pp. Free, one per ten students. Contains historical and contemporary information about the state. ms-hs.

Story of Illinois Series. Illinois State Museum Society. Springfield, IL 62706. A series of booklets written in nontechnical language on the natural history and prehistory of Illinois. Subjects include birds, flowers, mushrooms, insects, fossils, American Indians, and many others. Most cost under $1.00. Send for a complete listing. el-ms.

Tennessee. League of Women Voters of Tennessee. 1701 21st Ave. S. Nashville, TN 37212. Titles are:

►**International Trade: Tennessee's Window on the World.** 1981. 35 pp. 8½" x 11", spiral-bound. $4.00. A resource unit designed to enhance understanding of international trade and its effects on the personal lives of Tennesseans. G7-12.

►**Lobbying and the Tennessee General Assembly.** 1981. 22 pp. $2.00. A guide for citizen lobbyists and public interest groups. hs-ad.

On the Hill: A Guide to the Tennessee State Legislature. 1978. 8½"x 16" foldout. $4.00 per 50: Contains basic information on the composition, organization, and procedures of the State Assembly and a map of the Capitol Hill area. A useful guide for student field trips. el-ms.

►**This Is TVA: An Introduction.** 1982. 32 pp. $2.50. A comprehensive citizens' guide to the Tennessee Valley Authority—its history, organization, programs, and problems. Includes regional map. hs-ad.

Visual Geography Series. Sterling Publishing Co. 2 Park Avenue. New York, NY 10016. 64 pp. each. $2.95 each. Orders must be prepaid and include postage. Booklets discuss the land, history, people, government, and economy of each country. Illustrated with photographs and maps. ms. Sample titles are:

Alaska in Pictures

Hawaii in Pictures

Puerto Rico in Pictures

U.S.A. in Pictures

VOCATIONAL AND MANUAL SKILLS

►**Arc Welded Projects** (Vol. II). The James Lincoln Arc Welding Foundation. P.O. Box 17035. Cleveland, OH 44117. 1978. 272 pp. $5.00. Contains complete plans and instructions for over 100 projects. Separate sections on agricultural equipment, home and recreational equipment, shop tools and equipment, and trailers. hs-ad.

Arc Welding Teaching Aids Kit. The Lincoln Electric Co. 22801 St. Clair Ave. Cleveland, OH 44117. Free to welding teachers if requested on school stationery. Kit includes free-loan movie and free teaching aids information, wall charts, and teacher-student guides. hs.

Basic Texts. McKnight Publishing Co. 808 IAA Dr. Box 2854. Bloomington, IL 61701. Series of eight introductory textbooks in industrial arts which emphasize activities for students to explore the basic tools, skills, and materials used in the fields of drafting, graphic arts, photography, electricity, power mechanics, plastics, metalworking, and woodworking. G6-8 reading level. $3.96, softbound. Send for listing. Sample titles are:

Drafting. 1978. 92 pp. Covers the basics of freehand sketching, working drawings, mechanical and pictorial drawing, and drafting systems. ms.

Power Mechanics. 1978. 92 pp. Covers mechanical power, fluid power, electrical power, and small gas engine. ms.

Chilton Publications. Chilton Book Co. Radnor, PA 19089. Write for free brochures and catalogs concerning books about automobile repair and various technical and professional areas. hs-ad.

Delco Remy/Moraine Aids. Edu-Tech Publications. A Div. of Commerical Service Co. P.O. Box 2499. Anderson, IN 46018. Send for free publications list of training aids and service bulletins on electrical components of motor vehicles or the brake system. ad.

Flooring. Oak Flooring Institute. 804 Sterick Bldg. Memphis, TN 38103. Titles include:

Hardwood Flooring Finishing/Refinishing Manual. 7 pp. 50 cents. Describes methods and products to give a lasting finish to hardwood flooring and to restore beauty to old floors. hs-ad.

Hardwood Flooring Installation Manual. 8 pp. 50 cents. Explains installation of strip and plank flooring, and block and parquet produced from tongued and grooved strips. hs-ad.

Wood Floor Care Guide. 14 pp. 25 cents. A maintenance manual for hardwood flooring and finishes, including stain removal. hs-ad.

Furniture Projects. Hardwood Plywood Manufacturers Assoc. 1825 Michael Faraday Dr. P.O. Box 2789. Reston, VA 22090. Leaflets. 1-5 pp. 25 cents each. Titles are:

Do It Yourself With Hardwood Plywood: Bookcase-Room Divider

Do It Yourself With Hardwood Plywood: Planter, Desk, Hi-Fi

Do It Yourself With Hardwood Plywood: Saddle Seat Desk

Do It Yourself With Hardwood Plywood: TV Trays

General Shop Texts. Goodheart-Willcox Co. 123 W. Taft Dr. South Holland, IL 60473. 1978. $4.80 each; school price $3.60. Series of eight texts provides exploratory experiences in the use of tools, machines, and materials. Teacher's guide included. Sample titles are:

Electricity (#259-X). 1978. 120 pp. Contains 17 units and 25 electrical projects. Illustrated. ms-hs.

Power Mechanics (#307-3). 1980. 112 pp. Contains 12 units, glossary, and decimal and metric charts. ms-hs.

►**Printing and Graphic Arts** (SB-077). U.S. Gov't. Printing Office. Washington, DC 20402. 1981. 3 pp. Free. A list of many low-cost government publications.

►**Professional Resources.** National Center for Research in Vocational Education. The Ohio State University. 1960 Kenny Road. Columbus, OH 43210. Offers many publications and services of interest to professionals in vocational education. Write or call for brochures and listings. Toll free outside Ohio: 800-848-4815.

Standards for Vocational Automotive Service Instruction. Motor Vehicle Manufacturers Assoc. of the U.S.A., Inc. 300 New Center Bldg. Detroit, MI 48202. 1979. 114 pp. Single copies free; postage and handling charge on bulk orders. A manual for organizing and conducting an automotive training program. ad.

Vises and Clamps. Columbian Visc Div. c/o The Warren Group. P.O. Box 68. Hiram, OH 44234. Free. Titles include:

Clamps. 16 pp. A history of clamps and their uses, with a glossary. hs-ad.

Use and Care Chart. 8½" x 11". Also available in 16" x 22" wall size. Illustrates proper use and care of bench and woodworkers' vises. ms-hs.

►**Vocational and Career Education** (SB-110). U.S. Gov't. Printing Office. Washington, DC 20402. 1982. 17 pp. Free. A list of many low-cost government publications that may be used in the classroom.

►***Welding.*** American Welding Soc. 550 NW Le Jeune St. Miami, FL 33135. Request a free catalog of technical publications on various aspects of welding. ad.

WEATHER AND CLIMATE

Disaster Preparedness (NOAA/PA 76021). U.S. Dept. of Commerce. National Oceanic and Atmospheric Admin. Central Logistics Supply Center. 619 Hardesty St. Kansas City, MO 64124. Free. An annotated listing of publications available from the National Weather Service, the U.S. Dept. of Commerce, and the U.S. Government Printing Office. Materials deal with violent weather—tornados and hurricanes, winter storms, lightning and thunderstorms, and flash floods. el-ms-hs.

Forecasting. Taylor Instruments. Consumer Products Div. Sybron Corp. Arden, NC 28704. Free in classroom quantities; request on school stationery. Titles are:

> **How's Your Weather I.Q.?** 1974. 1 p. Contains a 7″ x 10″ chart for recording weather information such as temperature, barometric pressure, wind direction and speed, and for forecasting the next day's weather. el-ms.
>
> **Weather Forecasting With Your Taylor Stormoscope Barometer.** 1979. 12 pp. Explains basics of forecasting and the use of barometers. el-ms.

Forecasting Weather. C.C. Marketing. P.O. Box 1122. Glen Allen, VA 23060. Titles include:

> **Cloud Chart.** 11″ x 17″. $1.00 plus self-addressed envelope (#10). Larger chart: 18″ x 22″, $3.00; 2 or more, $2.50 each. Each chart contains 35 color photos with explanations of the weather different clouds bring. el-ms-hs.
>
> **What's the Weather Going to Be?** 12 pp. $1.00 plus self-addressed stamped envelope (#10). 16 cloud pictures and simple descriptions of the different types of clouds and the conditions they foretell. el-ms-hs.

How Weather and Climate Affect You (#533). Public Affairs Committee. 381 Park Ave. S. New York, NY 10016. 1976. 28 pp. 50 cents. Explains how winds, storms, humidity, air pressure, cold, and heat may impact on human behavior and health; how that may be detected in the body's metabolic and chemical processes; and how to weather-condition yourself. hs-ad.

►**Weather** (SB-234). U.S. Gov't. Printing Office. Washington, DC 20402. 1982. 7 pp. Free. A listing of many low-cost government publications which may be used in the classroom. ad.

WOMEN AND SEXISM

Bibliography of Suggested Readings on Non-Sexist Education. The Non-Sexist Child Development Project. Women's Action Alliance, Inc. 370 Lexington Ave. New York, NY 10017. 1978. 8 pp. Free. Gives publication data for more than 100 books on the subject. ad.

Employment. Business and Professional Women's Foundation. 2012 Massachusetts Ave., N.W. Washington, DC 20036. Order from: BPW Supply Serivce. 11722 Parklawn Dr. Rockville, MD 20852. Prepay orders. Titles include:

Educational Assistance. 1980. Chart, 17" x 22". Single copy free. Outlines the financial support programs of the Foundation. hs-ad.

Where the Jobs Are: An Annotated Bibliography. 1979. 12 pp. $1.35, postpaid. Reviews 29 publications. hs-ad.

►**Women and Poverty: A Research Report.** 1981. 4 pp. $1.00, postpaid. Summaries research findings on women's earnings and wage discrimination. hs-ad.

Women and Work in U.S. History. 1976. 128 pp. $1.25, postpaid. An annotated bibliography of recent literature dealing with women's work and its place in U.S. history. hs-ad.

Work Force Entry by Mature Women: A Review and Bibliography. 1977. 20 pp. $1.50, postpaid. Reviews 41 publications on the subject. hs-ad.

Feminist Resources for Schools and Colleges: A Guide to Curricular Materials. The Feminist Press. Box 334. Old Westbury, NY 11568. 1976. 80 pp. $2.50 postpaid. A selective guide to more than 500 sources of materials for teachers, students, and parents.

Growing Free: Ways to Help Children Overcome Sex-Role Stereotype. Assoc. for Childhood Education International. 3615 Wisconsin Ave., N. W. Washington, DC 20016. 1976. 32 pp. $2.00. A collection of seven reprints from *Childhood Education* supports the need for nonsexist curriculum and educational practice and gives practical guidance. Bibliographies. ad.

Guidelines for Sex-Fair Vocational Education Materials. Women on Words and Images. P.O. Box 2163. Princeton, NJ 08540. 1979. 40 pp. $3.00. Report to the U.S. Department of Education which includes guidelines for the development and evaluation of materials for both sexes in vocational education. ad.

A History of Women in America (#20762-8) Bantam Books, Inc. 666 5th Ave. New York, NY 10103. 1978. 400 pp. $3.95. True accounts of famous and anonymous women throughout U.S. history. hs-ad.

Issues. League of Women Voters Education Fund. 1730 M St., N.W. Washington, DC 20036. Titles include:

►**Pay Equity: Equal Pay for Work of Comparable Value** (#110). 1982. 2 pp. 20 cents. Presents a brief summary of a major civil rights concern of the 1982s—pay equity. Covers litigation, collective bargaining strategies, government actions, and job evaluations. hs-ad.

►**Public Policy on Reproductive Choices** (#286). 1982. 8 pp. $1.25. (members, 75 cents). Takes a brief look at the history of U.S. public policy on birth control and abortion. Discusses the impact of Supreme Court decisions, congressional and state efforts, and federal funding of family planning. hs-ad.

►**Women and Vocational Training: A Step Up or a Come Down?** (#408). 1982. 12 pp. $1.00. Discusses whether vocational education can train women for the skilled trades and high technology industries and reviews federal safeguards to women's opportunities. hs-ad.

Public Affairs Pamphlets. Public Affairs Committee. 381 Park Ave. S. New York, NY 10016. Titles are:

►**Men's Jobs for Women: Toward Occupational Equality** (#606). 1982. 28 pp. 50 cents. Presents a background to the inequality for women and the leading current efforts to counter the problem. hs-ad.

►**Woman's Changing Place: A Look at Sexism** (#509). 1974. 28 pp. 50 cents. How childhood conditioning, education, and other influences limit women's development and opportunities, and how women are working to effect changes. hs-ad.

►**Women and Abuse of Prescription Drugs** (#604). 1982. 28 pp. 50 cents. Explains reasons that the abuse of prescription drugs is a special problem for women and how to counteract it. hs-ad.

Publications of the Women's Bureau. Women's Bureau. Office of the Secretary. U.S. Dept. of Labor. Washington, DC 20210. 1980. 4 pp. Free; send a self-addressed return label. A listing of titles available of interest to women. Several are also in Spanish.

►**A Woman's Guide to Social Security** (#537J). Consumer Information Center. Pueblo, CO 81009. 1982. 15 pp. Free. Covers such vital concerns as how leaving the work force to raise a family, divorce, and husband's death affect future social security benefits. hs-ad.

WORLD OF COMPUTERS

►**Computer Information Resources.** National Council of Teachers of Mathematics. 1906 Association Dr. Reston, VA 22091. 1982. 4 pp. Single copy free. Gives references to articles that have appeared in recent issues of the *Arithmetic Teacher, Mathematics Teacher, Journal for Research in Mathematics Education,* and other NCTM publications. ad.

►**Computerms.** (C17). Computing Information Center HG-45. University of Washington. 3737 Brooklyn Ave., N.E. Seattle, WA 98105. 1981. 15 pp. $1.00. Gives non-technical definitions to common terms associated with computers and data processing. hs-ad.

►**Computers and Data Processing.** (SB-051). U.S. Gov't. Printing Office. Washington, DC 20402. 1982. 16 pp. Free. A list of many low-cost government publications in the field. ad.

►**Co-op Newsletter.** Micro Co-op. P.O. Box 714. St. Charles, IL 60174. Newsletter. Approx. 16 pp. First year subscription with $3.00 membership fee. Back issues, $1.00 each. Each issue gives narrative evaluations of selected software, a listing of discount software with ratings, and miscellaneous tips. Especially relevant to Apple microcomputers. ms-hs-ad.

►**Education News.** Apple Computer. 20525 Mariani Ave. Cupertino, CA 95014. Newsletter. Free subscription. A periodic publication for educators containing articles on developments related to Apple microcomputers. ad.

►**Edunet.** Educom. P.O. Box 364. Princeton, NJ 08540. Quarterly newsletter. 8 pp. Free subscription to members and interested individuals. Provides news articles on activities and projects to enhance instructional and research computing and to promote resource exchange within higher education. ad.

►**Computer Applications in Reading.** International Reading Assoc. 800 Barksdale Rd. P.O. Box 8139. Newark, DE 19711. 1979. 106 pp. $4.50 (members $3.00). A report on numerous school system experiments with computer-aided and computer-managed instruction from which assessment data have been gained. ad.

ERIC Bibliographies. ERIC Clearinghouse on Information Resources. School of Education. Syracuse University. Syracuse, NY 13210. Free for a self-addressed stamped envelope (#10). Titles are:

- ►**The Field of Educational Technology.** 1981. 4 pp. Lists specific sources of information for twelve frequently asked questions about educational and instructional technology. ad.
- ►**Information Resources on Microcomputers.** 1982. 4 pp. Annotated listing of documents and journal articles arranged in six categories, such as computer literacy, hardware, and software. ad.
- ►**Microcomputers: Some Basic Resources.** 1982. 4 pp. Provides references for researching eight general questions about microcomputers such as how to buy, how to get software, and how to keep up-to-date. ad.

Guide Booklets. AFIPS Press. 1815 N. Lynn St., Suite 800. Arlington, VA 22209. Three booklets published by the American Federation of Information Processing Societies for educators in secondary schools. Orders must be prepaid. Titles are:

- ►**Computer Education for Teachers in Secondary Schools—an Outline Guide.** 1971. 28 pp. 75 cents. Suggests content and methods for computer science courses to train teachers. ad.
- ►**Elements of Information and Information Processing for Teachers in Secondary Schools.** 1976. 35 pp. $1.00. Examines concepts and focuses on factors that govern the efficient handling of information. ad.
- ►**Use of the Computer in Teaching and Learning.** 1974. 23 pp. $1.50. Answers several basic questions on the use of the computer to assist in the learning process. ad.

►**A Guide to Computers in Education.** Atari, Inc. 60 E. Plumeria St. San Jose, CA 95134. 1982. 64 pp. Single copy free to educators. Reviews uses of computers in schools and learning, basics of the microcomputer, and factors in selecting and installing computers. Includes a checklist for comparing microcomputer features, resource information on software and support organizations, a glossary, and literature references. ad.

►**Guidelines for Evaluating Computerized Instructional Materials** (#122). National Council of Teachers of Mathematics. 1906 Association Dr. Reston, VA 22091. 1981. 32 pp. $3.75. Discusses issues unique to software evaluation, presents evaluation instruments, and outlines procedures for their use. Designed for users and creators of computer software; assumes no computer programming experience. ad.

IBM. IBM Educational Materials. International Business Machines Corp. Dept. 809. Armonk, NY 10504. Booklets of general information about computers and their present applications. Free to teachers in reasonable quantites. Titles include:

►**About Computers.** 1981. 16 pp. Explains basic concepts and functions of computers in non-technical terms. Cartoon illustrations. el-ms-hs.

Hexapawn: A Game You Play to Lose. 1969. Demonstrates how a simple principle can be used to program a computer so that past mistakes in problem-solving are not repeated. hs.

►**Introduction a la Computacion** (#21). Organization of American States. Dept. of Publications. 1889 F St., N.W. Washington, DC 20006. 1980. 86 pp. $3.50; send payment with order. Contains a basic description of how the computer is used for calculations. In Spanish. hs-ad.

Irwin Plaid Series. Dow Jones-Irwin. Div. of Richard D. Irwin, Inc. 1818 Ridge Rd. Homewood, IL 60430. Personal learning aids which may be used for self instruction. Titles include:

BASIC Programming Language. 1974. 77 pp. $4.95. Teaches the elements of writing instructions for computer applications using BASIC. Glossary. hs.

Introduction to Data Processing. 1979. 151 pp. $5.95. Provides familarily with equipment, systems, and procedures used in computer operations. Glossary. hs.

►**Layman's Guide to the Use of Computers in Education.** Assoc. for Educational Data Systems. 1201 16th St., N.W. Washington, DC 20036. 1982. 61 pp. $4.00; add $1.00 for postage for 1-10 copies. A booklet written to introduce educators to computing concepts and aquaint them with educational applications. Includes 8-page glossary of computer terms. ad.

►***MACUL.*** Michigan Assoc. for Computer Users in Learning. c/o Larry Smith. P.O. Box 807. Wayne, MI 48184. Membership fee, $5.00 yearly. An organization for educators and others interested in using computers to support instruction at all levels. Members receive the *Macal Journal* (annual) and *Checkpoint* newsletter (five yearly) and have access to diskettes of contributed software for the Apple II, Pet, Atari, and TRS-80 Model I microcomputers, ad.

►**Microcomputers . . . the Future Is Now** (VI, n.l). National Assoc. of Secondary School Principals. 1904 Association Dr. Reston, VA 22901. October 1979. 12 pp. 50 cents; send payment with order. An issue of *The Practitioner* providing an overview of microcomputers and their potential and actual uses in education. ms-hs-ad.

►**Microcomputers and the Media Specialist: An Annotated Bibliography** (IR-57). Informational Resources Publications. 30 Huntington Hall. Syracuse University. Syracuse, NY 13210. 1981. 70 pp. $5.25 postpaid. A selective listings of 250 recent books, articles, and other materials on microcomputers in education. Arranged in nine categories, such as hardware, software, computer literacy, and library applications. ad.

►**Microprocessor User's Guide.** Pro-Log Corp. 2411 Garden Rd. Monterey, CA 93940. 1979. 77 pp. 1-9 copies free; 10-99 copies $1.25 each. A collection of eight technical papers written by professional engineers on the design and architecture of microprocessors. ad.

PDK Fastbacks. Phi Delta Kappa. 8th and Union. Box 789. Bloomington, IN 47401. Prepay orders less than $5.00 or add $1.00 for handling. Titles are:

- ►**The Computer in the School** (#58). 1975. 42 pp. 50 cents. Covers the history of computers and their uses in schools, and addresses major questions about the future of computers in education. ad.
- ►**Computers in the Curriculum.** (#82). 1976. 42 pp. 50 cents. Discusses computer education for teachers and trends in training among school districts. ad.

Radio Shack. Many materials in the Educator Resource Series are available from local Radio Shack Computer Centers and stores. Some priced items may be available free in your area. Sample titles are:

- ►**Computer Discovery.** 1981. 127 pp. $4.50. A workbook designed for use with the TRS-80 Model III microcomputer to help students learn the essentials of computing. Available in junior high and senior high versions.
- ►**My TRS-80 Likes Me.** 1980. 26 pp. 8½" x 11". $2.50. Outlines a sequence of hands-on activities to help students learn how to read and understand programs written in BASIC language. el-ms.
- ►**TRS-80 Microcomputer Information Handbook for Educators.** 2nd ed. 1981. 32 pp. $2.50. Describes microcomputers and how they can be used in classrooms and in administration. Covers alternative systems, costs, courseware, environment, and other considerations involved in planning and decision making. ad.

►**Softswap.** Softswap. San Mateo County Office of Education. 333 Main St. Redwood City, CA 94063. Rev. periodically. Approx. 10 pp. $1.00 A catalog listing of educational software disks compiled for use with Apple, Atari, Compucolor, Pet, and TRS-80 microcomputers. Disks contain many programs, are in the public domain, and may be copied for educational purposes. el-ms-hs.

Teacher Aids. International Council for Computers in Education. Dept. of Computer and Educational Science. University of Oregon. Eugene, Or 97403. Offers publications designed for educators to promote instructional computing. Minimum order, $4.00; add $2.50 to total for billed orders. Quantity rates available. Sample titles are:

►**Evaluator's Guide for Microcomputer-Based Instructional Packages.** 1982. 48 pp. $2.50. Contains a summary of MicroSIFT's evaluation process, description of review components, review forms, and sample reviews. ad.

►**Precollege Computer Literacy: A Personal Computing Approach.** 1982. 25 pp. $1.50. Defines computer literacy for elementary and secondary students to guide educators in curriculum implementation. ad.

►**School Administrator's Introduction to Instructional Uses of Computers.** 1980. 48 pp. $2.50. Provides an overview of how computers are being used in schools and how they affect the curriculum. ad.

►**Teacher's Guide to Computers in the Elementary School.** 1981. 48 pp. $2.50. Designed to enable teachers to learn about several instructional uses of computers. ad.

Teacher-oriented Software. Innovations, Inc. P.O. Box 847. Carrollton, GA 30117. Two microcomputers programs that permit teacher input in their use. Titles are:

►**Test.** 1982. 3 pp. 40 cents. A computer program written in BASIC to build a test file, design multiple choice tests, administer the test, and record the results. Requires a computer that can work with a file program. ad.

►**Graph.** 1982. 1 p. 20 cents. A computer program written in BASIC to build graphs from raw data. Useful for science, math, and social studies classes. hs-ad.

►**Ten Pitfalls to Avoid in Buying a Small Computer System.** Assoc. of Computer Users. Research and Education Div. P.O. Box 9003. Boulder, CO 80301. May/June 1981. 15 pp. Free. Discusses mistakes that are made in computer purchasing and ways to avoid them. hs-ad.

Cross-Reference Index

Page numbers immediately after each subject head locate the main category in the book. Subsequent page numbers reference related materials within various other subject categories. The user should be aware that the pages cross-referenced often contain more than one listing related to the materials found in the main category.